THE GREAT TOURS
ENGLAND, SCOTLAND, AND WALES

PATRICK N. ALLITT

THE
GREAT
COURSES®

PUBLISHED BY:

THE GREAT COURSES
Corporate Headquarters
4840 Westfields Boulevard, Suite 500
Chantilly, Virginia 20151-2299
Phone: 1-800-832-2412
Fax: 703-378-3819
www.thegreatcourses.com

PATRICK N. ALLITT, PhD

Cahoon Family Professor of American History
Emory University

Patrick N. Allitt is the Cahoon Family Professor of American History at Emory University, where he also served as the director of Emory's Center for Teaching and Curriculum. He was raised in Mickleover, England, and he attended John Port School in the Derbyshire village of Etwall. After graduating from Hertford College at the University of Oxford, Professor Allitt earned his PhD in American History at the University of California, Berkeley. He was a Henry Luce Postdoctoral Fellow at Harvard Divinity School, where he specialized in American Religious History, and he was also a fellow at the Princeton University Center for the Study of Religion.

Professor Allitt is the author of five scholarly books: *A Climate of Crisis: America in the Age of Environmentalism*; *The Conservatives: Ideas and Personalities throughout American History*; *Religion in America Since 1945: A History*; *Catholic Converts: British and American Intellectuals Turn to Rome*; and *Catholic Intellectuals and Conservative Politics in America, 1950–1985*. In addition, he is the editor of *Major Problems in*

American Religious History and the author of a memoir about his life as a college professor, *I'm the Teacher, You're the Student: A Semester in the University Classroom*. He has written numerous articles and reviews for academic and popular journals, including book reviews in *The Spectator* and *The Weekly Standard*.

Professor Allitt's other Great Courses include *The Rise and Fall of the British Empire*; *The Conservative Tradition*; *American Religious History*; *Victorian Britain*; *The History of the United States, 2nd Edition* (with Professors Allen C. Guelzo and Gary W. Gallagher); *The American Identity*; *The Art of Teaching: Best Practices from a Master Educator*; *The Industrial Revolution*; and *The American West: History, Myth, and Legacy*.

Professor Allitt's wife, Toni, is a Michigan native. They have one daughter, Frances. ■

TABLE OF CONTENTS

Introduction

Lectures

Supplementary Material

Scotland
Northern Ireland
North Sea
Irish Sea
Ireland
England
Wales
English Channel
Celtic Sea

THE GREAT TOURS
ENGLAND, SCOTLAND, AND WALES

T his course is an introduction to England, Scotland, and Wales, aimed at both visitors from abroad and armchair travelers. It describes and illustrates the places and areas most deserving of visitors' attention, giving details of their history and anecdotes about the famous personalities associated with them.

The course begins with a set of historical lectures, introducing audiences to prehistoric, Roman, Anglo-Saxon, medieval, early modern, and modern Britain. Next comes a series of lectures on regions: two on Scotland, two on Wales, and one each on the English north, the Midlands, East Anglia, and the West Country. Two lectures are devoted to London, one to Oxford and Cambridge, and one to the Houses of Parliament and Buckingham Palace. A third group is dedicated to particular interests: four on literary Britain, and one each devoted to painting, seafaring, gardens, hiking, sports, and war memorials.

Certain themes are sustained throughout the course. One is the development of political stability, as a constitutional monarchy displaced the absolute monarchy of the Tudors and early Stuarts in the revolutions of the 17th century. Several lectures refer to the rise of democracy and the benefits it conferred on the British population. A second theme is the diversity of regional characteristics, which are reflected in strong local accents, a different living language in the case of Wales, and an intense loyalty to particular localities.

A third theme is the influence of powerful personalities, including Shakespeare, Queen Victoria, Winston Churchill, and Margaret Thatcher, each of whom is mentioned in several lectures. The course also emphasizes that there has never been a better time to visit Britain than now: The nation is fully aware of its rich heritage, preserves it very well, and has cleaned its cities, whose buildings until the 1970s were blackened by decades of soot from coal fires.

The course encourages visitors to be adventurous and not to confine themselves merely to the best-known places in Britain, such as Stratford, Stonehenge, Canterbury, and London. It begins and ends with practical advice on when to visit, how to get around, how to drive safely on the "wrong" side of the road, and various pitfalls to avoid. It encourages visitors to get out into the open as much as possible, to walk or cycle, and to interact with the people they meet. It also pays tribute to the radical improvement of restaurants in Britain since the nation opened its doors to immigrants from its former empire in India, Pakistan, and the West Indies, and (as a member until recently of the European Union) to immigrants from every part of Europe.

This course will give newcomers a real education in the main lines of British history, explaining the relationship of the island's three kingdoms, the significance of the British Empire to life in Britain itself, and the benefits of its increased wealth through the 20th and early 21st centuries. ■

1
WELCOME
TO BRITAIN

Great Britain is central to the history of civilization, has been heavily populated for centuries, and is full to the brim of fascinating landscapes, cities, castles, cathedrals, parks, gardens, and inventions. This lecture gives a broad overview of the region by looking at some of its key features and also provides some general travel tips if you plan on visiting.

Maiden Castle

Ancient Sites

Centuries of internal peace and a widespread interest in preserving the nation's heritage have ensured that evidence of all the ages of British life can still be found impressed on the landscape. It is possible to see superb examples of the ancient civilizations that lived there, including Maiden Castle, a great Iron Age hill fortress in the southwestern county of Dorset, and Stonehenge, the mysterious stone circle and earthwork in nearby Wiltshire.

Hadrian's Wall

Roman conquest in the first century of the Christian era also made a vivid and lasting impression. Best of the Roman remains is Hadrian's Wall, near the current border of England and Scotland; it marked the boundary between the Britons Rome had subdued and the wild men who lived further North.

Equally impressive are the Roman baths in the aptly named spa town of Bath in southwestern England. Its fashionable revival in the 18th century and its appearance in books like Jane Austen's *Persuasion* make Bath a popular and very worthwhile visitors' destination.

Roman baths

After the Romans

When the Romans left, Britain fragmented into petty chiefdoms and was invaded by Danish, Viking, and Anglo-Saxon tribesmen from Northern Europe. This was the era of the legendary King Arthur; several places in

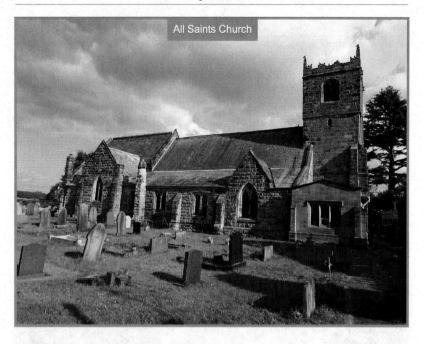
All Saints Church

England with scattered and picturesque ruins claim to be the original Camelot. It is not as easy to find Anglo-Saxon vestiges in Britain as Roman ones, but one incredible find is the Anglo-Saxon funeral longboat and treasure hoard, discovered at Sutton Hoo in the 1930s.

However, from the High Middle Ages in British history, the variety of objects still visible today is much larger. One example is the at All Saints Church in Mickleover, built in the early 1300s and extensively renovated in the Victorian era. Equally impressive are the medieval castles, which later lectures cover in detail.

Britain from 1500–1700

By looking at the great structures built in Britain between 1500 and 1700, it's possible to trace the rise of political stability in Britain. Henry VIII, who is notorious for having married six wives and killing two of them in the 1530s and 1540s, also managed to abolish private armies, which made internal warfare less frequent than it had been in the foregoing age.

A great civil war convulsed England in the 1640s, but after that, Britain enjoyed almost uninterrupted stability for the next three and a half centuries. The great houses from this era show a decline in the importance of fortifications and a new interest in comfort and luxury.

For most of its history Britain was far more rural than urban. Even today, despite a population of 65 million, it retains much wild country and large areas of farmland. Far back in time, the area was largely forested, but human demand for firewood and building materials meant that the forest was cut down nearly everywhere, surviving best when set aside from public use by kings and noblemen who wanted forest preserves for hunting.

Industrialization and the Sea

Eventually, industrialization was directly linked to cities, but the earliest industrial factories were built in hilly rural areas, where fast-flowing rivers

The Iron Bridge

powered water wheels linked to the machinery. In the Derwent Valley of Derbyshire, at Cromford, you can visit the world's first water-powered cotton spinning mill, built by Richard Arkwright in 1771.

A hundred miles southwest of there, in Shropshire, you can find Coalbrookdale, the valley where the great innovations of English iron making began. There, the world's first iron bridge, finished in 1779, still stands over the River Severn. Throughout this valley, a cluster of industrial museums has been created, beautifully preserving an important part of Britain's national heritage.

Britain was not only a rising industrial nation in the 1700s. It was also a great seafaring nation. It still bears many signs of its seafaring traditions. The obvious place to start is at Portsmouth on the South coast, where you'll find the notable ships HMS *Victory* and the *Mary Rose*. Equally engrossing are the clipper ship *Cutty Sark* at Greenwich in the Thames estuary and the pioneering oceangoing steamer *Great Britain* at Bristol.

HMS *Victory*

Important Sites in London

Many visitors from abroad devote much of their time in Britain to its capital, London. That's a pity in a way, because London is unrepresentative of the country as a whole. On the other hand, there's no denying what a treasure house it is of fascinating places and magnificent buildings. As its top three recommendations for a visit, this course makes the uncontroversial choices of the Tower of London, Buckingham Palace, and the Houses of Parliament. The city also features countless museums and art galleries.

Tips on Visiting Britain

Britain offers an immense number of places to visit, so this lecture now turns to practical tips on planning your visit. Have faith in your own convictions, go to see what you most want to see, and learn enough about it beforehand to make the visit worthwhile. Be prepared to change your plans at short notice if you see that a particular concert, play, or parade is taking place, even if it's outside your usual range of interests.

Britain has a mild climate; low winter temperatures rarely go below freezing, and high summer temperatures rarely go above 75 degrees Fahrenheit. It rains often, so it's a good idea to take waterproof clothing and an umbrella. Be ready to switch from planned outdoor to indoor activities.

Britain is a long way north of the equator, which means that the days are long and the nights short in summer. To go in winter, by contrast, is to face short days, where it's hardly light before 9:00 AM and getting dark again by 4:00 PM. The days are even shorter in Scotland.

Spring and autumn visits are likely to be less crowded than midsummer tours, when tens of thousands from all over the world are flocking in. If you rent a car, think carefully every time you get behind the wheel and have to drive on the left.

The great paradox of tourism is that no tourist wants to be jostled by thousands of other tourists. It's simultaneously possible to be one and to think that all the others are horrible. The two best ways to deal with the paradox are to go at times less likely to be crowded and to go to the countless beautiful but under-visited places of Britain.

Suggested Reading

Fraser, *The Story of Britain.*

Lonely Planet Great Britain.

Suggested Activity

1. Compare distances between major attractions in the UK and the US. For example, the distance from Stonehenge to Windsor Castle is 68 miles. The distance from Niagara Falls to the Grand Canyon is 2,193 miles. You'll be delighted at how compact Britain is.

WELCOME TO BRITAIN

Great Britain is central to the history of civilization, has been heavily populated for centuries, and is full to the brim of fascinating landscapes, cities, castles, cathedrals, parks, gardens, and inventions. Some of the most original and interesting people in world history lived there, including Shakespeare, Isaac Newton, Horatio Nelson, Isambard Brunel, Charles Darwin, Queen Victoria, and Winston Churchill. From Britain, thousands of enterprising people emigrated to settle other parts of the world, including the founders of the American colonies, Australia and Canada.

One of the less well-known emigrants is me! I was born in central England in the 1950s, grew up in the Derbyshire village of Mickleover, went to college at Oxford University, but then in the late 1970s traveled to America, where I studied for the PhD in history at the University of California, Berkeley. Through a series of happy coincidences, I ended up living and working in the United States, and became a US citizen in 2012. Still, I go back to England two or three times every year, and feel equally at home in both countries. I think my vantage point, with one foot in and one foot out of Britain has helped me gain some perspective on the country's history and on its immense value to our civilization. I love it, and love to be there.

Over the course of this and the next 35 lectures, I hope I'll be able to convey to you my enthusiasm for Britain and to point out some of the best places you should visit there when you have the chance to go. Even if you're just an armchair traveler, stay with me and learn about the history and culture of an island nation that has played an outsize role on the global stage.

Britain is the land where the Industrial Revolution began, and where many of the ideas central to our world originated—including ideas about democracy, individual rights, freedom of the press, and the rule of law. For at least 1,000 years its most articulate and literate people have been keeping detailed records, and for 1,000 years before that it was swept by the great movements of peoples across the ancient world.

Centuries of internal peace, and a widespread interest in preserving the nation's heritage, have ensured that evidence of all the ages of British life can still be found impressed on the landscape. It is possible to see superb examples of the ancient civilizations that lived there, including Maiden Castle, a great Iron Age hill fortress in the southwestern county of Dorset, and Stonehenge, the mysterious stone circle and earthwork in nearby Wiltshire. Roman conquest in the first century of the Christian era also made a vivid and lasting impression. Best of the Roman remains is Hadrian's Wall, near the current border of England and Scotland; it marked the boundary between the Britons Rome had subdued and the wild men who lived further North. Equally impressive are the Roman baths in the aptly named spa town of Bath, in southwestern England. It's fashionable revival in the 18th century and its appearance in books like Jane Austen's *Persuasion*, make Bath a popular and very worthwhile visitors' destination.

When the Romans left Britain, the country fragmented into petty chiefdoms and was invaded by Danish, Viking, and Anglo-Saxon tribesmen from Northern Europe. This was the era of the legendary King Arthur; several places in England with scattered and picturesque ruins claim to be the original Camelot. Eventually the Anglo-Saxons formed seven kingdoms, the "Heptarchy," and fought with one another for supremacy—each wanted to become the *bretwalda*, or king of the Britons. It's not quite so easy to find Anglo-Saxon vestiges in Britain as Roman ones—they're usually smaller and more fragile. On the other hand, an incredible Anglo-Saxon funeral longboat and treasure horde, found at Sutton Hoo in the 1930s, is one of the great archaeological sensations of the 20th century—maybe not quite the equal of Tutankhamun's tomb in Egypt, but not far off.

Once we reach the high middle ages in British history, the historical record, and the variety of objects still visible today, swells immensely. Front and center stand literally thousands of medieval churches. There are so many that some are shabby and neglected, even though they are 7-, 8-, or 900 years old. Many have been extensively renovated over the centuries, but they still give us vivid testimony of the powerful faith of Catholic England between the Norman Conquest of 1066 and the Reformation of the 16th century.

As a child I was a choirboy at All Saints Church in Mickleover—built in the early 1300s, extensively renovated in the Victorian era, wonderfully attractive, and yet too familiar to most English men and women to draw even a passing glance. One of the quintessential experiences of travel in England is to pass through the great oak door of a rural parish church like All Saints, and into the musty interior, where a brass-eagle lectern holds the Bible, where stained glass windows retell biblical stories, and where old grave markers commemorate the passing of village squires through the centuries.

The great cathedrals overshadow the parish churches, and draw the lion's share of visitors' attention. They nearly all date from the era 1100-1500, and I'll have much to say about them in the lectures that follow. The most famous of all are Westminster Abbey in London, where generations of kings and queens have been crowned, and Canterbury Cathedral, where the martyrdom of St. Thomas-a-Becket made it a great medieval pilgrimage, and which now serves as the world center of the Anglican church. Both, unfortunately, are now so popular that to visit them is to join a great scrum of other tourists, which makes it hard to appreciate their beauty. Ironically, the only time they are empty is during services, when the tourists temporarily step outside and give the remaining handful of British Christians their chance to worship. There's much to be said for visiting the equally magnificent, and much quieter cathedrals of Lichfield, Durham, Winchester, and many others.

Equally impressive are the medieval castles. Wonderful to visit today for people of all ages, they show in the clearest possible way just how dangerous and warlike life in Britain used to be. Our enjoyment is based on earlier generations' misery, fear, and eagerness to intimidate each other. There are dozens of examples, and I'll take you through several of them, including

Conwy Castle in Wales, Warwick Castle in central England, and Dover Castle on the South Coast.

By looking at the great structures built in Britain between 1500 and 1700, it's possible to trace the rise of political stability in Britain. Henry VIII, who is notorious to us for having married six wives and killing two of them in the 1530s and 40s, also managed to abolish private armies, which made internal warfare less frequent than it had been in the foregoing age, during the Wars of the Roses. A great civil war convulsed England in the 1640s but after that Britain enjoyed almost uninterrupted stability for the next three and a half centuries. The great houses from this era show a decline in the importance of fortifications and a new interest in comfort and luxury. They also bear witness to the fact that Britain was highly stratified by social class, with a small group of rich aristocrats and merchants right at the top who competed with each other for ostentation and magnificence. By our standards it was a horribly unjust world, and yet, in a paradoxical way, we benefit from that injustice now by having these great houses, gardens, and art collections available to visit and enjoy. Among them I'll introduce you to Chatsworth, Kedleston, and Calke in Derbyshire, Blickling in Norfolk and Melford in Suffolk. One of the characteristic emotions of visiting Britain's great houses, I think, is to be simultaneously impressed by the achievement and horrified by the colossal inequality they represent.

For most of its history, Britain was far more rural than urban. Even today, despite a population of 65 million, it retains much wild country and large areas of farmland. Go back far enough in history and you'll find a country almost entirely forested. Human demand for firewood and building materials meant that the forest was cut down nearly everywhere, surviving best when set aside from public use by kings and noblemen who wanted forest preserves for hunting. Today, the characteristic landscape of England's hill country, the Pennines, the Lake District, Dartmoor, and much of Scotland and Wales, is of deforested land, dotted with sheep and crisscrossed by dry stone walls. The hillsides have been bare of trees for so long, it's hard not to think of this as their natural condition.

None of them are high—Britain's highest mountain, Ben Nevis in Scotland, is only a shade over 4,000 feet—but they are steep and often wild, providing plenty of challenges to hikers and climbers. One of the very best ways to visit Britain is on foot. If you have time, I counsel you to walk part of one of the great network of footpaths that originated in ancient times and have been carefully preserved right up to the present. Among the greatest are, first, the Pennine Way. It begins in Derbyshire and leads north up the center of the country into the lowlands of Scotland. Second is the Pembrokeshire coastal path in Wales that will take you along clifftops and across broad estuaries. Third is the Ridgeway, across the chalk hills of central southern England, and based on ancient paths that have been trodden for thousands of years.

We think of industrialization as linked directly to cities, and eventually that was true, but the earliest industrial factories were built in hilly rural areas, where fast-flowing rivers powered water wheels linked to the machinery. In the Derwent Valley of Derbyshire, at Cromford, you can visit the world's first water-powered cotton spinning mill, built by Richard Arkwright in 1771. The great water wheel has gone, but the mill race that brought high pressure water to turn it is preserved. A hundred miles southwest of there, in Shropshire, you can find Coalbrookdale, the valley where the great innovations of English iron making began, and where the world's first iron bridge, finished in 1779, still stands over the River Severn. Throughout this valley, a cluster of industrial museums has been created, beautifully preserving an important part of Britain's national heritage.

Britain was not only a rising industrial nation in the 1700s. It was also a great seafaring nation, which projected its power across the world and built an empire on which the sun never set. No wonder it still bears so many signs of its seafaring traditions. The obvious place to start is at Portsmouth on the South coast, where you'll find, immaculately preserved, HMS *Victory*, flagship of Admiral Nelson, on whose deck he died at the climax of the Battle of Trafalgar in 1805. Nearby stands the hull of the *Mary Rose*, a ship of Henry VIII's navy that was launched in 1510 and sank in 1545. Its discovery and successful raising from the seabed in 1982 was a splendid feat of marine archaeology, while the thousands of artifacts recovered from it give us a richer picture of 16th century sailors' world than ever before. Equally engrossing are the fast sailing clipper ship *Cutty Sark* at Greenwich in the Thames estuary, and the pioneering ocean-going steamer *Great Britain*, at Bristol. The *Great Britain*, built in 1843 and, in its day, the world's longest and fastest ship, was restored to its former glory in the 1970s. These great ships, and many smaller ones in ports around the nation, bear witness to Britain's powerful association with the sea.

Many visitors from abroad devote much of their time in Britain to its capital, London. That's a pity in a way, because London is so unrepresentative of the country as a whole. On the other hand, there's no denying what a treasure house it is of fascinating places and magnificent buildings. If I had to single out three as particularly deserving of your attention, I would make the uncontroversial choice of the Tower of London, Buckingham Palace, and the Houses of Parliament.

The Tower was built by King William the Conqueror starting in 1078, and its history for the next seven centuries was directly linked to Royal affairs. It was a fortress, an armory, a garrison, a mint, but above all a prison, in whose dungeons languished suspected traitors, and on whose yards many were put to death, including Henry VIII's hapless queens Ann Boleyn and Catherine Howard. Incidentally, it's not a tower in the sense of being tall, thin, and cylindrical. Instead it's a massive series of fortifications, about which I'll have more to say later in the course.

Buckingham Palace is far more recent. Begun as a much smaller house in 1703, it was enlarged in the 1760s and again, much more extensively, in the 1820s. Only when Queen Victoria moved in on her accession in 1837, did it become the principal London residence of the monarchy. Just as it was being finished, the old Houses of Parliament burned down in 1834, and some government leaders suggested using Buckingham Palace as the seat of Parliament. One argument in favor of the idea was that the River Thames stank so badly from all the sewage and pollution it carried, and was so feared as the source of the recent cholera epidemic, that a site away from the River seemed like a much healthier alternative.

In the end, however, tradition prevailed, and the new Parliament was built on the same site as the old. A competition for the best design was won by

Charles Barry and Augustus Pugin, who had the idea of building it to echo the architecture of Westminster Abbey, just across the street. By making it look medieval, they emphasized the long continuity and stability of the British constitution, but they also took advantage of modern advances in structural iron and steam heating. The superb interior decoration of every part of the building makes it a continuing source of pride and pleasure. Likewise, the high quality of debate, especially the twice-weekly Prime Minister's Question Time, make a visit to Parliament a priority.

Just as the Houses of Parliament look older than they really are, so do many other parts of London and Britain's other cities. The bulk of the big public buildings are Victorian or Edwardian, constructed some time between 1830 and the beginning of World War I. That was an age of immense national confidence, in which British supremacy was embodied in brick and stone. Even the railway stations, which had a highly pragmatic reason for existence, became opportunities for fantastic elaboration, culminating in St. Pancras Station, whose iron and glass arch was one of the wonders of the age, and whose adjoining hotel, in decorated polychrome brick, remains one of the two or three most striking landmarks in all of London.

Equally engrossing are London's museums, many of which also date to the Victorian era, and which continue to show you something new even after dozens of visits. The grandest of them, all housed in palatial buildings, are the British Museum, whose entrance is reminiscent of the Parthenon in Athens; the Victoria and Albert Museum, named for the Queen and her husband Albert, whose premature death threw her into mourning for the rest of her long life; and the Museum of Natural History, a miraculously beautiful structure crammed to the rafters with interesting exhibits. There are also dozens of specialized museums, also on the grand scale. Among my favorites is the Imperial War Museum, filled with the weapons of the two world wars, uniforms, paintings, films, and dioramas. Another is the Science Museum, which traces British achievements in science and technology, and features the first steam locomotive ever to travel at 30 miles per hour.

Side by side with the museums are the art galleries, so extensive that to attempt a visit to all their rooms is a recipe for exhaustion. The grandest are the National Gallery, which fronts onto Trafalgar Square; the National Portrait Gallery, right next door; and the Tate Gallery. In recent years, a great converted power station on the South Bank of the River Thames has gained an excellent reputation as the Tate Modern. Even if you're lacking in sympathy for avant-garde art, you should visit it to see the breathtaking great hall which used to house a set of mighty turbines, and now offers a vast space for monumental art installations. Getting to the Tate Modern will also give you the chance to cross the Millennium Bridge, which opened in 2000 but had to close almost at once because of its alarming wobble. It's safer and more stable today, showing you the Tate Modern as you stride one way across it, and St. Paul's Cathedral as you saunter back toward the North Bank of the Thames.

Depending on who you are and what you like, you might want a tour of Britain linked to some special interest. In recent years, for example, some of the most picturesque castles and colleges have offered "Harry Potter" tours, showing the particular rooms and quadrangles where scenes from the *Harry Potter* movies were made. Of more durable interest, and already a centuries-old tradition, are literary tours. Certain authors are linked so strongly to particular landscapes that they are inseparable. Thomas Hardy transfigured the counties of Dorset, Wiltshire, and Somerset into "Wessex," and it's possible now to tour the sites he used as the originals for *The Mayor of Casterbridge*, *Far from the Madding Crowd*, and *Tess of the d'Urbervilles*, including the towns of Dorchester, Salisbury, and even Stonehenge itself. Similarly, Wordsworth and Coleridge tours will take you to the areas of the Lake District they loved best, and where they lived for many years. College tours in the old university town of Oxford will show you where J. R. R. Tolkien and C. S. Lewis lived and worked. The Lamb and Flag and the Eagle and Child, two pubs nearby, were the meeting places of their literary circle, the Inklings.

You've heard the old saying that "the pen is mightier than the sword." One of the places where you can believe it might be true is in the churchyard of Sutton Courtenay, a pretty village in Oxfordshire. Among the gravestones is that of Herbert Asquith, a powerful liberal politician of the early 20th century who was Prime Minister during the First World War. Last time I was there it was untended, half overgrown with weeds. But nearby is the simple black grave marker of George Orwell, the author of *Animal Farm* and *Nineteen-Eighty-Four*. It has become a shrine, at which fresh flowers are placed regularly by literary pilgrims, and when I was there it was surrounded by a small and appreciative crowd. It's all the more impressive in that the name "Orwell," which was a pen-name, is not even mentioned. The grave reads, simply: "Here lies Eric Arthur Blair" and the dates of his birth and death.

As you can see, there are many reasons for visiting Britain; some places that nearly every visitor is likely to want to see and others with more limited appeal. This series of lectures will approach the topic in three ways. First, I'll talk about the eras of British history, and we'll visit many fascinating sites associated with each of those eras. Second, I'll divide the country up into areas and point to the most engaging places to visit in those areas. Some will be geographic regions like the northeast, and in these I'm going to enlist the help of Paul Meier, who will give you an idea of what the local dialects sound like. Others will be more specific, such as the lecture devoted to the two ancient universities of Oxford and Cambridge, or the three lectures devoted entirely to London. And third, I'll present a set of thematic lectures, including four on literature, one on art and artists, one on sport, one on war memorials, and one on seafaring. There's a logic to the sequence, but you don't have to follow it; if one of the lectures strikes you as particularly appropriate to your interests, you will find it can stand alone, self-explanatory.

In addition to guiding you through these approaches to visiting Britain, I'll also offer some advice about how to plan a tour, when to visit, and how to choose among destinations when time is short. You should use this course in advance of travel, as a means of deciding why you want to visit, and what you want to see. It's easy to fall into the trap of thinking that you must check off a list of vital sites and events, which in England usually include the changing of the guard at Buckingham Palace, Stonehenge, and Shakespeare's birthplace in Stratford-on-Avon. There's nothing wrong with any of these, I suppose, apart from the mob of others who've all got the same idea, but Britain is so rich and varied that you might ask yourself whether alternatives—especially lesser known but equally interesting alternatives—might not be rewarding. The stone circle at Avebury, for example, is easily the equal of Stonehenge, and you won't have to fight the crowd to approach it.

As a college professor I often enjoy visits in my office hours from groups of students who say: "Hi, Professor Allitt. We're going to England this summer. What do you think we should see?" I answer: "That's wonderful news. I recommend you to avoid Stonehenge and Stratford and to go to places you haven't heard of, to get a sense of everyday life in a foreign country. Remember, it's a real country full of real people, not a quaint theme park. But if there's one place you really must not miss, it's the National Railway Museum in York. Promise me you'll go there." They leave, grinning. When I see them at the end of the vacation they tell me: "Hi, Professor Allitt. We had a great time in Britain. We saw Stonehenge, Stratford, the changing of the guard at Buckingham Palace, and the Cotswolds. It was fabulous." To which I answer: "I hope you didn't forget about the National Railway Museum." They giggle. "Didn't think you really meant that," and leave.

I admit that I'm far from immune to the "must see" impulse. On my first visit to Paris I literally couldn't avoid going to the Eiffel Tower—a magnetic force seemed to draw me there. On my first visit to Copenhagen I couldn't avoid going to see the Little Mermaid. Well, my verdict is yes to the Eiffel Tower but an emphatic no to the mermaid, which in my opinion is not worth a second glance. Have faith in your own convictions; go to see what you most want to see, and learn enough about it beforehand to make the visit a logical end point of your reading. And be prepared to change your plans at short notice if you see that a particular concert, play, or parade is taking place, even if it's outside your usual range of interests.

Here are a few practical tips. First, Britain has a mild climate; low winter temperatures rarely go below freezing, and high summer temperatures rarely go above 75 Fahrenheit, or 24 Celsius. It rains a lot, so it's a good idea to take good waterproofs or be ready to switch from planned outdoor to indoor activities. It's a long way north of the equator, which means that the days are long and the nights short in summer. One of the most exhilarating evenings I can remember was a late evening climb to Arthur's Seat, a beautiful hilltop overlooking Edinburgh, on midsummer's eve. Ten o'clock came and it still wasn't dark. Eleven o'clock came and the sky just dimmed a little. Even descending at midnight, there was still light enough to see. Those huge days are invigorating.

To go in winter, by contrast, is to face short days, where it's hardly light before 9:00 in the morning and getting dark again by 4:00 in the afternoon, even in the South around London, with an even shorter day in Scotland. On the other hand, spring and autumn visits are likely to be less crowded than midsummer tours, when tens of thousands from all over the world are flocking in, augmented further by Britons themselves, whose school summer holidays are usually the second half of July and all of August. And remember, if you rent a car, think very, very carefully every time you get behind the wheel and have to drive on the left.

The great paradox of tourism is that no tourist wants to be jostled by thousands of other tourists. It's simultaneously possible to be one and to think that all the others are horrible. The two best ways to deal with the paradox are to go at times less likely to be crowded, and to go to the countless beautiful but hitherto-neglected or under-visited places of Britain. I'm going to talk about some of the busiest and some of the most obscure sites in these lectures, but I promise you, the scope in Britain is inexhaustible.

2
PREHISTORIC BRITAIN

T his lecture gives an overview of sites remaining from prehistoric Britain. Key places discussed in the lecture include:

- The Stonehenge and Avebury stone circles.

- Hill Forts.

- The Uffington White Horse.

- The Great Orme copper mine in Wales.

- Skara Brae in Scotland.

Stonehenge

Stonehenge and Avebury

Located in Wiltshire in southwest England, the prehistoric monument of Stonehenge is now a UNESCO World Heritage Site, one of the most heavily visited places in the world. No one is allowed to walk among the stones—the collective impact of their trampling would quickly degrade the monument, so

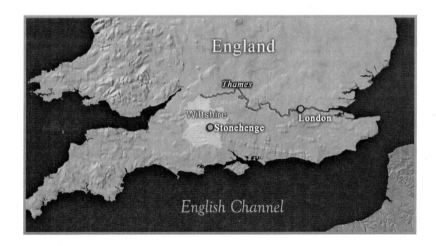

England

Thames

Wiltshire

London

Stonehenge

English Channel

they are kept at a safe distance, except for a select few on special occasions. Archaeologists using carbon dating estimate that Stonehenge is 50 centuries old.

For visitors, an alternate option to Stonehenge is the stone circle of Avebury, which is about 20 miles away. It is typically less crowded, and as of publication, it is possible to walk among the stones themselves.

Avebury

Hill Forts

The area of the old Anglo-Saxon kingdom of Wessex, covering Dorset, Wiltshire, Somerset, and part of Hampshire, is dotted with old hill forts, some of which date from the Neolithic era when hunters and gatherers were settling down to become farmers instead. Natural hilltops were made more secure against attack by the building of ditches and embankments. Inside them, communities could build their villages, gather the farm animals when under threat, and keep watch on the surrounding country.

The passage of time has gradually eroded many of these hill forts, but a few are still impressive, none more so than Maiden Castle. That location is south of Dorchester, the county town of Dorset. It is 430 feet high and part of a natural ridge, giving excellent views in every direction.

Archaeologists have shown that Maiden Castle was built over a long period of time. The cumulative effect is superb—a succession of great ditches, embankments, and ramparts enclosing a massive oval interior. It was extended and occupied continuously between the Neolithic era, more than 4000 years BCE, right through to the 6th century CE.

Maiden Castle

The Great Tours: England, Scotland, and Wales

Another impressive Iron Age hill fort is Cadbury Castle in Somerset, widely believed in former times to be the real site of King Arthur's Camelot. Excavations have shown evidence of a battle there at the time of the Roman invasion of Britain in about 43 CE. In addition to Maiden and Cadbury, the remains of other hill forts are scattered widely throughout the south of England.

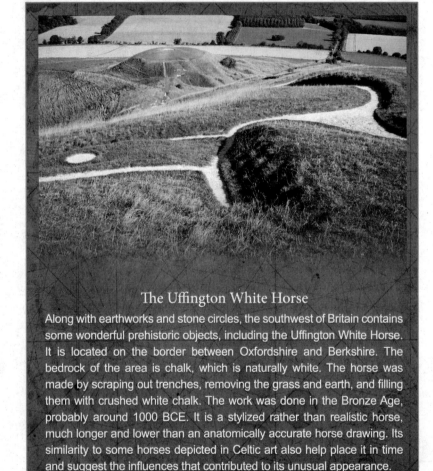

The Uffington White Horse

Along with earthworks and stone circles, the southwest of Britain contains some wonderful prehistoric objects, including the Uffington White Horse. It is located on the border between Oxfordshire and Berkshire. The bedrock of the area is chalk, which is naturally white. The horse was made by scraping out trenches, removing the grass and earth, and filling them with crushed white chalk. The work was done in the Bronze Age, probably around 1000 BCE. It is a stylized rather than realistic horse, much longer and lower than an anatomically accurate horse drawing. Its similarity to some horses depicted in Celtic art also help place it in time and suggest the influences that contributed to its unusual appearance.

Other Sites

Not all prehistoric sites in Britain are confided to Wessex, but if that's your principal interest and you have limited time, it's definitely the logical place to go. Across this district of great prehistoric riches lies the Ridgeway, an ancient route along the hilltops that since 1973 has been a recognized and government-protected national footpath.

In the hill country of Devonshire, Derbyshire, Yorkshire, and Cumbria, there are many more stone circles and remains of ancient earth works. Among the best are Castlerigg in Cumbria, part of the Lake District, where a circle of

Castlerigg

Great Orme Mines

40 stones create a ring in one of the most scenically dramatic areas of the district. Also impressive is Brisworthy in Devonshire, an oval of 24 standing stones. An enthusiastic local clergyman set most of them upright in 1909.

The best prehistoric site in Wales is the Great Orme copper mine, near Llandudno. One of the reasons Britain was in close contact with the rest of Europe, even in pre-Roman days, was the presence there of large copper deposits. The mine at Great Orme was dug out in the Bronze Age, probably beginning around 2000 BCE and continued to be worked over the course of 1,000 years or more.

Scotland's Prehistoric Sites

In Scotland, too, the remains of prehistoric cultures are widespread. Many are at or below ground level, where there isn't much to see, but more than 100 brochs still stand proud, albeit half ruined. Brochs are mysterious circular buildings, double walled and built using rocks without mortar, over which archaeologists have speculated and debated.

Scotland's best prehistoric site, Skara Brae, is on the Orkney Islands. These windswept treeless islands are among the most inaccessible places in Europe, but can be reached by plane or ferry boat by anyone with enough time, money, and determination.

Skara Brae probably dates back 4,000 years, to a period when the climate was rather warmer than it is now. The site was unknown until the 1850s, when a windstorm revealed the remains of old buildings. The local lord excavated four houses. Edinburgh University took over more systematically in the 1920s, and by now, eight low houses have been fully dug out, along with the stone passages that linked them.

The people who lived in them appear to have survived by a mixture of farming, herding, and fishing, to judge from recovered fragments. Stone furniture survives in several of the houses, and countless everyday objects have been discovered.

One contributor to the debate over Skara Brae, a museum curator from Glasgow named Julian Spalding, argues that such well-built stone objects show the site to have had a ritual rather than domestic purpose. He claims it was something like a sauna, heated by hot rocks immersed in water, around which people would gather for worship and story telling. As so often with prehistoric sites, it's impossible to be sure because the remains are so fragmentary.

Suggested Reading

Darvill, *Prehistoric Britain*.

Schama, *A History of Britain*.

Suggested Activities

1. Type "Stone circle, Britain" into Google. You will find more than 1,000 examples. Narrowing it down to the best eight or ten and locating them is a good way of learning about Britain's prehistoric heritage.

2. If you visit Stonehenge and Avebury from London, keep an eye open not just for the White Horse but also for more recent carvings into the chalk hillsides, including regimental insignia from World War I.

2

PREHISTORIC BRITAIN

The first time I saw Stonehenge, I was seven years old. It was a windy summer day in 1962. In those far-off times you could just stop your car by the side of the nearby road, walk over the fields, and wander among the great standing stones. That's what my family did—we were the only people there, and as my brother and I tried in vain to climb the vertical rock monoliths, my father explained that the Stonehenge had been there for thousands of years, but that no one was quite sure what it was, or why it had been built.

Those were the days! Located in Wiltshire, in South West England, Stonehenge is now a UNESCO World Heritage Site, one of the most heavily visited places in the world. Thousands of people can be seen there every day, and it's extremely difficult to find it unattended by crowds. Quite apart from the literally millions of tourists from around the world, an annual convergence of new age spiritualists surrounds it to pray and meditate during the summer solstice. In 1985, a group of them scuffled with police in an event remembered as the Battle of the Beanfield.

No one now is allowed to walk among the stones. The collective impact of their trampling would quickly degrade the monument, so they are kept at a safe distance, except for a select few on special occasions. Traffic management in the area is a big headache. For a while, I used to encourage Americans heading to the Southwest of England to visit the stone circle of Avebury instead, about 20 miles away, where it's still possible to walk among the stones themselves. At Avebury they could avoid the mob and get a sense of the awe the great standing stones evoke. But I admit that Stonehenge is, despite everything, a compulsively fascinating place.

Archaeologists using carbon dating now reckon that it's about 50 centuries old, begun around 3000 BCE and expanded often over the following millennia. The great trilithons, which feature one great stone laid like a lintel over two vertical stones, were probably set up when Stonehenge was already 1,000 years old. Was it a temple, a burial ground, an astronomical observatory, a healing center, or a royal dwelling place? Interested and ingenious people have been speculating for hundreds of years, and archaeological work in the Stonehenge area continues up to the present. What we lack, of course, are written records from the builders—every theory is based on fragmentary discoveries and deductions from limited evidence.

It's pretty clear, however, that tens of thousands of people were involved in its construction. The sheer size of the stones, and the fact that many of them were quarried in Wales at a site more than 100 miles away, bears witness to a phenomenal amount of hard work and a hierarchical social organization. Historical reenactors have tried dragging blocks of comparable weight on rollers or on greased tracks to see how long it would take and how many men it would involve. Moreover, what the casual visitor sees above ground is only the tip of the iceberg. For miles around in every direction are partially or wholly buried stones brought from elsewhere, other circles of post-holes, the remains of wooden henges, and hundreds of burial chambers, which provide the evidence that this was a bustling, highly organized, densely populated area for many centuries. Modern techniques like LIDAR enable us to picture the landscape above and below ground level more clearly than ever before.

The medieval chronicler Geoffrey of Monmouth, writing in the 12th century, suggested that Stonehenge was a site for healing. He believed that touching the stones had healing effects in his own time, and that it had been built by Merlin, King Arthur's magician. The first man to excavate at Stonehenge was the Duke of Buckingham, who dug a pit inside the central circle. John Aubrey, a 17th-century polymath, did a little more excavation and noticed a set of indentations in the ground that are now referred to as "Aubrey holes," possibly indicating additional structures beyond what is now visible above ground.

From 1720-1740, William Stukeley resumed the digging, and he was the first person to notice a great avenue leading east out of the henge toward the nearby River Avon. Stukeley was a doctor, a Freemason, an Anglican clergyman, and a friend and biographer of Isaac Newton—the kind of enterprising well-to-do gentleman of the Enlightenment who was interested in everything. Eager to travel and see as much as he could for himself, he became familiar at first-hand with many of the area's important sites. He was a founding member, and first secretary, of the Society of Antiquaries, which can be thought of as the first British group dedicated to archaeology. A fine draftsman, Stukeley made countless drawings of ancient sites that were later destroyed or damaged. Cooperating with the astronomer Edmund Halley, he theorized that Stonehenge had been built about 460 BC and that it was aligned with the Earth's magnetic North Pole. He also believed that it had been a worship-site for Druids, devotees of a patriarchal cult among the Celts, whom Julius Caesar encountered when the Romans first invaded Britain. Stukeley himself was nicknamed "The Arch-Druid" by friends who found his investigations amusing.

The situation improved a little in the late 19th century. By then, archaeology was becoming more systematic; the best survey to date was done in 1872 by William Flinders-Petrie, subsequently the leading British Egyptologist. He is credited with establishing the patient, systematic, and painstaking methods of 20th-century archaeology. At about the same time, Charles Darwin visited with his family for a picnic and later pointed out that the work of millions of earthworms, over thousands of years, would gradually shift everything at a site like this and cause the stones to sink into the ground and the embankment to diminish in size—an insight never forgotten by subsequent excavators.

In 1882, Parliament passed the legislation that recognized the need to protect Britain's ancient monuments. Stonehenge was put on the list right away, along with 67 other prehistoric sites. Government protection included the decision to return some fallen stones to the upright position. One of the great trilithons, which had fallen over in 1797, was restored in 1958.

It can be agonizing for modern archaeologists to read about, and see the evidence of, their predecessors' work because by current standards it was so primitive and destructive. Today's archaeologists dig carefully through every layer of ground with trowels, sift every ounce of soil, make meticulous drawings and photographic records of every stratum, and diagrams showing exactly where every find was made. Not so their predecessors, brawny workmen who often just shoveled the earth aside in the hope of turning up heaps of treasure. Only since the 1950s have archaeologists had radiocarbon dating, a technology that enables them to date organic finds more accurately than ever before. They are also caught in the paradox of knowing that they too are going to seem crude in the eyes of their successors, whose methods will presumably be even more refined. That makes them hesitate, lest their work in turn destroys evidence of the very thing they're hoping to recover.

Among the many theories about Stonehenge, one was advanced by the American astronomer Gerald Hawkins, in his 1963 book *Stonehenge Decoded*. In his view, Stonehenge was a kind of computer for predicting solar and lunar eclipses far into the future, a theory that other astronomers found convincing. It was already known that the henge was oriented to sunrise on midsummer's day and sunset on midwinter's day. Perhaps this was the key? Archaeologists, such as Richard Atkinson, who had been excavating there for the previous 15 years, didn't like the idea that their painstaking work was largely beside the point, and subjected Hawkins to some strenuous refutation. By now, however, the two disciplines have been linked in an academic specialization named archaeoastronomy. Peter Newham and Alexander Thom, following up on Hawkins's work, have demonstrated further ways in which the distribution of stones and local markers can be used to predict solar and lunar events. There's clearly some substance to these claims, even if Hawkins was wrong with some of the details.

When DNA analysis was added to radiocarbon dating, our ability to understand the human dimensions of Stonehenge in its heyday increased. Among the burials are people who came from the Mediterranean and from present-day Scandinavia; it appears to have been a Europe-wide destination long before the rise of the Roman Empire.

The work, and the wondering, continue. English Heritage, the agency that cares for Stonehenge, has to balance many interests and constituencies. The archaeologists want to excavate, the neo-Druids want to worship, the tourists from around the world want to see the site as undisturbed as possible, yet their own presence creates an immense and continuous disturbance. After protests against the poor quality of the visitor center and the surroundings, a new center opened in December 2013, which includes a fine museum exhibiting many of the best artifacts discovered at the site. From there, a bus takes you close to Stonehenge itself—no other traffic is allowed in the area, and the old road on which I first visited has now been closed.

I've spent a fair amount of time talking about Stonehenge, but if you're interested in exploring prehistoric Britain, Southwestern England has many other important sites. Avebury, which I mentioned earlier, is bigger than Stonehenge but slightly less impressive because it lacks any structures. There are no trilithons, and the great standing stones are not "dressed"—that is, not cut into neat blocks, but are irregular in shape. On the other hand, the number of stones at Avebury, and the height of the ditch and embankment surrounding them, is more impressive. A medieval village was sited there, and roads and dwellings still cut through the circle itself. Sheep graze among the stones to keep the grass short.

We know that in the Middle Ages many of the stones were deliberately knocked over by people who thought the circle was a site for Devil-worship. In the 1930s many of them were returned to their standing position by the archaeologist Alexander Keiller. Under one he found the skeleton of a man, whose pouch contained a pair of scissors, a probe, and a few coins that dated from the early 1300s. Keiller concluded from these tools that he might have been a barber, the man who in those days often doubled as the local surgeon. Had the unfortunate fellow been struck by the rock as it was knocked over, and thus entombed there? Or had he died earlier? In any event, this particular stone has been known as the Barber Stone ever since.

Keiller was heir to a great Scottish marmalade fortune (and incidentally, the company is still going strong and the marmalade still tastes great). Keiller devoted his money to acquiring land in the Avebury area to prevent its development. Working in the interwar years, he was one in a generation of archaeologists to realize the value of aerial photography. From the air, shapes and patterns that are invisible at ground level suddenly emerged, disclosing the presence of abandoned villages, the lines of ancient walls, and dozens of other places where the ground had clearly been modified by human actions. His book, *Wessex From The Air*, published in 1928, was the first British book on aerial archaeology and helped set in motion a revolution in the understanding of ancient Britain.

The whole of this area—Dorset, Wiltshire, Somerset and part of Hampshire, the area that Thomas Hardy called "Wessex,"—is dotted with old hill forts, some of which date from the Neolithic era when hunters and gatherers were settling down to become farmers instead. Natural hilltops were made more secure against attack by the building of ditches and embankments. Inside them, communities could build their villages, gather the farm animals when under threat, and keep watch on the surrounding country.

The passage of time has gradually eroded many of these hill forts, but a few are still impressive, none more so than Maiden Castle, just South of Dorchester, the county town of Dorset. It is 430 feet high, part of a natural ridge, giving excellent views in every direction, and an ideal defensive site. Hardy himself described it as "a heavy, high-shouldered presence . . . an enormous many-limbed organism of antediluvian time . . . lying lifeless and covered with a thin green cloth, which hides its substance."

Archaeologists have shown that Maiden Castle was built over a long period of time. The cumulative effect is superb—a succession of great ditches and embankments, ramparts enclosing a massive oval interior, giving wonderful views over the surrounding lowlands. It was extended and occupied continuously between the Neolithic era, more than 4000 years BCE, right through to the 6th century of the Common Era, or AD. The successive layers of ditches and banks are so elaborate that archaeologists speculate they might have been intended as decorative rather than strictly functional defenses, a way of declaring the supremacy of their chieftain. Mortimer Wheeler, the archaeologist who excavated Maiden Castle in the four summers between 1934 and 1937, and published a book about it in 1943, had a gift for publicity. He held regular press conferences, encouraged public visits to the site, and drew in more people to take an interest in this sometimes forbidding and recondite activity. His work helped establish the principle that Maiden and comparable hill forts were essential parts of the nation's heritage, as deserving of protection as castles, palaces, and cathedrals.

Another impressive Iron Age hill fort is Cadbury Castle in Somerset, widely believed in former times to be the real site of King Arthur's Camelot. Excavations have shown evidence of a battle there at the time of the Roman invasion of Britain in about 43 CE. In addition to Maiden and Cadbury, the remains of other hill forts are scattered widely throughout the south of England. At Old Sarum, near Salisbury, a later cathedral and a Norman castle were built inside the great perimeter of the earthworks. Even more striking, in its way, is Silbury Hill, because in this instance the hill itself was actually built by human labor. It is conical, almost 100 feet high, standing on otherwise level ground, and has a flat top with a 100-foot diameter. Archaeologists believe it to have been started in about 2400 BCE, probably by slave labor, and continued over a long period of time. But excavations show it not to have been a burial site. Subsequent use by later populations has modified the site. A Roman road swerved around it, confirming the point that the hill was already there when the Romans arrived.

Silbury Hill was a gathering place every Palm Sunday for people from the surrounding villages in the 17th and 18th centuries. As with Stonehenge and Avebury, however, its original purpose remains uncertain, despite plenty of plausible-sounding theories. Incidentally, this is another one I climbed in the days when it was still allowed; now it's off-limits, but still worth visiting, which is easy enough as it's only a few miles from Avebury and Stonehenge.

Along with the earthworks and stone circles, the southwest contains some wonderful prehistoric objects, including the Uffington White Horse, on the border between Oxfordshire and Berkshire. The bedrock of the area is chalk, naturally white, and the horse was made by scraping out trenches, removing the grass and earth, and filling them with crushed white chalk. The work was probably done in the Bronze Age, around 1000 B.C. It's a stylized rather than realistic horse, much longer and lower than an anatomically accurate horse drawing, and strangely modern in appearance. Its similarity to some horses depicted in Celtic art also help place it in time and suggest the influences that contributed to its unusual appearance. Every seven years, from the Middle

Ages right into the late 19th century, a local fair was held beside the horse, during which local people cleared away the grass which would otherwise have overgrown and obscured it.

Among the many puzzling aspects of the White Horse is that it's located in a place not easily viewed from any other place on the ground—all our best pictures of it come from the air. Surely such a spectacular design was meant to be seen by people as well as by the gods? Theories for this slightly inaccessible placement include the idea that the ground itself has slipped over the centuries, making its exact location different now than hitherto.

Later generations carried on the tradition. Among the best of later chalk drawings on the monumental scale is the giant of Cerne Abbas, also in Dorset. Made in essentially the same way as the White Horse, it depicts a man, presumably a warrior, holding aloft a great war-club, which is echoed by his great erect penis. Early antiquarians speculated that it too was prehistoric, or that it depicted the Roman god Hercules. Current theorizing, sadly, favors the idea that it was made only in the 1600s, because it is not mentioned in any older document. It might be a parody of Oliver Cromwell, the military dictator or "Lord Protector" of England in the 1650s. It too is difficult to photograph from ground level, and is best seen from the air. Like the older ones, however, its survival has also depended on generation after generation of local people keeping the outline distinct—otherwise the grass would quickly return to shroud it altogether.

Across this district of great prehistoric riches lies the Ridgeway, an ancient route along the hilltops that since 1973 has been a recognized and government-protected national footpath. It goes from the southwest, in Dorset, starting close to Stonehenge and Avebury, all the way to Buckinghamshire, on high ground nearly all the way. Historically, the advantage of a ridgeway was that the ground was unlikely to be swampy. On this high ground, travelers would be less vulnerable to ambush. To walk it from end to end, or just a few sections, is to enjoy superb views of this rich and still mostly rural part of England, and to encounter, one after the next, old burial mounds like Wayland's Smithy, hill forts, and patterns in the ground whose presence bespeaks ancient habitation and ritual life. Radiocarbon dating has shown that the Ridgeway has been in use for at least 5,000 years.

I don't want to give you the impression that prehistoric sites in Britain are confined solely to Wessex, though if that's your principal interest and you have limited time, it's definitely the logical place to go. In the hill country of Devonshire, Derbyshire, Yorkshire, and Cumbria, there are many more stone circles and remains of ancient earthworks. Among the best are Castlerigg in Cumbria, part of the Lake District, where a circle of 40 stones create a ring in one of the most scenically dramatic areas of the district. Last time I was there, rain pelted down and a ground mist rose around the ancient stones, giving a delicious sensation of being removed from everyday life. Also impressive is Brisworthy, in Devonshire, an oval of 24 standing stones most of which were set upright in 1909 by an enthusiastic local clergyman. There are hundreds of still-visible stone circles, around 1,300 in all, and every traveler can single them out with the help of an OS map.

OS stands for "Ordnance Survey." Starting in the mid 1700s, the British government's military department recognized the need for high quality maps, beginning in Scotland after Bonnie Prince Charlie's failed uprising was defeated at the Battle of Culloden Moor in 1746. The first map was made of the Scottish Highlands, but gradually the attempt to map the whole of Britain was extended, with the result that for more than two centuries now we have enjoyed access to phenomenally detailed maps of every part of Britain. All over OS maps of rural districts you'll find the word "tumulus," meaning an ancient earthwork or burial mound. They are innumerable, many are now nothing more than a cluster of rocks or a bulge in the landscape, but they remind passersby that people have been living and farming these lands for thousands of years.

The best prehistoric site in Wales is the Great Orme copper mine, near Llandudno. One of the reasons Britain was in close contact with the rest of Europe, even in pre-Roman days, was the presence there of large copper deposits. The mine at Great Orme was dug out in the Bronze Age, probably beginning around 2000 BCE and continued to be worked over the course of 1,000 years or more. The miners brought malachite to the surface, a greenish-blue copper ore from which the metal could be smelted. The miners must have used primitive candles or smoky lamps to light their way. By our standards their tools were primitive, either stone axes or pieces of antler, hundreds of which have been found in the mine. One of the pleasures of Great Orme is knowing that it was completely forgotten for hundreds of years before being accidentally rediscovered in 1987. Continuing exploration since then has disclosed a labyrinth of passages, making it almost certainly the largest prehistoric mine in Europe.

In Scotland too, the remains of prehistoric cultures are widespread. Many are at or below ground level, where there isn't much to see, but more than 100 brochs still stand proud, albeit half-ruined. Brochs are mysterious circular buildings, double-walled and built using rocks without mortar, over which (as with everything I have mentioned today) archaeologists have speculated and debated. Some scholars believe the brochs to be old fortifications; others say they were just strong farmhouses, and others again favor the idea that they were places of worship with ritual significance. They are mainly found in the extreme northeast of Scotland, one of the remotest parts of Britain, and in the even more inaccessible Shetland and Orkney Islands off the north coast. The best preserved of them all is at Mousa in Shetland, still about 40 feet high with an internal spiral staircase between the walls. On the mainland the two best, close to one another, are Dun Telve and Dun Troddan in Glenelg, on the coast of the Western highlands.

Scotland's best prehistoric site, however, Skara Brae, is on the Orkney Islands off the North Coast. These windswept, treeless islands are among the most inaccessible places in Europe, but can be reached by plane or ferry boat by anyone with enough time, money, and determination. Older than the pyramids of Egypt, older than Stonehenge, Skara Brae probably dates back 4,000 years, to a period when the climate was rather warmer than it is now. The site was unknown until the 1850s when a windstorm, even more scouring than usual, laid bare the remains of old buildings on what until then had seemed to be no more than an uneven earth mound. The local lord, or laird, excavated four houses. Edinburgh University took over more systematically in the 1920s, and by now eight low houses have been fully dug out, along with the stone passages that linked them.

The people who lived in them appear to have survived by a mixture of farming, herding, and fishing, to judge from recovered fragments. Stone furniture survives in several of the houses, and countless everyday objects have been discovered. One contributor to the debate over Skara Brae, however, a museum curator from Glasgow named Julian Spalding, argues that such well-built stone objects show the site to have had a ritual rather than domestic purpose. He claims it was something like a sauna, heated by hot rocks immersed in water, around which people would gather for worship and storytelling. As so often with prehistoric sites, it's impossible to be sure because the remains are so fragmentary. Archaeologists debate whether the settlement was abandoned in the face of a sudden catastrophe (one of the region's great storms, perhaps) or whether gradual climatic cooling made it steadily less habitable. In any case, it seems to have been abandoned around 2500 BCE, after about 600 years of continuous occupation.

Skara Brae's antiquity is a great point of emphasis among Scottish nationalists, who have campaigned in recent years for full independence from England, and did so with renewed vigor after the "Brexit" election of 2016. Skara Brae enabled them to claim that civilization came to Britain not from the classical south of Europe but from the north, making Scotland the earliest civilized site on the whole island. An even bigger site, the Ness of Brodgar, is now being excavated too, perhaps giving further substance to such claims.

Whichever site claims absolute primacy, collectively Britain's prehistoric remains make it an immensely rewarding place to visit. All the sites prompt you to consider the literally thousands of years in which men and women tried not just to stay alive to but to elaborate on the bare bones of existence with ritual, decoration, and architectural achievement.

3
ROMAN BRITAIN

This lecture covers sites that remain from the Roman era of Britain. Much more evidence remains from this era than the prehistoric one because the Romans were literate and commented on what they were doing. Key topics discussed in this lecture include:

- Hadrian's Wall.

- Roman baths.

- The remains of opulent villas.

- The notable amphitheater at Caerleon.

- Roman roads.

Background on the Romans

Roman ruler Julius Caesar visited Britain in 55 BCE and again in 54 BCE in the course of conquering Gaul. He fought against the local tribes there, exacting tribute from some and offering protection to others, but then withdrew.

About 90 years later, in 43 CE, the Romans returned under the emperor Claudius and conquered Britain. Claudius's army, led by Aulus Plautius, landed at Richborough in Kent, where the remains of a Roman fort can still be visited. The soldiers then fought their way into the island, overcoming tenacious native opposition.

Finally, in the year 60, they defeated the army of Boudica (or Boadecia), a mighty female warrior. Her statue on Westminster Bridge, installed in 1902, has often been used as the symbol of strong female leadership, such as that of Queen Victoria and Margaret Thatcher. Between the years 44 and 410, when Emperor Honorius withdrew the last troops, most of Britain belonged to the Roman Empire. The only area the Romans didn't subdue was the area they called Caledonia, today's Scotland.

Hadrian's Wall

Hadrian's Wall, near the current Anglo-Scottish border, is the best-preserved sign of the Romans' presence and one of the outstanding places to visit in contemporary Britain. It stretched from coast to coast, 73 miles, from Bowness in the west to the place now aptly named Wallsend in the east.

Hadrian's Wall

Even today, after nearly two millennia, large parts of it remain. It was about 15 feet high and 8 feet wide, made all the more daunting by the presence of a great ditch on each side that would put attackers at a huge disadvantage. Emperor Hadrian ordered its construction in the early 2nd century CE after deciding that the empire need grow no larger.

Historians at first assumed that the role of Hadrian's Wall was to stop invading tribes. More recent scholarship has modified the picture, suggesting that the wall should be thought of as a place where trade and tribal movements could be regulated rather than prohibited. It was never designed to be impermeable. Instead, the Romans could keep track of movements back and forth, charge tariffs to traders coming through, and close the gates and reinforce the garrison in times of crisis. Even so, attackers breached it on at least three different occasions, in the years 197, 296, and 367.

Vindolanda, part of Hadrian's Wall, is a grand archaeological site. It was a Roman garrison. A reconstruction of a section of the wall and one of the towers, as they would have been when in use, gives visitors an accurate sense of their height and solidity.

Another fort along Hadrian's Wall, at Chesters, was excavated in the early 19th century by the local landowner, John Clayton, who realized the historical importance of his estates. His house stood at the point where the wall crossed the River Tyne. To guard the crossing, the Romans built a fortress that was staffed for a century by Spanish cavalrymen.

Chesters

After excavating Chesters itself, Clayton went on to acquire several other fortresses and to buy lands that included lengths of the wall. It is in large part due to him that so much of Hadrian's Wall still exists.

The Roman Baths

The second great site of Roman Britain still visible is the Roman baths at the city of Bath in the southwest. It is a UNESCO World Heritage Site. Sulfurous

hot springs there, even though they smell and taste horrible, have long been taken to have healing properties. Research on recovered Roman-era skeletons shows that that arthritis and rheumatism were common ailments, which the waters were supposed to soothe. This was the basis of the town's growth.

An extensive and well-curated tour at Bath takes visitors through the main Roman sections, including the spring itself, the swimming pool, the temple, and a museum containing the best finds from the site.

Roman baths

Roman Villas

Evidence of the Roman presence is scattered throughout Britain, though more in England than in Wales and Scotland, where the Roman presence was more temporary. Villas, all in various states of ruin, are among the best of them. Some indicate that members of the British elite switched the style of their houses from circular wood-and-thatch houses to rectangular stone buildings in the Roman era. Chedworth, in the Cotswolds of Gloucestershire, is an extensive site and well worth a visit. Built between the 2nd and 4th

Chedworth

centuries, it must have been the home of a wealthy family, though scholars don't know whether they were Romans or Romanized Britons.

The villa was discovered by accident in 1864 by a gamekeeper. They were on the land of the earl of Eldon. The earl's uncle, James Farrer, an enthusiastic antiquarian, excavated it over the next few years. It features well-preserved mosaic floors and enough of the walls to give a sense of how magnificent it must once have been.

Another villa, at Woodchester, also in Gloucestershire, was excavated in 1793 by Samuel Lysons, a local enthusiast. He dug down to disclose a magnificent mosaic, more than

2,000 square feet in area, which made it one of the biggest and best-preserved Roman mosaics still in existence.

The Ampitheater at Caerleon

The best Roman site in Wales is the amphitheater at Caerleon, just north of Newport. The Romans had a fort here, which they called Isca Augusta. Along with the amphitheater, the barracks and bathhouse of Isca Augusta are also visible in outline. As for the amphitheater itself, it is oval in shape, with eight great entrances.

Roads

One way visitors sometimes become aware of the Roman mark on Britain is by driving on long, straight roads. Everywhere they went, the Romans built good roads to ensure rapid and effective military communications. The roads

Wade's Causeway

usually went straight over hills rather than contouring around them, ignoring older pathways that were more roundabout. The greatest of the Roman roads is the Fosse Way.

Very few stretches of unchanged Roman road are still visible. One is Wade's Causeway, which is located on high moorland in the North York Moors National Park. It has a high-quality surface made from sandstone slabs closely fitted together.

Suggested Reading

Branigan, *Roman Britain*.

Burke, *Roman England*.

De la Bedoyere, *Roman Britain*.

Suggested Activities

1. Walk a section of Hadrian's Wall or tour the baths in Bath. If you're an armchair traveler, open an atlas to trace the wall from coast to coast.

2. Read one of the many historical novels based on Roman Britain, such as Rosemary Sutcliff's *The Eagle of the Ninth* (1954).

ROMAN BRITAIN

A nyone who loves a mystery is going to enjoy the study of prehistoric Britain, because just about everything there remains mysterious. Once we come to the Roman era, by contrast, we're far better placed to unravel the mysteries and work out the puzzles. That's because the Romans were literate. They commented on what they were doing. We don't simply have Hadrian's Wall, the Roman Baths in Bath, and the remains of some opulent villas—we also have discussion of them in official correspondence to and from governors, and the help of dozens of lively writers. We know the names of literally hundreds of Roman Britons, along with the names of the tribal chiefs they displaced during their era of conquest.

The downside of visiting Roman Britain is just how fragmentary most of the remains are. Don't expect the Colosseum, Herculaneum, or Pompeii. One of the best historians of Roman buildings, Guy de la Bédoyère, admits that "for the most part, the surviving examples form disappointing chunks of shapeless masonry" and that "not a single Romano-British building has survived even nearly intact, though complete examples are not unknown elsewhere in the former empire." The upside of this situation is that researchers haven't been shy about digging into the scattered remains, because there's not much left above ground. Bédoyère points out that excavation reveals the sequence of buildings on a site, and shows that the Romans often built over older Bronze- and Iron-Age buildings. As he says: "it has been possible to learn far more about the buildings of Roman Britain than would ever have been possible had they been preserved much better."

Julius Caesar visited Britain in 55 and again in 54 BC in the course of conquering Gaul. He fought against the local tribes there, exacted tribute from some and offered protection to others, but then withdrew. About 90 years later, in AD 43, the Romans returned under the emperor Claudius and conquered Britain. For Claudius, who had recently succeeded Caligula, it was a way of gaining the prestige of a successful warrior and strengthening his grip on power. Trade over the preceding centuries had demonstrated that Britain was a prosperous place and a source of valuable copper, iron, and grain.

Claudius's army, led by Aulus Plautius, landed at Richborough in Kent, where the remains of a Roman fort can still be visited. The soldiers then fought their way into the island, overcoming tenacious native opposition. Finally, in the year 60, they defeated the army of Boudica, (or Boadecia) a mighty female warrior into whose mouth the author Tacitus put a stirring speech on the pride of warrior queens. Her statue, on Westminster Bridge, installed in 1902, has often been used as the symbol of strong female leadership, such as that of Queen Victoria and Margaret Thatcher. Between the years 44 and 410, when the Emperor Honorius withdrew the last troops, most of Britain belonged to the Roman Empire. The only area the Romans didn't subdue was the area they called Caledonia, today's Scotland.

Hadrian's Wall, near the current Anglo-Scottish border, is the best-preserved sign of their presence, and one of the outstanding places to visit in contemporary Britain. It stretched from coast to coast, 73 miles, from Bowness in the west to the place now aptly named Wallsend in the east. Even today, after nearly two millennia, large parts of it remain. It has nearly disappeared at each end because towns have grown up over its path, and even many of the high central sections have been pilfered through the ages. When you think of the labor required to cut stone with primitive tools into smooth-edged blocks, it's no wonder later generations cannibalized Hadrian's Wall and other Roman structures. The walls of the crypt at nearby Hexham Abbey still contain many Latin inscriptions, some of them sideways or upside-down, betraying the blocks' origins.

Luckily, enough of Hadrian's Wall is left to give us an accurate sense of its shape, size, and purpose. It follows the high ground across wild Pennine country, maximizing visibility for the men who patrolled it. It was about 15 feet high and eight feet wide, made all the more daunting by the presence of a great ditch on each side, 25 feet wide and eight feet deep, that would put attackers at a huge disadvantage. You can still see the ditch in places, though there's been a lot of land-movement since, and it's nowhere as deep as it was when first built. The fact that these ditches were built on both sides of the wall suggests to historians that the British tribes living south of the wall—the Brigantes—were also regarded by the Romans as a potential threat.

The Emperor Hadrian ordered its construction in the early 2nd century, after deciding that the empire need grow no larger. He was there in the year 122 when the work began—it was almost completed in just six years. At first, its western section was a great earth and timber rampart, but the whole thing was rebuilt as a much more durable stone structure from coast to coast in the early 3rd century, by order of the Emperor Septimus Severus. At every mile along its course stood a milecastle or miniature fortress, with a garrison of about 50 men, castles whose square foundations are still clearly visible. High quality reconstructions by artists give us a good sense of how they would have looked. At longer intervals stood bigger forts, holding 1,000 men each, ready to move quickly to the scene of any threat. It was patrolled mainly by soldiers who came from elsewhere in the empire, from Spain, Gaul, and Batavia (present-day Holland), and even from the far eastern reaches of the empire, in today's Turkey and Iraq.

As with prehistoric Avebury and the Ridgeway in Dorset and Wiltshire, so with Hadrian's Wall in Northumberland and Cumbria. If you possibly can, you should walk at least some of it, to get away from the modern roads and recreate for yourself the sensation of being in the wilds of the far North. It is forbidding moorland country. Countless historians have entertained themselves and their readers by imagining soldiers from the Mediterranean lands, even Syria and Persia, finding themselves stationed at this grim, wet, extremity of the empire. John Burke, writing in 1983, for example, speaks of "the wild background of hills and rock, the steely loughs, and the vast sky; and always there is the eerie rustling and moaning of the wind, sometimes rising to a howl like some barbaric battle cry."

The first person we know of to walk Hadrian's Wall from end to end was a certain William Hutton, in 1801. He came from my home town, Derby, and didn't attempt the walk until he was already 78 years old. What's more, he walked from the English midlands to the wall, making a round trip total of more than 600 miles. He doubted his own sanity, and in his book about the experience, *The History of the Roman Wall* wrote: "What can exceed the folly of that man, who at 78 walked 600 miles to see a shattered Wall." He also wrote: "Perhaps I am the first man that ever travelled the whole length of this Wall, and probably the last that ever will attempt it." I tipped my cap to him when, with my brother Malcolm, I walked just a four-mile stretch of the wall, there and back, on a day in 2017 that started out misty but ended in bright sunshine.

Historians at first assumed that the role of Hadrian's Wall was to stop invading tribes. More recent scholarship has modified the picture, suggesting that the wall should be thought of as a place where trade and tribal movements could be regulated rather than prohibited. It was never designed to be impermeable. Instead, the Romans could keep track of movements back and forth, charge tariffs to traders coming through, but close the gates and reinforce the garrison in times of crisis. Even so, it was breached by attackers on at least three different occasions, in the years 197, 296, and 367.

Vindolanda, part of Hadrian's Wall, is a grand archaeological site. It was a Roman garrison. A reconstruction of a section of the wall and one of the towers, as they would have been when in use, gives visitors an accurate sense of their height and solidity. Over the last few decades a long succession of marvelous finds there have rewarded the archaeologists' hard work. The anaerobic, or oxygen-free soil, has prevented decay of organic materials that would normally have perished centuries ago. Excavations of a rubbish dump created between the years 97 and 103 have brought up leather from shoes, horses' bridles, and even written documents that bring to life the rhythms of everyday life along the wall. Many of these finds are on display at an excellent onsite museum.

We know that women as well as men lived in Vindolanda and similar forts— plenty of their combs and hairpins have been found, and even written notes, shopping lists, and a birthday invitation from one lady to another. To date, the site has yielded up about 400 such notes, which are collectively known as the Vindolanda tablets. Most of the notes are preserved in the British Museum and were recently voted Britain's most popular archaeological discovery, but a selection of them are also on view at the Vindolanda museum itself.

These written notes were made not on paper but on very thin pieces of wood, usually birch or alder bark, hardly thicker than cardboard. The usual method was to write the message in ink, then fold the bark sheet in half, writing the name of the intended recipient on the outside. Archaeologists have found that it's possible, by carefully unfolding the tablets and shining infrared light on them, to read the handwriting. At first, experts in Latin epigraphy were baffled by it—it is a previously unfamiliar style of cursive script. Most of them are lists of items needed by the garrison—one of them shows that Roman soldiers did wear underpants! In another note, a soldier named Masculus writes to his commander Cerialis saying there is no beer, and asking him to send for more. The soldiers' diet was based on grain baked into bread, but a wide variety of foodstuffs are mentioned in the tablets, including olives and wine—which must have been imported from southern Europe—and even pepper. The Vindolanda tablets also make it clear that the soldiers were jacks of all trades. Many of them worked at building and maintaining the wall itself. Others were shoemakers, waggoners, brewers, and armorers. Fortunes could be made in supplying the garrisons too. One letter, detailing the various business activities of two energetic brothers, Octavius and Candidus, includes the following passage:

> Make sure that you send me some cash so that I may have ears of grain on the threshing room floor . . . I have already finished threshing all that I had. A messmate of our friend Frontius has been here. He wanted me to allocate him some hides, and that being so, was ready to give cash. I told him I would give him the hides by the Kalends of March. He decided that he would come on the Ides of January. He did not turn up, nor did he take the trouble to obtain them since he had hides. If he had given the cash, I would have given him them. I hear that Frontinius Julius has for sale at a high price the leather ware which he bought here for five denarii apiece.

As you can see from these excerpts, there's nothing elevated or literary in the Vindolanda tablets—no hint here of Cicero or Tacitus. The very ordinariness of them is what makes them precious to historians, of course, bringing the details to light of how massive forces, thousands of miles from Rome, were kept fit, well-supplied, and in fighting order. They're the nuts and bolts of a big bureaucracy in action.

Another fort along Hadrian's Wall, at Chesters, was excavated in the early 19th century by the local landowner, John Clayton, who realized the historical importance of his estates. His house stood at the point where the wall crossed the River Tyne. To guard the crossing, the Romans built a fortress that was staffed for a century by Spanish cavalrymen. Chesters includes the remains of the soldiers' barracks, the commander's home, and the strong room in which the garrison's funds would be kept. The strong room still has its original roof, one of very few such places in Britain. The remains of the bathhouse are visible, including the changing room that contains the niches in which visitors would leave their clothes, and the well-preserved *sudatorium*, or sweating room.

After excavating Chesters itself, Clayton went on to acquire several other fortresses and to buy lands that included lengths of the wall—it is in large part due to him that so much of Hadrian's Wall still exists. The artist William Bell Scott's romantic painting *The Romans Cause a Wall to be Built* is dominated by a centurion whose face is modeled on Clayton's own.

Clayton himself gathered together hundreds of stones bearing inscriptions and other items of interest that his workmen turned up. A museum at Chesters was built in 1895 to house the whole lot, and it presents a crowded, jumbled appearance. Curators recently made the decision to leave it like that rather than rearrange it according to contemporary museological standards. They repainted the interior with bright red paint, aiming to duplicate its appearance in the first decade of the 20th century. This is a super idea, I think, giving visitors today the chance to see a kind of double-museum, which draws your attention not only to the Roman objects, but also to the history of thinking about history.

At another museum, Arbeia, in South Shields on the east coast, part of a Roman fortress has been reconstructed. The replica includes a Roman gateway, which provides a sense of the fort's original scale and grandeur.

The original structure would have served as a crucial link in the defense of the northern frontier. It was the port to which food and military supplies were shipped from southern England or continental Europe, and from which they were sent to garrisons along the wall. Among the best items in the Arbeia museum are monuments recalling the lives of two Britons who began life as slaves and were freed. One of them, Regina, married a merchant originally from Palmyra, in modern-day Syria, whose grave also stands nearby and provides further evidence of the variety of people who ended up in the north of Britannia. The name Arbeia may signify "place of the Arabs," a reference to the fact that the first soldiers there had previously been stationed on the Tigris River in present-day Iraq.

Under Hadrian's successor, Antoninus Pius, in the year 142, the Romans advanced 100 miles further into Scotland and built a second wall, the Antonine Wall, at the narrowest crossing point of Scotland from west to east, about 39 miles. An earth and timber rampart on stone foundations, it took 12 years to complete. Less of it remains than of Hadrian's Wall, partly because it was not built of stone, and partly because the outskirts of two great cities have overrun it—Edinburgh to the East and Glasgow to the West. But several central sections have been preserved and can still be visited. Slabs carved by the soldiers who did the hard work on the wall read like this: "For the Emperor Caesar Titus Aelius Hadriano Antoninus Augustus, father of his country, a detachment of the Sixth Legion Victrix Pia Fidelis, built the rampart for 3240 feet." The Antonine Wall fell into disuse in the later 2nd century, was briefly reoccupied in the early 200s, but then abandoned once and for all, apparently because the Caledonians were just too difficult to subdue.

Along with Hadrian's wall, the second great site of Roman Britain still visible, and with lots to see, is the Roman baths at the city of Bath in the Southwest. It is a UNESCO World Heritage Site. The Romans called it Aquae Sulis. Sulphurous hot springs there, even though they smell and taste horrible, have long been taken to have healing properties. We know from research on recovered Roman-era skeletons that arthritis and rheumatism were common ailments, which the waters were supposed to soothe. This was the basis of the town's growth.

The name Aquae Sulis derives from Sulis, a local Celtic goddess, and the springs were already sacred to the people who lived in the area before the Romans arrived. The Romans had a tolerant approach to the religions of the people they dominated, often blending their own gods with those they found locally. So it's not surprising that the Romans dedicated the baths jointly to Sulis and Minerva, the Roman goddess of healing.

An extensive and well-curated tour at Bath takes you through the main Roman sections, including the spring itself, running hot just as it did 2,000 years ago, the swimming pool, the temple, and a museum containing the best finds from the site. Generations of modification, especially from the late 1800s, sometimes require you to work out what's original and what's a later addition, but the mood of the place is still ancient—highly addictive. Roman visitors threw coins and bracelets into the waters to propitiate the gods. The best of them are on display. Among the finds was a curse tablet, written backwards, asking the goddess to destroy the people who had stolen away a woman named Vilbia, and even naming a few of them.

Baths were a central element of daily life for the Romans. Villas often had private baths of their own, but nearly all the major Roman cities included large public baths, to which even relatively poor people had access. They were centers of social life and exercise as well as cleanliness, and were ingeniously provided with underfloor heating and pools of various temperatures—the cold *frigidarium*, the warm *tepidarium*, and the hot *caldarium*—along with sweating chambers and massage rooms. Many were lavishly decorated with mosaic floors, and were so well-built that they're among the most durable of Roman remains.

Bath itself, supplied by a hot spring, is slightly different, and one of only a handful of Roman baths in which it was actually possible to swim, rather than merely soak. There was a similar arrangement at two other Roman sites we know of, Buxton in Derbyshire, and Wroxeter in Shropshire. The main pool at Bath, like the water pipes supplying it, was clad with lead sheeting and about six feet deep. Bathers stepped down into it to immerse themselves in water that flowed in at 115 degrees Fahrenheit, or 46 Centigrade.

Evidence of the Roman presence is scattered throughout Britain, though more in England than in Wales and Scotland, where the Roman presence was more temporary. Villas, all in various states of ruin, are among the best of them. Some indicate that members of the British elite switched the style of their houses from circular wood-and-thatch houses to rectangular stone buildings in the Roman era. Chedworth, in the Cotswolds of Gloucestershire, is an extensive site and well worth a visit. Built between the 2nd and 4th centuries, it must have been the home of a wealthy family, though we don't know whether they were Romans or Romanized Britons.

The villa was discovered by accident in 1864 by a gamekeeper, when his hunting dogs rooted up a few mosaic tiles. They were on the land of the Earl of Eldon. The Earl's uncle, James Farrer, an enthusiastic antiquarian, excavated it over the next few years. It features well-preserved mosaic floors and enough of the walls to give you a sense of how magnificent it must once have been. It had underfloor heating too. A spring, providing fresh water to the villa, is also preserved—its elaborate stonework shows it to have been a shrine, not just a well. On summer weekends, local craftsmen at Chedworth demonstrate how the Romans wove, made arrows, smelted iron, and other practical trades. The building dominating Chedworth, ironically, is a Victorian house, built by the first excavators as a museum for their finds—an outrageous intrusion by today's archaeological standards.

Another villa, at Woodchester, also in Gloucestershire, was excavated in 1793 by Samuel Lysons, a local enthusiast. There was nothing visible above ground but he dug down to disclose a magnificent mosaic, more than 2,000 square feet in area, which made it one of the biggest and best-preserved Roman mosaics still in existence. Its central figure is Orpheus playing his lyre. Tantalizingly, it's not currently on view. The last time it was shown was in 1973. So many people came to see it—141,000 in 50 days—that the village was jammed with traffic. The local people decided it was more trouble than it was worth and voted to cover it up again, and it's been buried ever since. At least we have good photographs of it, along with a replica, containing 1.5 million mosaic pieces, made by two local craftsmen. For a while the replica was on display in a local abbey, but it was auctioned off in 2010 and is also now unavailable. There's something very English about this story. It's a great illustration of the fact that one man's priceless treasure is another man's pain in the neck. The fact that the situation remains like this is also testimony to just how many other Roman remains are available to visit as alternatives.

The best Roman site in Wales is the amphitheater at Caerleon, just north of Newport. The Romans had a fort here, which they called Isca Augusta, and, besides the amphitheater, the barracks and bathhouse of Isca Augusta are also visible in outline. As for the amphitheater itself, it is oval in shape, with eight great entrances. Prior to the 20th century, it was known to the local folk as "King Arthur's Round Table." But excavations in 1926 confirmed its Roman origins. It was built about AD 80 for audiences of up to 6,000, and was twice rebuilt during the occupation. Only in imagination, alas, can you see it as a distinguished provincial variant of the Colosseum in Rome.

The highest still-standing Roman building in Britain, incidentally, is the shell of a lighthouse at Dover Castle. It's a great thick lumpy cylinder, right next to a church—originally Anglo-Saxon—that has been extensively renovated and modernized. Its location is matchless, on one of the highest points of the fort, overlooking the English Channel.

One way you sometimes become aware of the Roman mark on Britain is by driving on long, straight roads. Everywhere they went, the Romans built good roads to ensure rapid and effective military communications—they usually went straight over hills rather than contouring around them, ignoring older pathways that were more roundabout. The greatest of the Roman roads are the Fosse Way, marking a very straight line between Bath and Lincoln, Ermine Street from London to York, and Watling Street, a Roman adaptation of an even earlier road that made a continuous line between Richborough in Kent, across the Thames, and on to Wroxeter near the Welsh border.

Replacing old dirt tracks that became impassable in wet weather, the Romans built elevated roadways, paved with crushed rock or, occasionally, dressed stone, and built drainage ditches on each side to keep the roads themselves free from swamping. About every four miles would be a staging post so that dispatch riders with urgent messages could change horses regularly and maintain a high speed. These roads were so good, and so superior to anything else, that they were used continually for centuries after the Romans left in 410, and in places they became the basis for the national road system right up to the present.

Very few stretches of unchanged Roman road are still visible. One is Wade's Causeway, on high moorland in the North York Moors National Park. It has a high quality surface made from sandstone slabs closely fitted together, is elevated, and has the characteristic drainage ditches on each side. I walked a mile of it recently, felt very Roman, and only discovered afterwards that there are now some academic doubts about its provenance. It's not quite straight enough, say the doubters, and might be from a later era. Perhaps the slight deviations from straight are due to subsequent earth movements over the centuries? We have no hard evidence, but Wade's Causeway is certainly built in the same general style as Roman roads, and gives you an inkling of how the roads must have looked as the legions marched along them.

This survey of Roman remains in Britain is not comprehensive—to include everything would turn it into a mere list. St. Albans near London, and Chester near Liverpool also have significant Roman remains; and nearly all important historical sites in southern Britain contain Roman traces. These traces may not be as impressive as the Colosseum or the Pantheon in Rome, but they are important reminders of a presence that shaped the course of Western history. To be in almost any place of continuous habitation in Britain is to be in one of the places the Romans lived, worked, fought, and prayed together during their nearly 400 years of occupation.

4

ANGLO-SAXON AND VIKING BRITAIN

This lecture looks at key sites that remain from the Anglo-Saxon and Viking eras of Britain. The lecture also provides some background information on both groups. Key topics of the lecture include:

- Offa's Dyke.

- English churches and crosses.

- The Sutton Hoo ship burial.

- Notable Viking-related locations.

Background on the Anglo-Saxons

In the last days of Roman Britain, Germanic tribes began to migrate to England across the North Sea. The power vacuum that followed the Romans' evacuation of Britain in 410 accelerated this migration. From Jutland in present-day Denmark came the Jutes, while from present day northern Germany came the Angles and the Saxons. The name England means "land of the Angles."

The Edict of Thessalonica (380) mandated Christianity as the Roman Empire's official religion. Roman remains in Britain indicate the popularity of Mithraism, a form of sun worship, but there are also scattered vestiges of Roman Christianity. The Anglo-Saxons were pagans, but between the 5th and 8th centuries, they too gradually adopted Christianity.

For much of the period between the 5th and 9th centuries, Anglo-Saxon England was divided into seven kingdoms, which are known to historians as the Heptarchy. Northumbria was the most northerly of these kingdoms, while

the middle of England was the kingdom of Mercia. East Anglia, as its name suggests, was the land of the eastern Angles. Sussex and Essex, which have survived into recent times as county names, are the lands of the southern and eastern Saxons, while Wessex was the land of the western Saxons. In the southeast of England was Kent. The kings of these seven territories were chronically at war with one another, as each strove to become the dominant king.

Offa's Dyke

The biggest and most visible Anglo-Saxon object in Britain is Offa's Dyke. Offa was king of Mercia from the mid-750s to 796. He built a continuous barrier on his western frontier, probably as a guard against Welsh raiders. Radiocarbon dating has found evidence that some parts of the dyke are earlier, so Offa may have completed a job already partly done by his predecessors.

Crossing land most of which is still farmed, it fades from view in places but is still distinct in others. The best place to visit it is at Knighton, where an

Offa's Dyke

Offa's Dyke visitor center explains its significance and where well-preserved sections are visible. Since 1971, hikers have also been able to walk Offa's Dyke Path, which is a national trail that runs for 177 miles along the Anglo-Welsh border.

English Churches and Crosses

In addition to earthworks, several English churches survive from the 7th, 8th, and 9th centuries. One well-preserved example is tiny St. Laurence's Church in Wiltshire. Equally well kept is the chapel of St. Peter-on-the-Wall in Essex. Built around 660, it recycled Roman bricks and cut stones. A third and much bigger example is All Saints Church in Brixworth, Northamptonshire. It too is largely unchanged since its construction in the 680s. Only the tower and spire are subsequent additions.

Carved crosses from the Anglo-Saxon period are also widespread in England, though usually very worn by centuries of weathering. Probably the best is the Ruthwell Cross, now protected from the elements inside Ruthwell parish church, just north of the Scottish border.

The Sutton Hoo Ship Burial

In the 20th and 21st centuries, archaeologists have been excited by major Anglo-Saxon finds. The most spectacular was the Sutton Hoo ship burial in East Anglia, east of Ipswich. In 1937, the local landowner, Edith Pretty, decided to excavate the numerous oddly shaped mounds on her property. She hired a self-taught archaeologist named Basil Brown. He uncovered a wonderful Anglo-Saxon ship burial. Mrs. Pretty's gardener and a local gamekeeper also joined in the painstaking work of uncovering the find.

When archaeologists from Cambridge University and the British Museum realized the significance of the discovery, they took over the work in 1939. Before the excavations could be completed, World War II began, so the site was not fully explored until the 1960s.

Sutton Hoo Ship Burial

The timbers of the Sutton Hoo ship had rotted away over the centuries, but its impression was clearly shown by the excavators. This had been a real seagoing ship, with places for 40 oarsmen and evidence of periodic repairs. Its benches and mast had been removed, and a central area enclosed to receive the body.

The ship had then been dragged up out of the river and lowered into an excavated chamber. After the interment, probably of King Raedwald of East Anglia, a great mound was heaped up over it.

Background on the Vikings and Lindisfarne

In the 790s, Britain endured another round of invasions. This time, the intruders were from Scandinavia—the warlike Vikings. In British history, they are usually called the Danes.

The Vikings' first appearance in Britain was their attack on the island monastery at Lindisfarne off the northeastern coast. It was the first of many ruthless attacks on eastern England. The raiders seized everything of value, killed the poor men, carried the women off into slavery, and took the richest men for ransom.

Lindisfarne is today one of the most enchanting places in England. Just a few miles south of the Scottish border, it's only accessible when the tide is low. It features the ruins of the area's attacked monastery and a superb castle.

Viking Names

The Vikings had magnificent names. One of the first major Viking kings was Harald Fairhair. His son was Eric Bloodaxe. Some of their names corresponded to the individual's father's name. Hence, the son of Erik the Red was Leif Eriksson, and his daughter was Freydis Eriksdottir.

After the initial raid on Lindisfarne, Viking depredations became a regular fact of life in the 800s, especially along the east coast of England. Viking ships were the best in the world at that time, combining the capacity to sail long distances with a shallow draft that enabled them to sail

Lindisfarne

far up England's rivers and attack inland communities. A combination of sails and oars also made them maneuverable in a wide variety of conditions.

Alfred the Great

In 865, a Viking army landed in East Anglia, intent not just on raiding but on conquering Anglo-Saxon Britain. It was led by the unforgettably named Ivar the Boneless, and is remembered in English history as the Great Heathen Army. It marched north, sacked Whitby, captured York, and seemed all set to dominate the whole of Britain. Opposition came from two kings of Wessex: Aethelred and then his brother Alfred the Great, who ruled from 871 until 899.

Alfred's achievement was to prevent Viking conquest of the whole country. At one point, he was forced into hiding in the marshlands of Athelney, Somerset, where a monument to him still stands. Archaeological work at Athelney has shown that this was the site of an Iron Age fort. Signs of metalworking in the area also suggest that Alfred and his followers cast weapons there in

King Alfred's Tower

preparation for their counterattack on the Vikings.

Alfred's army won a decisive victory against the Viking general, Guthrum, at Edington in 878. Guthrum was forced to become a Christian with Alfred acting as his godfather. England was partitioned into a Viking-dominated east, known as the Danelaw, and an Anglo-Saxon-dominated west under Alfred.

The traditional site of the battle is Egbert's Stone, an unobtrusive marker. At Stourhead nearby, however, commanding the surrounding country, is King Alfred's Tower, a striking triangular tower completed in 1772 to celebrate England's victory over France in the

King Alfred

Seven Years' War (or, as Americans call it, the French and Indian War). It is 160 feet high and includes a statue of King Alfred and an inscription. There are also statues of Alfred in Wantage (in Oxfordshire), Pewsey (in Wiltshire), and Winchester, all from the late 19th and early 20th centuries.

In the centuries after Alfred's reign, the various populations of England gradually merged through coexistence, intermarriage, and trade. Anglo-Saxon and Viking artistic traditions also persisted and interacted with those of the Normans after 1066.

Suggested Reading

Brown, *Anglo-Saxon England*.

Care-Evans, *The Sutton Hoo Ship Burial*.

Higham and Ryan, *The Anglo-Saxon World*.

Loyn, *The Vikings in Britain*.

Suggested Activities

1. Work out what your name would be if you were a Viking. For example, course instructor Patrick Allitt would be Patrick Ericsson because his father is Eric. His sister would be Deborah Ericsdottir.

2. Find a book or web site explaining British place names. You can then trace the western boundary of the Danelaw by watching how place names change.

4

ANGLO-SAXON AND VIKING BRITAIN

I n the last days of Roman Britain, Germanic tribes began to migrate to England across the North Sea. The power vacuum that followed the Romans' evacuation of Britain in 410 accelerated this migration. From Jutland, in present-day Denmark came the Jutes, while from present day northern Germany came the Angles and the Saxons. The name "England" means "land of the Angles." Say "Angle-land" rapidly a few times and you'll get "England."

The Edict of Thessalonica of 380 mandated Christianity as the Roman Empire's official religion. Roman remains in Britain indicate the popularity of Mithraism, a form of sun worship, but there are also scattered vestiges of Roman Christianity. The Anglo-Saxons were pagans, but between the 5th and 8th centuries they too gradually adopted Christianity. The best book describing this process is the Venerable Bede's *Ecclesiastical History of the English People*, from the year 731. Bede himself, sometimes referred to as "the father of English history," was a monk at Jarrow, near Newcastle-upon-Tyne. The chancel of the Anglo-Saxon church at Jarrow, St. Paul's, where he worshipped, is still well preserved, and a few fragments of 8th-century stained glass discovered nearby have been integrated into the church windows. Standing in the chancel, it's therefore possible to experience the same light, through the same glass, between the same walls, as Bede himself.

His *History* is a guide to the Anglo-Saxon kings, their wars, their holy men and women, and the gradual spread of Christianity. Its heroes are the saintly monks and nuns who preached Christianity, and the kings who accepted it and lived by its principles. Its villains are the stubborn warriors who refused to convert, or who slipped back into paganism. Of King Oswald of Northumberland, for example, Bede writes:

> Oswald, the most Christian king of the Northumbrians, reigned for nine years if we include the fatal year made abhorrent by the callous impiety of the British king Cadwalla, and the insane apostasy of the English kings Osric and Eanfrid; for it has been generally agreed that the names of these apostates should be erased from the list of Christian kings and the year of their reign ignored.

He goes on to say that after good King Oswald's death in battle, so many people took dust from the ground where he had fallen that, "as the earth was gradually moved, a pit was left, in which a man could stand." No wonder—this dust had miraculous healing powers! Bede's writings, when combined with archaeological research, enable us to reconstruct many aspects of Anglo-Saxon British history in detail. On the other hand, the material remains are fragmentary and ambiguous.

For much of the period between the 5th and 9th centuries, Anglo-Saxon England was divided into seven kingdoms, which are known to historians as the "Heptarchy." Northumbria was the most northerly of these kingdoms, while the middle of England was the kingdom of Mercia. East Anglia, as its name suggests, was the land of the eastern Angles. Sussex and Essex, which have survived into recent times as county names, are the lands of the southern and eastern Saxons, while Wessex was the land of the western Saxons. In the southeast of England was Kent. The kings of these seven territories were chronically at war with one another, as each strove to become Bretwalda, the dominant king or "Britain-Ruler."

Religious division accompanied this political division. Christianity introduced from Scotland and Ireland differed in several ways from the Christianity brought from Rome. One of the great set pieces of Bede's *Ecclesiastical History* is his account of the Synod of Whitby, a 7th-century meeting that tried to reconcile these differences. Bede was not there himself (he was born just a few years after the synod) but he knew several monks who did attend; and historians think his account is fairly reliable. King Oswy of Northumbria oversaw the synod, which decided that the Roman way of selecting the date of Easter each year should prevail, and that Northumbrian monks should have the same tonsure (the distinctive monastic haircut) as those further south.

Whitby itself, scene of the synod, is one of the most attractive little coastal towns in the whole of Britain. Now a fishing village and vacation spot, it was historically a major monastic foundation of both monks and nuns. The splendid ruins of the abbey overlook the whole town in one direction, and the North Sea in another. Admittedly, they're the ruins of an abbey that was built centuries after the Synod, but still, the actual location is the same. It has a haunted aspect. A dramatic stone staircase leads you from the remains of the abbey down to the port itself.

The biggest and most visible Anglo-Saxon object in Britain is Offa's Dyke. Offa was king of Mercia from the mid-750s to 796 who built a continuous barrier on his western frontier, probably as a guard against Welsh raiders. It was a ditch or trench on the Welsh side, with the displaced earth thrown up into a rampart on the Mercian side. Its existence is testimony to the organizational powers of Mercian kings, who presumably used conscripted labor to get such a massive project finished. As two recent historians wrote:

> The dyke must have been a powerful ideological statement, inviting comparisons between Offa and Roman rulers of the past who had undertaken similarly grand construction projects—the Hadrianic and Antonine Walls being the most obvious examples.

Radiocarbon dating has found evidence that some parts of the dyke are earlier, so Offa may have completed a job already partly done by his predecessors. Crossing land most of which is still farmed, it fades from view in places, but is still distinct in others. The best place to visit it is at Knighton, where an Offa's Dyke visitor center explains its significance, and where well-preserved sections are visible. Since 1971, hikers have also been able to walk Offa's Dyke Path—a National Trail that runs for 177 miles along the Anglo-Welsh border.

In addition to earthworks, several English churches survive from the 7th, 8th, and 9th centuries. Probably the least altered is tiny St. Laurence's Church, at Bradford-on-Avon in Wiltshire. Only in the 19th century was its significance recognized, as one of very few 8th century buildings that had not been modified over the following generations. Equally well-kept is the chapel of St. Peter-on-the-Wall in Bradwell-on-Sea in Essex. Built even earlier, around 660, it recycled Roman bricks and cut stones. Standing half a mile from the nearest road, a simple barn-like box, its quiet, rural setting makes it magically evocative of antiquity. A third and much bigger example is All Saints Church in Brixworth, Northamptonshire. It too is largely unchanged since its construction in the 680s. Only the tower and spire are subsequent additions.

Let me just pause at this point to explain one of the traditions about place names in Britain, such as Bradford-on-Avon or Bradwell-on-Sea. There are several places called Bradford, so the addition of "on Avon" is a way of distinguishing which one is being discussed. The Avon is a river. Stoke-on-Trent and Newcastle-upon-Tyne are similar examples, identifying the rivers Trent and Tyne. Of course, in the days before there were railways or good roads, rivers were the principal means of transport, so they were the obvious items to mention in identifying a town.

Carved crosses from the Anglo-Saxon period are also widespread in England, though usually much worn by centuries of weathering. Probably the best is the 7th- or 8th-century Ruthwell Cross, now protected from the elements inside Ruthwell parish church, just north of the Scottish border. It was smashed by iconoclastic Presbyterians in the 1640s, but the fragments, lying around the graveyard, were reassembled by a 19th century vicar. An indoor apse was purpose-built for it in 1887. It is 18 feet high and includes elaborate carvings of Jesus, along with poetry in both Latin and runic. A similar cross at Bewcastle in Cumbria appears to come from the same era, and possibly even the same craftsmen. Unfortunately, its head is missing. It too has elaborate carvings, featuring vines and mythical beasts, birds and saints, and might once have been part of Jarrow Monastery, where the Venerable Bede lived and worked. A third Saxon cross the Easby Cross, is now kept in the Victoria and Albert Museum, in London.

In the 20th and 21st centuries, archaeologists have been excited by major Anglo-Saxon finds. The most spectacular was the Sutton Hoo ship burial in East Anglia, east of Ipswich. In 1937, the local landowner, a widow and spiritualist named Edith Pretty, thought she had seen a ghost from her upstairs window. Deciding to excavate the numerous oddly-shaped mounds on her property, and speculating that the ghost might be linked to them, she hired a self-taught archaeologist named Basil Brown. He uncovered a wonderful Anglo-Saxon ship burial. Mrs. Pretty's gardener and a local gamekeeper also joined in the painstaking work of uncovering the whole thing. When archaeologists from Cambridge University and the British Museum realized the significance of the discovery, they took over the work in 1939, amid squabbles and personality clashes. John Preston's 2007 novel *The Dig* uses the real names and creates a fine dramatization of these events. Before the excavations could be completed, World War II began, so the site was not fully explored until the 1960s.

The timbers of the Sutton Hoo ship had rotted away over the centuries but its impression, or "ghost," was clearly shown by the excavators. This had been a real seagoing ship, with places for 40 oarsmen and evidence of periodic repairs. Its benches and mast had been removed, and a central area enclosed to receive the body. The ship had then been dragged up out of the river, lowered into an excavated chamber, and, after the interment—probably of King Raedwald of East Anglia—a great mound heaped up over it. Luckily, earlier treasure hunters and grave robbers had failed to get at the heart of the burial.

Treasures from inside the ship, surrounding the body, came not just from East Anglia but from many parts of Britain and Europe; one item from as far away as Byzantium. They bear witness to the complex trade patterns of the 7th century, despite the political fragmentation of post-Roman Europe. A warrior helmet was perhaps the most impressive find. It has a full-face mask, highly decorated, cheek flaps, and a neck protector. The royal armories made a superb replica, and it exudes an ancient ferocity. Other objects found at the site include buckles, belts, clasps, dishes and spoons, and a decorated shield, with minutely detailed engraving and brightly colored enamels. A coroner's inquest awarded all the discoveries to Mrs. Pretty—in England, a coroner is an agent of the Crown. She was generous enough to donate them all to the nation.

There are 17 other mounds at Sutton Hoo, though most have eroded over the centuries, some to the point of near invisibility. Mound 2, also a ship mound, was restored to its probable original height and shape in 1992 as a way of testing erosion rates. In Mound 17, archaeologists found another undisturbed grave. This was a young man buried along with his horse and a cluster of personal items, including a hair comb made of bone. Most of the items from Sutton Hoo were carried off to the British Museum where they are still on display. A museum at Sutton Hoo itself contains excellent descriptions and photographs of the mounds, the history of the excavation, and high-quality replicas of the finds. This is the place to see them, on-site. In London, though well-cared-for, the originals feel out of context, and have to contend with the vestiges of other mighty cultures.

Sutton Hoo is a great story about uncovering buried treasure. Recent developments in metal detection have led to new discoveries. In the year 2009, for example, near the village of Hammerwich in Staffordshire, an Anglo-Saxon treasure hoard was discovered by Terry Herbert, a metal-detector enthusiast working in a recently ploughed field. He filled 244 bags with his finds before contacting the relevant authorities to announce this discovery. The farmer, Fred Johnson, then permitted qualified archaeologists to undertake a systematic survey and excavation of his field.

In all there are around 4,000 objects, making it the biggest hoard ever collected from one site. Most of the objects come from the 7th century and nearly all are military, including sword hilts, buckles, and knife handles, but they don't appear to be connected to a burial, and this is not a battlefield. It's almost as though their owner, worried for their safety, dug a hole for them, marked it, but was never able to return and recover his stash. Some of the garnets might have come from as far away as Sri Lanka! I saw some of the items Herbert had found, at the City of Birmingham Museum, mainly gold fragments, garnets, and broaches. What impressed me about them were their brightness—many are brilliantly enameled—and the extremely sophisticated and detailed decoration. Several of the items were shown under magnifying glasses, to give visitors the chance to see their full intricacy. Other parts of the horde are on display at Stoke-on-Trent, Tamworth, and with a touring exhibition.

In the 790s, Britain endured another round of invasions. This time, the intruders were from Scandinavia—the Vikings. They didn't have helmets with horns (that's a Victorian invention from the 1870s), but they were warlike and ruthless. The word "Viking" means "raiding," and is sometimes used as a verb, rather than as the name for a group of people. In British history, they are usually called "the Danes."

They had magnificent names. One of the first major Viking kings was Harald Fairhair. His son was Eric Bloodaxe. In the first paragraph of one of the Icelandic sagas, which are great sources for understanding Viking culture, we meet Ketil Flatnose, Eystein the Rattler, Thorfinn the Skullcleaver, Thorbjorg the Ship-Breasted, and Eijof the Foul. Viking names have two elements— one is nicknames like "skullcleaver" and "ship-breasted," while the other corresponds to the individual's father's name. Hence, the son of Erik the Red was Leif Eriksson, and his daughter was Freydis Eriksdottir.

The Vikings' first appearance in Britain was their attack on the island monastery at Lindisfarne, or Holy Island, off the northeastern coast. Here's how the *Anglo-Saxon Chronicle* describes what happened:

> AD. 793. This year came dreadful fore-warnings over the land of the Northumbrians, terrifying the people most woefully: there were immense sheets of light rushing through the air, and whirlwinds, and fiery dragons flying across the firmament. These tremendous tokens were soon followed by a great famine: and not long after, on the sixth day before the ides of January in the same year, the harrowing inroads of heathen men made lamentable havoc in the church of God in Holy-island, by rapine and slaughter.

It was the first of many ruthless attacks on eastern England. The raiders seized everything of value, killed the poor men, carried the women off into slavery, and took the richest men for ransom. The shock was profound.

After several centuries of relative peace, at least for the church, suddenly everything seemed vulnerable.

Lindisfarne, site of the attack, is today one of the most enchanting places in England. Just a few miles south of the Scottish border, it's only accessible when the tide is low. The Venerable Bede described it like this: "As the tide ebbs and flows, this place is surrounded by sea twice a day like an island, and twice a day the sand dries and joins it to the mainland." Today, you must follow a winding road to get to the causeway, read the tide tables carefully, and drive slowly across to the island, after which you need to keep in mind throughout your visit just how much time is left before the waters close over the road. Otherwise you'll be stuck.

As with most English monasteries, the site of the Viking raid is now just a ruin, albeit a very picturesque one. It had been founded by Saint Aidan, an Irish Christian and evangelist, in the 630s, 150 years earlier. There's now a modern statue of him, on site, necessarily speculative because we have no idea what he actually looked like. The monastery had also been the home of Saint Cuthbert. Alcuin of York, a learned monk who lived nearby, wrote:

> Lo it is nearly 350 years that we and our fathers have inhabited this most lovely land, and never before has such terror appeared in Britain as we have now suffered from a pagan race, nor was it thought that such an inroad from the sea could be made. Behold the church of St. Cuthbert spattered with the blood of the priests of God, despoiled of all its ornaments; a place more venerable than all in Britain is given as a prey to pagan peoples.

A biography of Cuthbert, written at Lindisfarne, is the oldest work of history in England to have survived. The Vikings must have been delighted to find such a rich target so close to the shore, undefended.

Lindisfarne is also the site of a superb castle on a vertical rock that dominates the island. Built in the 1500s because of the chronic problem of Scottish raids, it was allowed to fall into ruin, but was restored and rebuilt in the early 20th century by the architect Edwin Lutyens. It's not big inside, especially by comparison with nearby Bamburgh, but there can't be more than a dozen buildings in the world that provoke such an instant emotional reaction. It's England's answer to Mont St. Michel in France, another great building on top of a striking, isolated rock.

After the initial raid on Lindisfarne, Viking depredations became a regular fact of life in the early 800s, especially along the East coast of England. The Vikings were still pagans; their three main gods were Odin, Thor, and Frey, after whom we name Wednesday, Thursday, and Friday. Odin was the one-eyed god of wisdom and guile. Thor was the god of thunder and war. Frey was the god of fertility, farming, and sex. Viking ships were the best in the world at that time, combining the capacity to sail long distances out of sight of land, with a shallow draft that enabled them to sail far up England's rivers and attack inland communities. A combination of sails and oars also made them maneuverable in a wide variety of conditions. The Norwegian counterpart of Sutton Hoo is the Gokstad Ship, discovered near Oslo in 1880. A replica built in 1893, the *Viking*, made an Atlantic crossing, which confirmed the plausibility of the story that Leif Eriksson had been the first European to visit the Americas around the year 1000.

For the first time in 865, an actual Viking army landed in East Anglia, intent not just on raiding but on conquering Anglo-Saxon Britain. It was led by the unforgettably named Ivar the Boneless, and is remembered in English history as the Great Heathen Army. It marched north, sacked Whitby, captured York, and seemed all set to dominate the whole of Britain. Opposition came from the kings of Wessex, Aethelred, and then his brother Alfred the Great, who ruled from 871 until 899. Alfred is the only English king ever to be called "the great." His achievement was to prevent Viking conquest of the whole country. At one point, he was forced into hiding in the marshlands of Athelney, Somerset, where a monument to him still stands. Seeking shelter with an old peasant woman, according to legend, she asked him to keep an eye on the cakes she was baking. Preoccupied by his precarious military situation, he forgot, the cakes got burned, and the woman berated him, only to discover moments later that she was boxing the ears of her king.

Archaeological work at Athelney has shown that this was the site of an Iron Age fort, that Athelney was an island often surrounded by flooded fields, and that a causeway led from it to nearby East Lyng. Signs of metalworking in the area also suggest that Alfred and his followers cast weapons there in preparation for their counterattack on the Vikings.

Another legend has Alfred cleverly disguised as a minstrel, spying on the Viking camp. Whatever the merits of the legend, it is true that his army won a decisive victory against the Viking general, Guthrum, at Edington 878. Guthrum was forced to become a Christian, with Alfred acting as his godfather. England was partitioned into a Viking-dominated east, known as the "Danelaw," and an Anglo-Saxon-dominated west under Alfred. G. K. Chesterton's epic poem, *The Ballad of the White Horse* tells the whole story in verse, as a triumph of Christianity over paganism.

The traditional site of the battle is Egbert's Stone, an unobtrusive marker. At Stourhead nearby, however, commanding the surrounding country, is King Alfred's Tower, a striking triangular tower completed in 1772 to celebrate England's victory over France in the Seven Years' War—or, as Americans call it, the French and Indian War. It is 160 feet high, and includes a statue of King Alfred and an inscription that reads:

> ALFRED THE GREAT. AD 879 on this Summit Erected his Standard Against Danish Invaders. To him, We owe The Origin of Juries, The Establishment of a Militia, The Creation of a Naval Force. ALFRED, the Light of a Benighted Age, Was a Philosopher and a Christian, The Father of his People, The Founder of the English MONARCHY and LIBERTY.

There are also statues of Alfred in Wantage in Oxfordshire, Pewsey in Wiltshire, and Winchester, all from the late 19th and early 20th centuries.

In the centuries after Alfred's reign, the various populations of England gradually merged through coexistence, intermarriage, and trade. Anglo-Saxon and Viking artistic traditions also persisted and interacted with those of the Normans after 1066. Look at the church doorway of Kilpeck, in

Herefordshire near the Welsh border, built in about 1140. Norman themes predominate but there's an elaborate and playful set of Anglo-Saxon beasts and abstract patterns around the south door, including dragons swallowing their own tails.

One of the best archaeological finds from Viking England is a treasure hoard found in 1840 in Cuerdale, Lancashire. Workmen were strengthening the embankment on the River Ribble when they unearthed a box containing 88 lbs. of coins, bracelets, and decorated chains, mostly made of silver. Some of the coins were from the Danelaw, some from Wessex, and some from remote parts of Europe. The workmen were given one coin each, and the rest passed to the Crown. They are displayed partly in the British Museum and partly in the Ashmolean Museum in Oxford. No one knows who buried this treasure, or why, but a probable date seems to be around the year 910.

More recently, metal detector enthusiasts have been improving our understanding of the Vikings as well as the Anglo-Saxons. In 2007, for example, a metal detectorist named David Whelan and his son Andrew found a hoard of about 600 coins and other items near Harrogate in Yorkshire. They were enclosed in a decaying lead case, and stored inside a highly decorated silver and gold pot. Similarly, in 2011, a hobbyist named Darren Webster located the Silverdale Hoard, in Lancashire, with his metal detector. Both these hoards included items that appear to have been made nearby along with items from present-day Turkey and Uzbekistan, as well as many European centers.

The British Treasure Act of 1996 says that if you find anything over 300 years old you have to report it to the authorities, and that a coroner will then decide who gets it. Usually the landowner and finder share it, while museums compete to buy the finds. For example, the Harrogate Hoard was valued at over a million pounds and was purchased jointly by the British Museum and the York Museums Trust. That meant quite a payout for David and Andrew Whelan!

There is a love-hate relationship between the archaeologists and the metal detectorists. Any man with a metal detector who suddenly encounters a pot of gold is likely to see himself as the rightful possessor. Pots of gold in the ground, and sudden vaults from poverty to wealth, have long been staples of folklore and daydreams. Archaeologists, by contrast, want the metal detectorists to stop the instant they see the glint of ancient metal, to alert the authorities, and then to just go away. The BBC ran a comedy TV show, *Detectorists*, in 2014, making fun of hobbyists' delusions of grandeur. But the issues are serious; metal detectors are getting better all the time, and more treasure is being discovered. It is of course possible that much of it is not being reported.

Luckily, the 1996 Treasure Act does provide an incentive for amateurs and enthusiasts to report their finds—it guarantees an impartial valuation and opens the door to above-board purchases from institutions with a mission to preserve and curate Britain's past. And surely, on the balance, it's much better to find than not find these hoards, which have the collective effect of giving us a better understanding of material culture in Anglo-Saxon and Viking Britain.

5

BRITAIN'S MEDIEVAL CASTLES

This lecture focuses on medieval castles in Britain, built between 1066 and 1500 for military reasons. The lecture provides some background on castle design and then moves on to discuss specific castles, including:

- Caerphilly in Wales.

- The castles of Edward I.

- Four castles that are particularly interesting to visit, at Bamburgh, Dover, Warwick, and the Tower of London.

Note that while this lecture highlights many notable castles, Britain contains hundreds more in various states of repair.

Dover Castle

The Evolution of Castles

The Norman king William the Conqueror (r. 1066–1087) used castles from the outset to assert his authority and create strongpoints in his kingdom. The earliest were motte-and-bailey castles, in which a wooden keep was set up on a mound, or motte. An area around the motte, known as the bailey, would be fenced in with a stout palisade. The next stage in castle design was the square stone keep. Several built in the 1100s survive, including those at Dover, Orford, and the Tower of London.

The logical next step was to build an outer wall around the keep, making it more difficult for attackers even to approach it. This development is visible in many of the great fortifications of the 1200s. The Tower of London, for example, was made safer and stronger by having the keep enclosed by an outer wall during the reign of King Henry III. When a second wall was added by his son Edward I, it became stronger still.

The superiority of multiple defensive layers led to the development of concentric castles, designed from the outset to present attackers with a succession of obstacles to overcome. Concentric castles also included refinements such as towers bulging out from the line of the outer wall, so that attackers would never find shelter from defenders' fire. A notable concentric castle in Britain is Caerphilly in Wales. It was built not by the king but by an extremely powerful baron, Gilbert de Clare, struggling in the 1270s to assert his power against the Welsh rebel Llywelyn ap Gruffyd.

Caerphilly Castle

Edward I was England's preeminent castle builder. He consolidated his grip on Wales in the 1280s and 1290s by building four massive ones: Conwy, Caernarfon, Harlech, and Beaumaris. They were built for strength, to overawe Welsh onlookers, to assert Edward's claim to the throne, and to provide him with places to live safely and comfortably when he was in the area. His architect, James of Saint George, came from Savoy, the area of the Western Alps where France, Italy, and Switzerland meet. Edward honored him with high pay and generous estates.

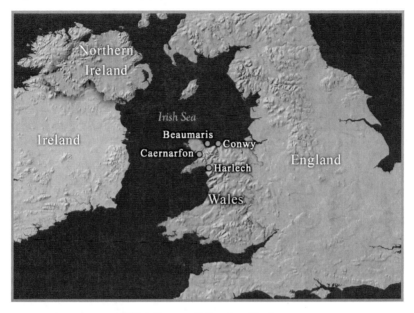

The State of Castles Today

Most of Britain's castles are ruins today, and for nearly three centuries, owners and visitors have enjoyed seeing them in that state. The romantic appeal of a ruined castle matches the romantic appeal of a ruined monastery. Some are ruins simply because no one looked after them after their original military functions ceased. Many more, however, are in ruins because they were deliberately wrecked, or slighted. This sometimes occurred in the reign of Henry VIII, the king who abolished private armies, but most of all at the end of the English Civil War.

The parliamentary armies of Thomas Fairfax and Oliver Cromwell devoted a lot of energy to besieging Royalist-held castles. They wanted to make sure, after the fighting ended, that they would never have to do so again. Slighting consisted of damaging them badly enough to make their restoration impossibly expensive, especially for Royalists who were forced to pay heavy fines for having been on the wrong side.

Castles that are not ruins today are well preserved either because they were converted into aristocratic dwellings or because regiments of the British army continued to use them as military bases. The Edinburgh and Dover castles, for example, were working military bases until the 1920s and 1950s respectively, before being turned into visitor attractions. Warwick, Bamburgh, and Cardiff were turned from ruins into residences by wealthy families, inspired by the idea of living in medieval surroundings.

Four Notable Castles

This lecture closes by suggesting four castles that are particularly fascinating to visit: Bamburgh in the north, Dover in the south, Warwick in the Midlands, and the Tower of London.

Bamburgh is just a few miles south of the Scottish border. Perched on high ground overlooking the North Sea, it has a magnificently romantic profile. Founded by the Normans on the site of a much older fort, it was besieged

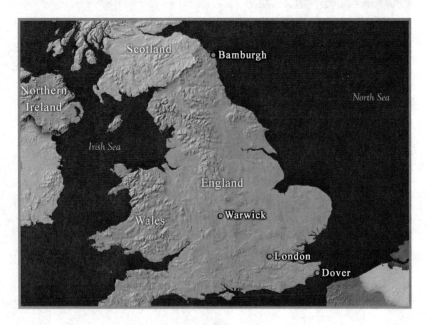

by King William II in 1095 when its owner, Robert de Mowbray, rebelled. The castle was bought by businessman William Armstrong in 1894 and restored to more than its former glory.

One of the biggest castles in Britain is at Dover, and it is also one of the best to visit. It sits atop the white cliffs where the English Channel is at its narrowest, and it looks superb if you're approaching England on a cross-channel ferry from France. Every generation has added new elements to Dover Castle, but the boldest and strongest medieval parts still stand out clearly.

Warwick Castle is another crowd pleaser. Right in the heart of the kingdom, it looks like a child's drawing of a medieval castle. Like so many others, it started as an ancient defensive site on which a Norman motte-and-bailey castle was built by William the Conqueror. Warwick has an immense collection of arms and armor.

Warwick Castle

Finally, the Tower of London the single most popular tourist attraction in the whole of Britain. Be prepared for the crowds, but go anyway. If you plan ahead, you can book tickets to the ceremony of the keys, which officially closes the tower every evening. Over time, the tower has served as a royal residence, a safe house for the crown jewels, a mint, and a prison. Now, it is largely a tourist attraction, but a splendid one.

Suggested Reading

Cormack, *Castles of Britain*.

Jones, *Tower*.

Morris, *Castle*.

Questions to Consider

1. How did medieval commanders prepare to resist a siege? What factors led to their success or failure?

2. What does the survival of so many castles tell us about British historical self-awareness? Did they sometimes survive simply because they were too sturdy to be demolished?

5

BRITAIN'S MEDIEVAL CASTLES

P rehistoric, Roman, and Anglo-Saxon vestiges are widespread in Britain, but you need to know a lot of history, and something about archaeology, to work out what's what. It gets much easier after the Norman invasion of 1066, because there are so many big, impressive medieval buildings in Britain. The castles and the cathedrals are the most striking of all, bearing witness to the era's two great obsessions: war and Christianity.

There are hundreds of buildings in Britain whose names include the word "castle." But beware of the word—some are earthworks, like Maiden Castle in Dorset, with nothing visible above ground level. Others are 19th century sham castles, like Riber Castle in Derbyshire, which was built in 1862 by industrialist John Smedley. Smedley liked the idea of living in a medieval castle and so he had one built to order, though the local people, who called it "Smedley's folly," were evidently unimpressed. Castle Drogo in Devonshire looks even older but is actually even younger, started in 1910 and not finished until about 1930. Eilean Donan in Scotland, which could compete strongly for the prize of most scenically impressive castle in the world, was built around a few ancient fragments in the 1920s and early 1930s. These examples remind us that for the last 200 years at least, castles have stimulated the romantic imagination and tempted generations of rich men to build their own. In this lecture, however, I want to concentrate on actual medieval castles, built between 1066 and 1500 for military, not scenic, reasons.

William the Conqueror used castles right from the outset to assert his authority and create strongpoints in his new kingdom. The earliest were motte-and-bailey castles, in which a wooden keep, or stronghold, was set up on a mound, or motte, sometimes man-made. An area around the motte, known as the bailey, would be fenced in with a stout palisade and contain barracks, stables, a well, a chapel, storehouses, and the other necessities of a garrison. Ideally, a ditch or moat outside the palisade would create added difficulties for potential attackers. No such wooden castles survive, but Britain still has several in which the original wooden keep was later replaced by a stone keep. At Cardiff Castle, for example, in the grounds of a much later building, stands the circular motte with a strong stone tower, or "shell keep," on top.

The next stage in castle design was the square stone keep. Several built in the 1100s survive, including those at Dover, Orford, and the Tower of London. The Tower, begun in 1070, is almost a cube: 107 by 118 feet at the base, and 90 feet tall. As the historian Marc Morris says: "Construction on this scale had not been witnessed in Britain since the time of the Romans. The Normans were well aware of this, and seem to have been deliberately styling themselves as new Romans, come a-conquering in imperial style." The walls of these stone towers are often 10 feet thick, meaning that they feel oddly smaller inside than they look from outside. The benefit, of course, was that no siege engine could knock down a structure so immensely strong. The armies of the day lacked explosives to destroy them. Only by tunneling beneath was it sometimes possible to provoke a cave-in that might partially destroy such a keep.

The logical next step was to build an outer wall, or curtain wall, around the keep, making it all the more difficult for attackers even to approach it. This development is visible in many of the great fortifications of the 1200s. The Tower of London, for example, was made safer and stronger by having the keep enclosed by an outer wall during the reign of King Henry III. When a second wall outside that one was added by his son Edward I, it became stronger still. The Tower is one of many places where you can see the development of these stages and where, in general, the outer layers are more recent than the inner.

The superiority of multiple defensive layers led to the development of concentric castles, designed from the outset to present attackers with a succession of obstacles to overcome, and making it likely that any who broke through the first ring would be subjected to devastating fire from the second. Concentric castles also included refinements, such as towers bulging out from the line of the curtain wall, so that attackers would never find shelter from defenders' fire.

Probably the greatest concentric castle in Britain is Caerphilly, in Wales. It was built not by the king but by an extremely powerful baron, Gilbert de Clare, struggling in the 1270s to assert his power against the Welsh rebel Llywelyn ap Gruffyd. Not only does it have a concentric design, it's further secured by sitting in the midst of an artificial lake, making it difficult even to approach. A causeway across one of the two dams that created the lake could be heavily-defended. By the time it was finished, however, Wales lay securely in English hands, so the castle was never put to the test. A distinctive aspect of Caerphilly is that one of its towers stands at a crooked angle, far off the vertical. It was probably blown up during the English Civil War, but we have no documentation to prove it. In any case, Caerphilly, just a few miles north of Cardiff, is superb. The historian Patrick Cormack describes it as "quite simply one of the greatest buildings of the Middle Ages, equal in importance to any of Britain's major cathedrals. There never was a more triumphant assertion of power and magnificence by any noble subject."

Refinements of various kinds are also apparent in concentric castle designs. Because the gatehouse was a potential weak point, with wooden gates more vulnerable to battering rams than walls, they might be protected by being approached over a drawbridge that could be hoisted in times of danger. Similarly, a portcullis, a thick iron-banded gate that descended from above, added strength to gateways. "Murder holes" overhead, through which hot liquids, rocks, and fire could be thrown down on attackers, are common in these gatehouses, though I've never found a reference to boiling oil being used, except in fiction

Edward I was England's castle-builder par excellence. He consolidated his grip on Wales in the 1280s and 1290s by building four massive ones: Conwy, Caernarfon, Harlech, and Beaumaris. They were built for strength, to overawe Welsh onlookers, to assert Edward's claim to the throne, and to provide him with places to live safely and comfortably when he was in the area. His architect, James of Saint George, came from Savoy, the area of the western Alps where France, Italy, and Switzerland meet. Edward honored him with high pay and generous estates. Caernarfon's walls are made of different-colored banded stones. This is an echo of the walls of Constantinople, the Byzantine capital, which Edward had visited when he went on crusade. He sited Caernarfon at the place where the Romans had established their local headquarters, Segontium. In both these ways, Edward was not merely building a stronghold: he was also implying a continuity between the old Roman overlords and himself as the new one.

In the days when castles were useful to the degree they could be defended, it's worth asking how successful they were in resisting sieges and safeguarding their defenders. The answer is that they worked well so long as the defenders were resolute and well-led, and so long as they had supplies of food and fresh water. Poor leadership, famine, epidemics, and internal treason could all provoke failure among defenders. Harlech, for example, garrisoned by only 37 men, withstood an entire Welsh army besieging it in 1294. Harlech also held out for seven years in the 1460s as a stronghold for the Lancastrian side in the Wars of the Roses, though admittedly it wasn't under continuous threat. When you visit Harlech today, you find it about a mile inland, with the sea visible in the middle-distance across an open plain. When it was built, by contrast, the castle was actually on the coast, and could be resupplied by sea.

Most of Britain's castles are ruins today, and for nearly three centuries owners and visitors have enjoyed seeing them in that state. The romantic appeal of a ruined castle matches the romantic appeal of a ruined monastery. Some are ruins simply because no one looked after them after their original military functions ceased. Many more, however, are in ruins because they were deliberately wrecked, or "slighted," sometimes in the reign of Henry VIII—the king who abolished private armies—but most of all at the end of the Civil War in the 1640s. The parliamentary armies of Thomas Fairfax and Oliver Cromwell devoted a lot of energy to besieging Royalist-held castles, and wanted to make sure, after the fighting ended, that they would never have to do so again. Slighting consisted of damaging them badly enough to make their restoration impossibly expensive, especially for Royalists who were forced to pay heavy fines for having been on the wrong side.

Castles that are not ruins today are well preserved either because they were converted into aristocratic dwellings, or because regiments of the British army continued to use them as military bases. Edinburgh and Dover Castles, for example, were working military bases until the 1920s and 1950s respectively, before being turned into full-time visitor attractions. In fact, part of Edinburgh is still in use by the army and off limits to visitors. Warwick, Bamburgh, and Cardiff were turned from ruins into residences by wealthy families, inspired by the idea of living in medieval surroundings.

It would be easy to do a dozen lectures on Britain's castles, and I will return to many important castles, such as Conwy and Edinburgh, when we tour the various regions of Britain. For the rest of today, however, let me suggest four castles that are particularly fascinating to visit: Bamburgh in the North, Dover in the South, Warwick in the Midlands, and finally the most famous of the lot, the Tower of London.

First, Bamburgh is phenomenal. Just a few miles south of the Scottish border, and perched on high ground overlooking the North Sea, it has a magnificently romantic profile. Founded by the Normans on the site of a much older fort, it was besieged by King William II in 1095 when its owner, Robert de Mowbray, rebelled. Robert was captured, but his doughty wife refused to surrender, and the royal army could not break down the defenses. The king finally told her that Robert would have his eyes torn out if she did not surrender, at which point she relented. After many years of resisting Scottish raids, and enduring another siege during the Wars of the Roses, Bamburgh fell into decay. Partially restored as an asylum, a girls' school, and hostel for shipwrecked sailors, the castle was bought by William Armstrong in 1894 and restored to more than its former glory. Armstrong was an engineer and munitions manufacturer, one of Britain's most successful businessmen in the late 19th century, whose other house, Cragside, was the first dwelling in the world to be lighted by hydroelectric power.

Armstrong created a medieval fantasy world inside Bamburgh. The great hall features a hammer-beam roof. Life-size portraits and ancient weapons decorate the high walls above the ground-level wooden paneling. High windows admit light through the immensely thick outer walls. Porcelain vases and great globes complete the decoration—another barrel-vaulted room is given over entirely to a collection of arms and armor. The succeeding rooms are decorated with comparable lavishness. On the battlements, great old cannons face out toward the North Sea below. Armstrong died before the renovation could be completed, but his successors held onto the castle right up to the present. In one of the annexes stands a museum of the weapons he designed and built.

One of the biggest castles in Britain is at Dover, and it is also one of the best to visit. It sits atop the white cliffs where the English Channel is at its narrowest, and looks superb if you're approaching England on a cross-channel ferry from France. The town of Dover is unremarkable, but take the steep hill that zig-zags out of town and you'll soon be on the clifftops. Every generation has added new elements to Dover Castle, but the boldest and strongest medieval parts still stand out clearly.

The high, central stone keep, the "Great Tower," comes from the reign of Henry II and was built in the 1180s. It is now displayed, by its owners, English Heritage, as if for a king's visit. Inside, on the ground floor, the medieval kitchens are littered with pots, jars, trestle tables and vats suitable to the era. Upstairs in the royal reception rooms are banquet tables laid out for the king and his men, whose banners are displayed on the walls. Above that is the throne room, a great stone chamber adorned in rich red fabric as it might have looked when the king held court there. Beside it is the king's private chapel, elaborately decorated and with its own miniature stained-glass window.

The walls are 20 feet thick in places, several "mural rooms" are contained within the walls, and two spiral staircases run from top to bottom of the tower. A 300 foot well was sunk in the 1180s, which confirms that the castle was designed to withstand siege if necessary. In the event, it was necessary. In 1216, the rebellious English nobles, who had just forced King John to sign Magna Carta, invited Prince Louis of France to become their king. He quickly seized most of the southern towns and besieged Dover Castle. His men undermined one of the great stone gatehouses, which crashed to the ground, but the defenders were able to plug the breach with heavy beams stripped from inside the keep.

These defenders, led by a resolute Hubert de Bergh and 140 knights, were well-supplied. Louis's siege engines flung rocks and fireballs against the keep but couldn't make even a dent in such thick walls. In the end, after three months' fruitless fighting, Louis was forced to call a truce, and the besieged garrison survived. Louis tried again the following year, this time with a great trebuchet named Malvoisine, but still could not break down the walls. Harassed by English guerrillas outside the castle, his siege failed again after only 10 days.

At nearby Rochester Castle, the previous year, King John had been the attacker and one of the rebels its defender. The outcome was the same: the attacker couldn't get in. The closest King John came was when his men tunneled under one of the towers, keeping up the roof of his tunnels with great wooden props. They then lit a fire, using the fat from 40 pigs to make it burn hot, destroy the props, and cause the castle to cave in. Down came the tower, sure enough, but that wasn't enough to get John's army inside the keep. The defenders retreated behind a stout dividing wall and carried on fighting. Only when they were starving, after two more months, did they finally give up.

Since we're on the subject, let me say a word about the siege engines used to attack castles. Trebuchets like Malvoisine have a great wooden arm, spring loaded, and attached to a sling. When properly primed, it can fling a rock or a ball of burning material a couple of hundred yards, with a maximum speed of 150 miles per hour. The ballista is a giant crossbow, while the mangonel is a huge catapult. Siege towers are wooden structures on wheels, designed to be rolled up to the enemy battlements, and from which attackers can jump onto the walls or fire arrows from just above. Battering rams, sometimes roofed over for their users' protection, are designed to break down gateways. All were tried until the arrival in western Europe of gunpowder in the early 1300s, after which siege cannons began to displace them.

The two elements older than the keep at Dover are the Anglo-Saxon church, and right beside it, the Roman-era lighthouse. The maze of other fortifications all around you mark modifications made to Dover Castle through the centuries as offensive weapons became more powerful and the defenders were forced to adapt. These later additions include 17th-century star-shaped abutments and massive earthworks from the First World War era to absorb the impact of incoming naval shells.

Beneath the castle there's a honeycomb of passages and chambers, which have also done different duties through the ages. At one point, they were a prison for French soldiers and sailors captured during the Napoleonic Wars. Later they became a wartime hospital, where underground operating rooms provided safety against potential aerial attack. Dover's most critical moment in modern times came in May 1940, when the Nazi blitzkrieg had forced the British army in France into a headlong retreat to Dunkirk. From these tunnels under Dover castle, Admiral Bertram Ramsay masterminded their evacuation. There is a statue of him on site.

His command post can still be seen, stark and businesslike. The operation involved thousands of volunteers, private boat owners who crossed the channel at great risk to their lives, to help get stranded soldiers off the beaches of France and onto deep-draft vessels offshore. The unexpected success of this venture, rescuing 330,000 men, led to exaggerated British claims of victory. That in turn prompted the new prime minister, Winston Churchill, to issue in Parliament the dry reminder: "Wars are not won by evacuations."

The last use of Dover's tunnels, before becoming a visitor attraction, was as one of 12 potential seats of government in the event of a nuclear war. Filled with provisions after the Cuba Missile Crisis of 1962, the tunnels were finally decommissioned in the mid 1980s.

Warwick Castle is another great crowd pleaser. Right in the heart of the kingdom, it looks like a child's drawing of a medieval castle. Like so many others, it started as an ancient defensive site, on which a Norman motte and bailey castle was built by William the Conqueror. The motte is now called Ethelfleda's Mound. Extensive fortifications were added in the 1300s and 1400s. There's a great high route around the walls and battlements, whose highest point, Guy's Tower, is vertigo-inducing. You can look through the murder holes over the gateway, next to the workings of the portcullis, and you can visit the dungeons where unfortunate prisoners languished. Warwick was held by a Parliamentarian loyalist in the Civil War and successfully withstood a Royalist siege. After the Restoration, it was turned into a stately home and was never subsequently put to military uses.

Warwick has an immense collection of arms and armor. Last time I was there, an eloquent guide explained that the most elaborately worked suits of armor were worn only on ceremonial occasions rather than for battle. He also distinguished the different ways in which the many weapons on display were supposed to be used. They included various hacking, chopping, and spearing motions—all lethal. The best items on display are a suit of horse armor, and the armor worn on ceremonial occasions by a teenage boy, possibly the young Prince who later became King Charles II.

Warwick, still in private hands rather than being run by the National Trust or English Heritage, has not kept itself immune from commercialization. There are wax figures of famous residents and visitors, provided by Madame Tussauds. Lusty wenches in colored tents hawk ale, tell bawdy tales, and sell tickets to the jousts that are held on summer afternoons. Demonic laughter and shrieks of horror issue from the dungeons. A bird of prey show has eagles and condors swooping overhead to astonish the children. There's more than a hint of Disney about the presentation, especially during the school holidays. Whether that's a good or a bad thing is a matter of taste. I've been there often with groups of American teenagers, nearly all of whom have lapped it up enthusiastically and uncritically, which confirms their suspicion that I might be a bit stuffy! I must also speak up in favor of the great trebuchet, which is demonstrated every day in summer.

Moving south, let's return to the Tower of London. Great black ravens hop about the battlements and lawns at the Tower. According to tradition, if they ever leave, the kingdom will fall. Several million visitors each year make the Tower the single most popular tourist attraction in the whole of Britain. Be prepared for the crowds, but go anyway. If you've thought far enough ahead, you can book tickets to the ceremony of the keys, which officially closes the tower every evening at 10:00. At the ceremony, one of the red-garbed beefeaters advances, accompanied by soldiers. A sentry, also in red dress uniform, shouts: "Halt, who comes there?" The beefeater, or yeoman warder, replies, "The keys." "Whose keys?" "Queen Elizabeth's keys." "Pass then, all's well."

A full history of the Tower could constitute a pretty good history of England itself over the last millennium, with an emphasis on its more violent elements. It was a royal residence until the 1600s, often an arsenal, a mint where the national coinage was made, a safe-house for the storage of the crown jewels, a zoo (the "Royal Menagerie"), but above all, a prison. Most of London's Jews were imprisoned there in 1278 on trumped-up charges of degrading the currency. Edward I then expelled the whole Jewish community from England in 1290.

A crisis came during the Peasants' Revolt of 1381, menacing the young king Richard II. A great mob surged into the Tower, stole as many of the jewels as they could find, seized Simon Sudbury, the Archbishop of Canterbury, who had taken shelter in the chapel, and chopped off his head. Here at the Tower were killed the two young Princes in the Tower—Edward V and his brother Richard, Duke of York—by King Richard III, in 1483. See Shakespeare's *Richard III* for a dramatic reenactment, but don't forget the offsetting claims of Richard's champions, who say he didn't do it.

Here too were imprisoned and killed King Henry VI, and two of Henry VIII's wives, Anne Boleyn and Catherine Howard. Also, Henry VIII's former minister Thomas More, an event superbly fictionalized in *Wolf Hall* by Hilary Mantel. Also, Lady Jane Grey, only 17 years old, who briefly asserted a claim to the throne in 1553 before being ousted by Mary I. Also, Sir Walter Raleigh, who spent long enough in prison between arrest and execution to be able to write a history of the world. There is some elaborate graffiti, much of it 3- and 400 years old, on the walls of the old prison chambers, now carefully preserved. Sixty people are buried in the grounds of St. Peter ad Vincula, the church inside the Tower grounds. Fifty-one of them were beheaded. On a brighter note, some of the Tower's prisoners went on to successful later lives. Elizabeth I is one notable example.

Visitors have been coming to the Tower since the mid 1500s. By now it's almost entirely a tourist attraction. There's a lot to see: first of all, the buildings themselves, but also exhibits on the Tower's history, the unequalled armory, and the splendidly attired beefeaters—all of them veterans of the British military with at least 22 years' service and a good conduct medal. Above all other attractions rank the Crown Jewels, 141 crowns, maces, scepters, orbs, coronets, and other jeweled objects still used in royal ceremonies such as the coronation and the annual state opening of Parliament. One of them, the Sword of Mercy, was made in 1626 for the coronation of King Charles I and has been used at every coronation since then. Visitors are conveyed by a moving walkway deep in the vaults to view these precious items; the surroundings immediately emphasize their rarity, value, and symbolic significance to the nation.

In this lecture, I have mentioned just a few of the best castles in Britain, but I want to emphasize that there are hundreds more, some still in good condition, others in fragments and ruins. Around most of them cluster legends, and haunting tales of the knights who died defending them, along with true stories of bravery, treachery, and hardship. They are awe-inspiring, not least because of the scale they achieved in an age when most buildings were low wooden shacks or wattle-and-daub huts. Their high watchtowers can still induce vertigo, even though we're accustomed to multistory buildings. How much more impressive they must have seemed to the soldiers who manned them, and how much more daunting to the men who were ordered to attack them! Along with the cathedrals, to which we will turn next, they are the most distinctive and instructive relics of medieval Britain.

6

BRITAIN'S MEDIEVAL CATHEDRALS

Britain's 26 medieval cathedrals are among its most famous buildings. Some are over 1,000 years old and others are approaching that milestone. Elegant, majestic, and massive, they bear witness to their founders' determination to build something that would last for generations. This lecture provides background on cathedrals in general and highlights several of them in particular, including.

- Provincial cathedrals at Durham, Wells, and Llandaff.

- Westminster Abbey.

- Notable cathedrals at Canterbury, Lichfield, and Wells.

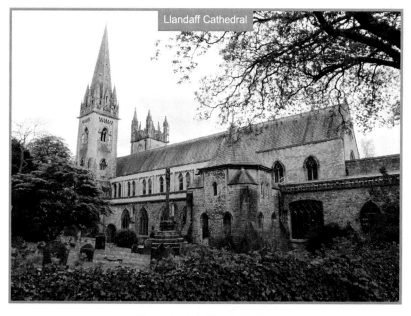

Llandaff Cathedral

Provincial Cathedrals

Note that the most popular cathedrals—such as Westminster Abbey, York Minster, and Canterbury Cathedral—are hard to visit except as part of a crowd. If you want a less-crowded visit, this lecture recommends the provincial cathedrals, which can still be seen in quietness and solemnity.

In particular, at Durham, Wells, Lichfield, and Llandaff, relative quiet still reigns at most times of the year. Around each of these provincial cathedrals stands a cluster of almshouses and old administrative buildings, set in beautifully kept grounds.

Background on Cathedrals

Cathedrals stand at the center of dioceses, the administrative districts of the Church of England. Each diocese has a bishop. Canterbury and York, the most senior, have archbishops. A *cathedra* is a bishop's throne. The dean is the clergyman who takes care of the daily and weekly services at the cathedral itself, and is usually assisted by a crowd of subordinate clergy. The bishop, by contrast, has responsibility for all the churches and clergy in the diocese.

The English cathedrals have a superb musical tradition, and to many of them are attached choir schools where young boys and girls with treble voices sing the liturgy every day. The choir schools have preserved distinctive ways of singing religious music.

Styles of Cathedrals

The earliest medieval cathedrals were built in the Norman or Romanesque style, with heavy columns supporting great rounded arches. They generate a feeling of dark, massive solemnity. Durham Cathedral in northeast England is perhaps the best example of the Norman style in Britain.

Durham Cathedral

In the 12th century, the gothic style began to displace Romanesque. Architects accepted the challenge of creating a sense of vertical soaring, with spaces much higher than they were wide, leading the eye up to remote

vaulted ceilings and pointed arches. The most distinctive features of gothic cathedrals are wide, bright windows with elaborate tracery, brilliantly colored stained glass, and flying buttresses, spires, and pinnacles.

Unfortunately, hardly any of the medieval stained glass remains. Even where it does, as at York, it has faded from its former glory. The best and most brilliant stained glass in English cathedrals today is mainly Victorian, from the mid- and late 19th century.

Notable Cathedrals

This lecture closes by looking at several notable cathedrals, starting with Westminster Abbey, which is right across the road from the Houses of Parliament in London. Every monarch has been crowned there since 1066, and it has also served of the site of numerous royal weddings and burials.

About 60 miles southeast of London is the cathedral city of Canterbury, the seat of the archbishop. Canterbury Cathedral achieved notoriety in the year 1170 when Archbishop Thomas Becket was murdered there. Three

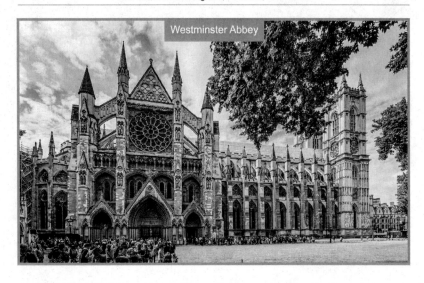

Westminster Abbey

years later, Pope Alexander III named Becket a saint, and the scene of his martyrdom became one of the great pilgrimages of Europe.

Lichfield Cathedral

In Staffordshire, there is a lovely gothic cathedral in the city of Lichfield. It's a distinctive structure, as it is the only medieval cathedral with three spires. Building at Lichfield began in 1195 on the site of an older cathedral. It took about 135 years to complete, with stylistic adjustments along the way. It was damaged by war in the 1640s but restored in the 19th century.

In the county of Somerset in southwest England is the city of Wells, featuring the Wells Cathedral. The structure is from the late 12th and early 13th centuries, but many of the details come from each of the subsequent centuries. Notable at this site are the structure's strainer arches, which were installed in the late 1300s because pillars were sinking under the weight of the tower above them.

If the strainer arches make Wells distinctive, a 20th-century statue of Jesus has the same effect at Llandaff, the cathedral for the Welsh city of Cardiff. Built in the 1100s, Llandaff Cathedral has sustained repeated severe damage, including from the German air force in World War II. After the German air raid, the roof was rebuilt. Jacob Epstein, a prominent sculptor, was commissioned to make the 16-foot rendering of Jesus.

Suggested Reading

Jenkins, *England's Cathedrals*.

Johnson, *Cathedrals of England, Scotland, and Wales*.

Suggested Activities

1. Compare pictures of the towers and spires of any five of the cathedrals. Though they are superficially similar, they become increasingly varied and inventive the more closely you look.

2. In each of the cathedrals you visit, try to find the names of the men and women whose bequests made the building and its adornment possible. What were their motives?

6

BRITAIN'S MEDIEVAL CATHEDRALS

Britain's 26 medieval cathedrals are among its most famous buildings. Many are approaching, or have celebrated, their 1,000 birthdays. Elegant, majestic, and massive, they bear witness to their founders' determination to build something that would last for generations. Even today they shame nearly every other building around them. Think how much more spectacular they must have been in an age when most people lived and died in thatched huts or squat stone cottages.

Something strange has happened to the cathedrals over the last century. They have become less and less places of worship, more and more tourist venues. The most popular, including Westminster Abbey, York Minster, and Canterbury Cathedral, are emptiest during the religious services that were the rationale for their creation. The advantage of this change in fortune is that they will survive—visitors' money pours in, enabling their caretakers to repair the roof, shore up sagging beams, and repoint the stonework. Their poor country cousins, England's thousands of medieval parish churches, are in far greater danger of neglect and decay because they are so numerous and so needy.

The downside of the famous cathedrals' popularity is that they are now hard to visit except as part of a crowd, especially during the summer, when immense numbers of visitors from all over the world surge through by the thousands. More than a million people visit Westminster Abbey every year. If you can possibly do so, visit a few of the provincial cathedrals, which still tower over their surroundings as they did centuries ago, and which can still be seen in quietness and solemnity. Among my favorites are Durham, Litchfield, Wells, and Llandaff, where relative quiet still reigns at most times of the year. Around each of these provincial cathedrals stands a cluster of almshouses and old administrative buildings, set in beautifully kept grounds that are known collectively as "the close."

America is proud of the First Amendment that separates church and state. Most Britons for centuries, by contrast, assumed the rightness of church-state unification. The Church of England, or C of E, has sordid origins in the divorce politics of Henry VIII and Catherine of Aragon, and has been trying to make up for it ever since. Anglicans speak of "the beauty of holiness," the distinctive mood, mixing faith and aesthetics, that the cathedrals generate. Anthony Trollope uses the idea brilliantly in his series of novels *The Barchester Chronicles*, about the lives and tribulations of Victorian-era clergymen. In the first book of the series, *The Warden*, about a decent man who profits from a corrupt institution under threat of radical reform, he wrote:

> Who would not feel charity for a prebendary when walking the quiet length of that long aisle at Winchester, looking at those decent houses, that trim grass-plat, and feeling, as one must, the solemn, orderly comfort of the spot! Who could be hard upon a dean while wandering round the sweet close of Hereford, and owning that in that precinct, tone and colour, design and form, solemn tower and storied window are all in unison, and all perfect! Who could lie basking in the cloisters of Salisbury and gaze on Jewel's library and that unequalled spire, without feeling that bishops should sometimes be rich!

As always with Trollope there's a mischievous gleam in his eye; he knows how to say one thing while implying its opposite, and the book's dramatic tension comes from his placing the morally justified, yet joyless characters against the morally indefensible, yet lovable traditionalists.

Cathedrals stand at the center of dioceses, the administrative districts of the Church of England. Each diocese has a bishop—Canterbury and York, the most senior, have archbishops. A *cathedra* is a bishop's throne. The dean is the clergyman who takes care of the daily and weekly services at the cathedral itself, and is usually assisted by a crowd of subordinate clergy. The bishop, by contrast, has responsibility for all the churches, and all the clergy, in the diocese, and spends much of his time traveling among them. Until quite recently bishops also held seats in the House of Lords.

The English cathedrals have a superb musical tradition, and to many of them are attached choir schools where young boys and girls with treble voices sing the liturgy every day. The choir schools have preserved distinctive ways of singing the communion service every Sunday, Evensong late each afternoon, and a repertoire of chanted psalms, hymns, and anthems. Just as it's easy to think of cathedrals more as works of art than as houses of prayer, so it's easy to think of their choirs as the providers of concerts rather than worship. The Church of England is at its best architecturally and musically; its theology and its sermons are far less impressive. These are the pros and cons of having a state church.

The earliest medieval cathedrals were built in the Norman or Romanesque style, with heavy columns supporting great rounded arches. They generate a feeling of dark, massive solemnity. The usual plan was a cross shape, with a long nave at the western end, a shorter but elevated chancel at the east culminating in the altar, with north and south transepts, all four elements meeting at the crossing. Running the length of a Romanesque nave you'll typically find three series of arches. At the base is the arcade, which defines the nave. Above this is a second set of arches, called the triforium, and above the triforium is yet a third set of arches, the clerestory, whose pillars lead up to the ribbed or vaulted ceiling. To each side of the nave run aisles, sometimes featuring chapels or side altars. Outside, towers mark the western entrance, which often has an elaborately carved doorway, or tympanum.

Durham Cathedral, in North East England, is perhaps the best example of the Norman style in Britain. Dedicated to Saint Cuthbert and begun in 1093, the cathedral occupies a dramatic and strategic hilltop site above the River Wear. For centuries, the bishop had military as well as religious authority, living as he did in territory that was continuously raided by border bandits, the "reivers," and Scottish plunderers. Inside, along the nave, its massive stone columns are decorated with strong yet simple designs of crisscrossing lines and zigzags. Great stained glass windows tell stories, either Biblical or of the saints, abbots, and warrior chieftains who founded and defended Durham.

Saint Cuthbert was a monk of Lindisfarne who died in 687, already an ancient memory by the time the current cathedral was founded on the site of an even older church. It housed his relics and became a pilgrimage site until the Reformation. Durham was a monastic foundation, and a superb set of cloisters adjoins the cathedral. Cloisters are the covered walkways in which the monks would exercise, and are a feature of many of the great cathedrals.

In the 12th century, the Gothic style began to displace Romanesque, or Norman. Architects accepted the challenge of creating a sense of vertical soaring, with spaces much higher than they were wide, leading the eye up to remote vaulted ceilings and pointed arches. They also accepted the challenge of making their interiors as light as possible, altering the glass-to-masonry ratio without compromising their structural integrity. The most distinctive features of Gothic cathedrals are wide, bright windows with elaborate tracery, brilliantly colored stained glass, flying buttresses, spires, and pinnacles, all of which seem fanciful yet each of which contributes to their structure's stability and aesthetic completeness. Unfortunately, hardly any of the medieval stained glass remains. Even where it does, as at York, it has faded from its former glory. The best and most brilliant stained glass in English cathedrals today is mainly Victorian, from the mid- and late-19th century.

It comes as something of a shock to realize that we don't know the names of the great gothic cathedrals' architects. Living as we do in an age that celebrates exceptional creative individuals, we look back 7- or 800 years to a world in which the designers and master-builders had less opportunity to single themselves out. It's important to remember, besides, that building a cathedral by hand was a project that could easily take 100 years or more. Several of the most famous were clearly redesigned during building, so that their lower sections exhibit different architectural styles than the later, higher sections. At Norwich Cathedral, for example, begun in the same era as Durham in the Norman style, the upper levels of the chancel have pointed Gothic windows and fine window tracery, demonstrating a much later date of completion than the lower levels.

Among the distinctive features of many cathedrals are elaborate carvings, sometimes of scenes from Jesus's life, sometimes of the saints and martyrs of the church. Built when England was still a Catholic country with no inhibitions about iconography, they are often accompanied by gargoyles, grotesque figures of devils, but also angels. Nearly everyone was illiterate then, so the statues and pictorial windows had a didactic function, illustrating for ordinary folk the stories on which their faith was founded. They were perhaps particularly necessary since the liturgy was all said or sung in Latin. To add to the sensory vividness, the interiors of the cathedrals were painted, often brightly. Only after the Reformation in the 1530s were the walls stripped of paint or whitewashed over. In some of the cathedrals, many of the best statues were smashed or disfigured by militant Protestants who thought they were idolatrous. To get a sense of how their interiors might have looked before this transformation, you need to visit the great Catholic cathedrals of France, Spain, and Italy.

Westminster Abbey, right across the road from the Houses of Parliament in London, is probably the most celebrated of all the gothic cathedrals. Every monarch has been crowned there since 1066—17 of them are buried there too, and it has been the site of 16 royal weddings. In its present form it was begun in the middle 1200s, on the site of an older monastery, and was consecrated in 1269. At the East end, behind the high altar, is the exquisite Henry VII Chapel, whose ceiling exhibits one of the most perfect examples of fan vaulting, among the last great achievements of Gothic architecture. The chapel was consecrated in 1516, shortly before the Reformation.

The tomb of Henry VII itself, centerpiece of the chapel, was carved by an Italian sculptor, Pietro Torrigiano, who was a superb craftsman. Torrigiano is best remembered not for his sculptures but for an assault on Michelangelo in Florence, possibly provoked by jealousy. Giorgio Vasari, in his *Lives of the Artists*, describes it like this:

> Torrigiano, having formed an intimacy with Michelangelo, and becoming envious of his distinction in art, one day, when jeering our artist, struck him so violent a blow in the face that his nose was broken and crushed in a manner from which it could never be

recovered, so that he was marked for life; whereupon Torrigiano was banished from Florence.

Benvenuto Cellini, the era's greatest silversmith, recalls in his wonderful autobiography that he was invited to accompany Torrigiano on a trip to England but was so horrified by this attack that he declined to go. Whatever his shortcomings as a gentleman, however, Torrigiano was a brilliant sculptor, and his statue on Henry's tomb stands among his masterpieces.

Westminster Abbey is also famous for Poets' Corner, where many of Britain's most famous writers have been buried or commemorated. It's fun to read along the walls there and to single out the names, which include Geoffrey Chaucer, Edmund Spenser, John Dryden, Jane Austen, Charles Dickens, Robert Browning, Thomas Hardy, and Rudyard Kipling. Controversy often attends the placing of a new plaque, depending on the writer's status or conduct. Lord Byron was such a scandalous fellow in life, despite his great poetry, that he wasn't given a plaque until 1969, 145 years after his death. If, as many feminists believe, the 20th-century poet Ted Hughes drove his poor wife Sylvia Plath to suicide, was it right that he should be honored at Poet's Corner, right next to T. S. Eliot? Even Shakespeare, who is buried in Stratford-on-Avon, didn't get his plaque until 1741, 125 years after the fact!

About 60 miles southeast of London is the cathedral city of Canterbury, the seat of the Archbishop, who is also primate of the world-wide Anglican communion. Another dazzling gothic structure, Canterbury Cathedral achieved notoriety in the year 1170 when Archbishop Thomas à Becket was murdered there. Becket, a thoroughly political man, had been Chancellor to, and a close friend of, King Henry II. On becoming archbishop, however, he turned to asceticism and renounced his worldly loyalties, now standing up for the church's rights as against the king's. After an escalating series of conflicts, the king made an impatient declaration, variously remembered as, "Who will rid me of this troublesome priest?" or "What miserable drones and traitors have I nourished and brought up in my household, who let their lord be treated with such shameful contempt by a low-born cleric?" Whatever the exact words, four of the king's knights entered the cathedral and hacked the archbishop to death, a violation of the tradition of sanctuary. A single candle burns today at the spot where his shrine was erected.

Three years later, Pope Alexander III named Becket a saint, and the scene of his martyrdom became one of the great pilgrimages of Europe. It is best commemorated in Geoffrey Chaucer's *Canterbury Tales*, written in the late 1300s, a series of stories told by pilgrims as they make their way from London to Canterbury, apparently not in very pious frame of mind.

If we travel to Staffordshire, in England's West Midlands, we'll find another lovely gothic cathedral in the city of Lichfield. It's a distinctive structure—in fact, the only medieval cathedral with three spires. Building at Lichfield began in 1195 on the site of an older cathedral. It took about 135 years to complete, with stylistic adjustments along the way. Strongly pro-Royalist in the Civil War of the 1640s, the cathedral was bombarded by parliamentary forces, lost nearly all its stained glass, and fell into partial ruin. The town itself changed hands repeatedly during the war. Only in the 19th century was it fully restored, by confident builders who believed they could improve on the medieval original. The whole thing is immense and impressive, but it's also full of superb little things, from every generation of its history. Last time I visited, it was hosting about 100 junior-school children on an educational outing. The place was full of life, and sending a timely reminder that cathedrals are meant to be places of community life, not museum pieces.

In the chapter house, the place where the pre-Reformation monks would gather to discuss community affairs, is now kept a celebrated 8th century copy of the scriptures. Also displayed there is the Lichfield Angel, a carving fragment that was discovered during excavations in 2003 and probably dates from the year 672. It led to a great surge of interest in Lichfield, and a spike in visitor numbers. A section of the old south wall still bears a fragment of the fresco painting that once covered all the walls, but were whitewashed over at the Reformation or vandalized by parliamentary soldiers in the Civil War. The east window contains Flemish stained glass from the 1530s, not original to the cathedral but instead brought in during the Napoleonic Wars from an abandoned monastery in Belgium.

Countless statues and monuments give you plenty to admire at Lichfield, as in most of the cathedrals. Probably the best and most touching is *The Sleeping Children*, an 1817 statue by Francis Chantrey, showing two sisters asleep in each other's arms. Both had died, one in a fire, the other of illness, soon after the premature death from tuberculosis of their father, a cathedral clergyman. The bereaved mother commissioned the statue. Chantrey himself was among the most prominent sculptors of the Regency era, and in this work he made a moving statement about childhood that still speaks in a loud, clear voice. Other tombs, such as that of Henry Howard, another of the cathedral clergy, are also works of great brilliance and power.

The man in charge of the Victorian restoration of Lichfield Cathedral was George Gilbert Scott, one of the big names of his era. Under his supervision, a superb wrought-iron rood screen was installed at the entrance to the chancel. A rood screen marks off the nave from the chancel—traditionally they had been made of carved wood or stone, so this was an innovation. At the same time, magnificent tiles were installed on the chancel and altar floors. It's often a good policy in English churches and cathedrals to look down—decorative tiles were a specialty of the Victorians, nowhere better than here, except possibly in the Houses of Parliament. Some are copies of medieval fragments that the restorers found; others are tributes to Queen Victoria and King Charles I. Together they add to the richness and splendor of the ensemble.

The south transept contains memorials to three renowned Lichfield natives: Dr. Samuel Johnson, the pioneer lexicographer; Erasmus Darwin, poet and physician; and David Garrick, the most famous actor in 18th-century Britain. Most of this space is given over to military memorials, however, especially to members of the Staffordshire Regiment who lost their lives in campaigns of the last 300 years. Battle flags, some thinned out almost to transparency, still hang proudly over the south entrance. A memorial book to men of the diocese who died in the First World War is on display, created and gilded with the same care as the illuminated manuscripts of the middle ages. Nineteenth-century regimental memorials often distinguish between officers, men, and noncommissioned officers, preserving gradations of rank and social class even in death.

Moving from Staffordshire to the county of Somerset in southwest England, we come to the city of Wells, nestled just below the lovely Mendip Hills. In Wells Cathedral, as in Lichfield, the structure is "Early English," from the late 12th and early 13th centuries, but many of the details come from each of the subsequent centuries. There too you soon realize that you're not beholding a once-and-for-all statement in stone, but a long process of people alive and at work, dying, commemorating each generation, and reshaping their surroundings according to new ideas.

By the time you enter your third or fourth English cathedral, you're familiar with the basic shape and the relative position of nave, choir, pulpit, lectern, and altar. Now your eye seeks out interesting variations on the theme. Instantly notable at Wells is a great set of four strainer or scissor arches, installed in the late 1300s because the pillars supporting the crossing were sinking under the weight of the tower above them. An earthquake, very rare for England, had also weakened them, such that a super-strong remedy was needed. These strainer or scissor arches may be functional but they are also attractive, drawing your eye up to the triforium and giving the cathedral a distinctive badge all of its own.

A long flight of worn stone steps leads up to the chapter house at Wells, and the chapter house itself is elegant and cool. All over Wells cathedral, as at Lichfield, are grave markers and remembrances of the intervening centuries. A striking black wooden chest in one corner, shaped like a quarter circle, bears an explanatory card: "Cope chest made of local oak about 1120 and still in use." That's right: a 900-year-old chest, still in daily use. A bronze lectern nearby carries this inscription: "Dr. Robert Creyghton, upon his return from fifteen years' exile, with our sovereign Lord King Charles the 2nd, made Dean of Wells, in the yeare 1660, gave this brazen desk with God's holy word thereon to the said Cathedral church." That carries us 500 years forward from the making of the cope chest, but still 400 back from our own times, to the fraught years of the Civil War, when a loyal clergyman might go into exile rather than submit to Cromwell's military dictatorship.

A pair of grave markers in the cloisters tell a tale of their own, and by reading between the lines you can imagine what actually happened. The first is to

Robert Foster, a priest of the cathedral who died in 1836. After paying tribute to his theological orthodoxy, the inscription continues:

> His eye sight, weak from his birth, waxed more and more dim with advancing years, till at length those that look out of the windows were darkened. But a light sprang up in the darkness, while those around him shed the silent tear, contemplating his painful loss. A Holy joy would brighten up his countenance so that of him it might be truly said: 'He kissed the rod that smote him.'

Beside it is this tribute to his wife, Joanna, who is praised for her "humbleness of mind, benevolence of heart, placidity of temper, ... [and] untiring watchfulness." She's also remembered for "anticipating the wants and alleviating the trials of a beloved husband when his sight had become darkened." Don't you get the feeling that he became increasingly cranky as he went blind, and that she was infinitely long-suffering on his behalf?

Next door to the cathedral is the bishop's palace, and at Wells you could be forgiven for thinking it was a fortress. It has crenellated walls and a moat, and looks as though it could withstand a siege. The bishop in question, Ralph of Shrewsbury, a worldly 14th-century builder, was resented by the local people for imposing taxes on them to get his ambitious projects completed. That's another worthwhile reminder: that a lot of human vanity and an incredible expenditure were wrapped up in the making of the cathedrals. The last time this Wells drawbridge was used was in 1831 when riots broke out in nearby Bristol over the failure of Parliament to reform itself. Fearing the worst, the bishop sequestered himself inside until the situation calmed down.

If the strainer arches make Wells distinctive, a 20th-century statue of Jesus has the same effect at Llandaff, the cathedral for the Welsh city of Cardiff. Another beautiful medieval structure, built in the 1100s, Llandaff Cathedral sustained repeated severe damage: first from Owen Glendower's rebellion in 1400; then from parliamentary troops in the Civil War, who turned part of it into a tavern and another part into a livestock barn; then from a severe storm in 1703; and then from the German air force in 1941. A rough-hewn stone marker, placed where the bomb landed, recalls the damage it did to the cathedral. Somehow, Llandaff is still there after these plunges into decay and the vigorous restorations that ensued. The Victorians got it back on its feet after years of neglect, with the Pre-Raphaelite artists Dante Gabriel Rossetti, Ford Madox Brown and Edward Burne-Jones playing a prominent role, while funding came from the fabulously wealthy Marquis of Bute, Cardiff's greatest public benefactor.

After the German air raid, the roof was rebuilt. And Jacob Epstein, a prominent sculptor, was commissioned to make the statue I mentioned a moment ago—a 16-foot rendering of *Christ in Majesty*, which stands atop a great concrete arch in the middle of the nave. It looks out of place to me, a defiantly 20th-century addition to an otherwise medieval building. On the other hand, it's much less bad than most 20th century church architecture in Britain.

Llandaff has the usual regimental side chapel, in this case to the Welch Regiment. Among its battle honors, recorded in a wall inscription, are those of the War of 1812, including battles at Detroit and Niagara that are scarcely acknowledged in American historical accounts. In the main body of the church is a superb recessed grave to Henry Thomas, a local judge. The sculptor has depicted Solomon, looking very much the eastern potentate, judging the famous case of the baby between two women, suggesting it should be cut in half. That's just the right image for commemorating a good judge. There's also a full-size funerary statue of Sir David Mathew, right hand man of King Edward IV during the Wars of the Roses, and a staunch supporter of the Yorkists against the Lancastrians. He's shown in full armor and, as is common in such statues, his feet rest on a dog, the symbol of fidelity.

The painted ceiling of the chancel is Victorian, and some of the stained glass was done by the Pre-Raphaelite artist Ford Madox Brown. The reredos, which is to say, the painting behind the altar, was by Dante Gabriel Rossetti, another Pre-Raphaelite, though it has now been removed to a side chapel near the west entrance. Here, as in so many of the cathedrals, the Victorians were all-important. There was a great religious revival in the Victorian era, there was more money available than ever before, and there was a revival of interest in Britain's architectural heritage. The cathedrals as we see them today are far more impressive, well-kept, well-floored, and well-decorated than they were in 1800.

I could easily rhapsodize at length about Lincoln, Ely, Winchester, Norwich, Salisbury, and many more of the medieval cathedrals. For those of you who'd like to pursue this topic in greater depth, I can strongly recommend Professor William Cook's 24-lecture series *The Cathedral*, which includes several sites that will enrich any trip to England. But let me reiterate a point I made earlier: the cathedrals are fascinating, but you shouldn't feel the obligation to visit them all. When you do enter one, look for interesting curiosities from the different centuries as well as marveling at the great designs the buildings embody, which still today have so much power to impress.

7
TUDOR BRITAIN

K ing Richard III died at the Battle of Bosworth Field in 1485, defeated by Henry Tudor. This was the last battle in the Wars of the Roses. For more than half a century, the Lancastrians and the Yorkists, all descended from Edward III, had exchanged blows in their struggle for the throne. Henry Tudor, now crowned as Henry VII, was a shrewd, tight-fisted king from the Lancastrian side. He pacified England, married a Yorkist princess, and made a clever dynastic alliance with the king of Spain. At his death in 1509, he passed the kingdom to his talented and warlike son, Henry VIII. This lecture looks at sites remaining from the Tudor reign over Britain, which lasted until Elizabeth I's death in 1603. Sites discussed include:

- Bosworth Field, where Henry Tudor achieved victory.

- Hampton Court Palace.

- English places of worship, especially after Henry VIII began attacking religion.

- Sites relevant to later rulers Mary I and Elizabeth I.

- Tudor houses.

Bosworth Field

Bosworth Field in Leicestershire is largely farmland today, but a visitor center, a museum, and a set of footpaths enable visitors to walk over the ground where the soldiers fought and died. Though one group of historians continues to claim that the location is wrong by about two miles, the exhibits give a lively sense of the participants, the immense class gulf that separated knights from men-at-arms, and the way the armies had moved to their rendezvous over the preceding weeks.

Hampton Court Palace

Henry VIII became king in 1509 at the age of 18. For a taste of royal opulence in Henry's reign, visit Hampton Court Palace in southwest London. It was designed and built by Cardinal Wolsey, a worldly churchman who was Henry's chief advisor in the 1510s and 1520s. He aimed to show foreign ambassadors and papal envoys that, as a cardinal, he enjoyed the same high style as the cardinals in Rome itself.

Italian workmen accomplished much of the detailed work. Hampton bears witness to the truth that red brick can be just as impressive as stone when it

Hampton Court Palace

comes to building monumental houses. It has a series of superb gatehouses, handsome quadrangles, and a wonderful astronomical clock.

English Places of Worship

In 1534, Henry VIII declared himself head of the English church, separating English religious life from Rome and the popes. He then abolished shrines to the saints throughout England, closed the monasteries, appropriated all their property to himself, and put a stop to pilgrimages.

Today, there are more than 800 ruined abbeys, priories, and monasteries across Britain. Many are imposing, even as ruins. At Rievaulx Abbey in Yorkshire, for example, enough of the complex remains to give a vivid sense of its extent and magnificence.

Rievaulx Abbey

Another among the picturesque monasteries dissolved by Henry is Tintern Abbey, on the Welsh side of the River Wye. Founded in the 1100s, it grew to

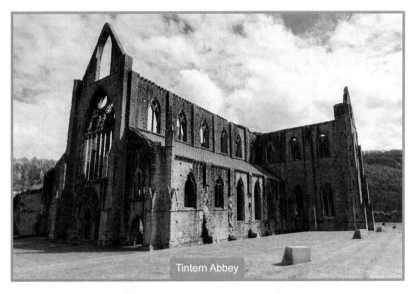
Tintern Abbey

cathedral dimensions in the late 13th century. Henry VIII dismissed the abbot at Tintern and gave the site to a courtier in 1536, after which it gradually decayed.

Mary I and the Martyrs' Memorial

On Henry VIII's death in 1547, nine-year-old Edward VI, the son of Jane Seymour came to the throne. He lasted only six years. At the age of 15, Edward VI, recognizing that his death was near, nominated his cousin, 15-year-old Lady Jane Grey, to succeed him because she was a Protestant.

Her reign lasted only a week before 37-year-old Mary Tudor, Henry VIII's oldest daughter, marched on London from Framlingham, in Suffolk, with her sister Elizabeth and a large military contingent to displace her. The intelligent and well-educated Jane Grey was imprisoned, later tried for treason, and ultimately beheaded at the Tower of London. Mary became Queen Mary I, often known to posterity as Bloody Mary.

Mary persecuted and killed several of England's Protestant leaders, including three bishops—Cranmer, Latimer, and Ridley—who were burned at the stake in Oxford. Their willingness to die for their faith demonstrated that there was more than cold political calculation involved in the English Reformation. The Martyrs' Memorial in Oxford that commemorates them is Victorian, from about 1840.

Martyrs' Memorial in Oxford

Elizabeth I

Mary's death in 1558, at the age of 42, made way for her younger half-sister, Elizabeth I. Elizabeth took the throne, reigned for 45 years, persecuted Catholics where Mary had persecuted Protestants, and carefully avoided marriage.

Among the Catholics who suffered at Elizabeth's hands was Mary Stuart, queen of Scotland, whom she imprisoned for 18 years and finally executed in 1587. Today, travelers can visit many of the places where Mary Queen of Scots was imprisoned, including Carlisle Castle near Hadrian's Wall and Bolton Castle in Yorkshire. Little remains of Fotheringhay Castle, where Mary was put to death, but the site is marked by a bit of masonry from the castle's keep along with some commemorative markers.

Carlisle Castle

One Catholic response to Elizabethan persecution was the so-called priest hole. Families still loyal to the Catholic faith knew that their priests were in danger for their lives. At several country houses, secret rooms were built where the priest could hide when the priest hunters came searching. An excellent example is Harvington Hall in Worcestershire, where visitors can peer into a series of priest holes, including an attic hiding place that is accessed via a false fireplace.

Tudor Houses

Priest holes aside, the design of English houses changed radically between 1485 and 1603. Henry VIII's abolition of private armies and the end of the Wars of the Roses created a situation in which fortification was no longer necessary.

The best Tudor houses in England have much bigger windows than the old castles, and they conspicuously do not have curtain walls, moats, drawbridges, and portcullises. Some of them might still be called castles, but really they are mansions.

One fine example of the new Tudor house is Wollaton Hall in Nottingham, designed in the 1580s by Robert Smythson and owned by Sir Francis

Wollaton Hall

Willoughby. Willoughby had made a fortune in coal mining and hoped to entice the queen to visit him by creating a spectacular setting that she would enjoy. (She never actually visited.)

Another fine example of the Tudor country house is Hardwick Hall. Built on a hilltop, close to the ruins of an earlier hall, it belonged to Bess of Hardwick, a larger-than-life redheaded businesswoman who somehow managed to outlive four husbands, three of them rich, each of whom bequeathed to her another fortune. Visit Hardwick if you possibly can; it has some of the grandest staircases in the kingdom.

Hardwick Hall

Melford Hall in Suffolk is a striking example of a Tudor house built on formerly monastic lands; in fact, its cellars were part of the monastery, and the current house was built right on top of them. It is a red brick structure with six impressive towers, topped by onion-shaped domes. They are echoed in its imposing gatehouse. Queen Elizabeth I visited in 1578 as a sign of favor to the Cordell family, the owners and builders.

Just over a mile from Melford stands Kentwell, another fine house from the same era, built in the same style. The parish church of Long Melford, Holy

Melford Hall

Kentwell Hall

Trinity, lies between the two houses, and it is among the most spectacular churches in the whole kingdom.

A smaller scale Tudor house is Sulgrave Manor in Northamptonshire, which has a special significance for American visitors. The land, part of a monastic estate, was bought in 1539 by Lawrence Washington, formerly mayor of Northampton.

The house stayed in his family for the next century until, in 1656, John Washington emigrated to the colony of Virginia, after which his English relatives sold the house. John Washington was the great-grandfather of George Washington—the planter, soldier, revolutionary, and first president of the United States.

Suggested Reading

Ackroyd, *The Tudors*.

Girouard, *Hardwick Hall*.

Knowles, *Bare Ruined Choirs*.

Questions to Consider

1. Why is the story of Henry VIII and his six wives so inexhaustibly interesting? Is it possible to sympathize with Henry in his long marital drama?

2. Why were the Tudors able to achieve internal peace in England after the long Wars of the Roses?

TUDOR BRITAIN

King Richard III died at the Battle of Bosworth Field in 1485, defeated by Henry Tudor. This was the last battle in the Wars of the Roses. For more than half a century, the Lancastrians and the Yorkists, all descended from Edward III, had exchanged blows in their struggle for the throne. Henry Tudor, now crowned as Henry VII, was a shrewd, tight-fisted king from the Lancastrian side. He pacified England, married a Yorkist princess, made a clever dynastic alliance with the king of Spain, and at his death in 1509 passed the kingdom to his talented, handsome, and warlike son, Henry VIII.

Bosworth Field in Leicestershire, the site of his victory, is largely farmland today, but a visitor center, a museum, and a set of footpaths enable you to walk over the ground where the soldiers fought and died. There's a historians' controversy over whether you're in quite the right place—one group continues to claim that it's wrong by about two miles. Never mind: the exhibits give you a lively sense of the participants, the immense class gulf that separated knights from men at arms, and the way the armies had moved to their rendezvous over the preceding weeks. Henry, with an army from France, had landed in southwest Wales, at Mill Bay in Pembrokeshire, near his birthplace, then marched slowly east and north, picking up recruits along the way. One of the keys to the battle was the arrival at Bosworth of Thomas Stanley, a nobleman with his own private army. Stanley watched to see which side appeared to be winning, then intervened on Henry's side.

The loser of the Battle of Bosworth Field, Richard III, had been king of England for only two years. Most people know Richard through Shakespeare, who depicts him as a malicious hunchback who did evil for its own sake.

There has always been an offsetting pro-Richard faction, whose views are well-expressed in Josephine Tey's 1951 novel *The Daughter of Time*. Its hero, a detective stuck in a hospital with a broken leg, goes over all the evidence to conclude that Richard was a good and blameless man, scapegoated by Tudor propaganda, and that the actual villain was Henry VII.

Everyone with a dog in this fight was fascinated to learn in 2012 that the body of a hunchbacked man had been discovered beneath a parking lot where Greyfriars Church had once stood in the city of Leicester. DNA testing proved that it was in fact Richard, and that at least one part of the Shakespearean version was true. Analysis of the remains showed that severe blows to the head had killed him, after which his body had apparently been stabbed and hacked. A squabble then broke out over whether, as a king, he should be buried at Westminster Abbey, or perhaps, as a Yorkist, at York. The mayor of Leicester, recognizing the publicity benefits for his city, declared: "These bones leave Leicester over my dead body." In the end, he got his way. A reinternment ceremony took place at Leicester Cathedral, with the Archbishop of Canterbury officiating but with members of other Christian denominations in attendance. Sure enough, his grave has become a tourist attraction.

Henry VIII became king in 1509, at the age of 18. His older brother, Prince Arthur, had died prematurely in 1502. Henry married his brother's widow, Catherine of Aragon just after ascending the throne, and remained married to her until he was 40. Her inability to give him a surviving male heir sparked the political and religious crisis that ended with his marriage to Anne Boleyn and the English Reformation. The story of his six wives is one of the most famous in English history. Almost equally well-known is the story of Henry's ministers, Cardinal Wolsey, Thomas More, and Thomas Cromwell, whose fortunes rose and fell with Henry's marriage gambits.

For a taste of royal opulence in Henry's reign, visit Hampton Court Palace, in southwest London. It was designed and built by Cardinal Wolsey, a worldly churchman who was Henry's chief advisor in the 1510s and 1520s. He aimed to show foreign ambassadors and papal envoys that, as a cardinal, he enjoyed the same high style as the cardinals in Rome itself, and that he had impeccable taste. Italian workmen accomplished much of the detailed work.

Hampton bears witness to the truth that red brick can be just as impressive as stone when it comes to building monumental houses. It has a series of superb gatehouses, handsome quadrangles, and a wonderful astronomical clock. The Great Hall, added by Henry VIII in the 1530s, has a marvelous hammer-beam roof, and is vast. The kitchens, greatly extended by Henry, who seized the house after Wolsey's fall from grace, often had to feed 1,000 people per day.

Hampton was extended by Christopher Wren in the 1690s for King William III, so that the façade facing the gardens looks very different from the Tudor front. William, and his queen, Mary II, spent much of their time at Hampton Court. The painting gallery and the great murals around one of the staircases date from their era. The gardens, facing Wren's baroque façade, are a mixture of formal and informal designs, and there's a famous maze made up of hedges, that's surprisingly challenging. When I visited Hampton Court as a 10-year-old, this was the highlight of the whole visit. Returning at the age of 60, I found it far less labyrinthine than memory had made it, but still a good challenge.

In 1534, Henry VIII declared himself head of the English church, separating English religious life from Rome and the popes. He then abolished shrines to the saints throughout England, closed the monasteries, appropriated all their property to himself, and put a stop to pilgrimages. These actions had the effect of making him wealthier than any previous English king, and also potentially more powerful, because there was no longer any question of sharing spiritual and temporal power. All power was now concentrated in himself. By distributing lands seized from the church to his loyal followers, Henry created a class of retainers with an immediate personal debt of gratitude to himself.

From our vantage point it's difficult to recall just how widespread and how powerful the English monasteries had become. There are more than 800 ruined abbeys, priories, and monasteries across Britain. Many are imposing, even as ruins. At Rievaulx Abbey in Yorkshire, for example, enough of the complex remains to give you a vivid sense of its extent and magnificence. Aelred, abbot from 1147-1167, was determined to make the place spectacular. There were, in all, 72 buildings serving 140 monks and 500 lay brothers at the height of its prosperity. The ruined sanctuary of their church shows it to have been a place comparable to the great cathedrals. Founded by the Cistercians in 1132, Rievaulx was meant to be a place dedicated to asceticism and mortification, remote from the temptations of the world, but the passage of time led to a gradual relaxation of the rules. The monks bred sheep for wool, and mined for lead and iron.

When Henry VIII dissolved the monasteries, he dispersed the remaining 23 monks and handed the whole estate over to Thomas Manners, the Earl of Rutland. A later owner, Thomas Duncombe, recognized the scenic possibilities of the site. In 1758 he built a terrace, overlooking the picturesque Rievaulx ruins. It is a curving, high-level path, marked at its north and south ends by classical temples. By then, the fact of the abbey being a ruin was one of its chief attractions, making it a point of special interest rather than a mere remnant of old Catholic England. Fountains Abbey nearby, a comparable ruin, was similarly valued for its decrepitude.

Another among the picturesque monasteries dissolved by Henry is Tintern Abbey, on the Welsh side of the River Wye. Founded in the 1100s and also growing to cathedral-dimensions in the late 13th century, it too was Cistercian, though its remains don't bring to mind poverty, chastity, and obedience so much as drama and ostentation. Henry VIII dismissed the abbot at Tintern and gave the site to a courtier in 1536, after which it too gradually decayed. In the late 1700s, however, it became the centerpiece of a vogue for paintings and rambles in wild settings. In another lecture I'll say more about the poet Wordsworth, who wrote one his best-known poems about a reverie beside Tintern Abbey. And in still another lecture, we'll meet the artist William Gilpin, who popularized the concept of "the picturesque" and named Tintern, in its wooded valley, as the perfect example.

On Henry VIII's death in 1547, nine-year-old Edward VI, the son of Jane Seymour, came to the throne. He lasted only six years, during which the kingdom faced the distressing and unfamiliar fact that a queen, rather than a king, was likely to be his successor. This wasn't simply a question of gender bias; kings were supposed to be warrior leaders, and the inability of queens to lead armies—along with the expectation that they would be dominated by whomever they married—led to fears of intrigue and political instability. That was a serious matter to Britons who could clearly remember the Wars of the Roses. The 15-year-old Edward VI, recognizing that his death was near, nominated his cousin, 15-year-old Lady Jane Grey, to succeed him because she was a Protestant. Her reign lasted only a week before the 37-year-old Mary Tudor, Henry VIII's oldest daughter, marched on London from Framlingham, in Suffolk, with her sister Elizabeth and a large military contingent, to displace her. The intelligent and well-educated Jane Grey was imprisoned, later tried for treason, and ultimately beheaded at the Tower of London. Mary became Queen Mary I, often known to posterity as Bloody Mary.

The new queen had a strong claim to the throne: She was the daughter of Catherine of Aragon, Henry VIII's first wife, but her accession was bound to cause trouble because she was an outspoken Catholic. Her plan to marry Philip II of Spain made the situation worse, as it threatened to yoke England to Spain, then the world's strongest power, and to the papacy. Parliament specified that English soldiers would not have to fight in Spanish wars, and that no Spaniards could be appointed to English offices. Philip landed on the South Coast of England in July 1554 and married Mary two days later at Winchester Cathedral.

Mary persecuted and killed several of England's Protestant leaders, including three bishops, Cranmer, Latimer, and Ridley, who were burned at the stake in Oxford. Their willingness to die for their faith demonstrated that there was more than cold political calculation involved in the English Reformation. The Martyrs' Memorial in Oxford that commemorates them is Victorian, from about 1840, but its design is strongly reminiscent of the Eleanor Crosses that Edward I had set up in England to commemorate his wife in the 1290s.

Mary's persecution of Protestants explains her unpopularity. One Protestant who fled from England to save his life, John Foxe, later wrote a book about the whole episode. Foxe's *Acts and Monuments*, popularly known as *Foxe's Book of Martyrs*, became a Protestant classic, widely read in England and America right into the late 1800s, depicting Mary as a monster and the Protestants as Christ-like in their willingness to die for their faith. The first edition, lavishly illustrated with woodcuts, was one of the biggest publication projects in English history up to that date, and later editions expanded on the first, making it the equivalent of one of today's blockbuster book releases.

Mary's death in 1558 at the age of 42 made way for her younger half-sister, Elizabeth I, daughter of Anne Boleyn. Elizabeth took the throne, reigned for 45 years, persecuted Catholics where Mary had persecuted Protestants, carefully avoided marriage, and became a legend in her own lifetime. Among the Catholics who suffered at Elizabeth's hands was Mary Stuart, queen of Scotland, whom she imprisoned for 18 years and finally executed in 1587. Today, you can visit many of the places where Mary Queen of Scots was imprisoned, including Carlisle Castle near Hadrian's Wall and Bolton Castle in Yorkshire. Little remains of Fotheringhay Castle, where Mary was put to death, but the site is marked by a bit of masonry from the castle's keep, along with some commemorative markers.

One Catholic response to Elizabethan persecution was the "priest hole." Families still loyal to the old Catholic faith knew that their priests were in danger for their lives, so at several country houses secret rooms were built where the priest could hide when the "pursuivants," or priest-hunters, came searching. An excellent example is Harvington Hall in Worcestershire, where you can peer into a series of priest holes, seven in all, including an attic hide that is accessed via a false fireplace. Some of the hiding places at Harvington were designed and built by the Jesuit lay brother Nicholas Owen, who kept busy at this task for nearly 30 years before being captured and tortured to death in 1606.

Priest holes aside, the design of English houses changed radically between 1485 and 1603. Henry VIII's abolition of private armies, and the end of the Wars of the Roses, created a situation in which fortification was no longer necessary. The best Tudor houses in England have much bigger windows than the old castles, and they conspicuously do not have curtain walls, moats, drawbridges, and portcullises. Some of them might still be called castles, but really they are mansions: more comfortable, lighter, and less communal than their predecessors. The craze for building bigger and better houses was a status contest, much commented-on at the time. In 1577 an Essex clergyman wrote: "Everie man almost is a builder and he that hath bought any small parcall of ground, be it never so little, will not be quiet till he have pulled down the old house (if anie were there standing) and set up a new after his own devise." By our standards, the work was agonizingly slow because there were no machines to expedite the process, and even getting the materials to the site could take years.

One fine example of the new Tudor house is Wollaton Hall in Nottingham, designed in the 1580s by Robert Smythson and owned by Sir Francis Willoughby. Willoughby had made a fortune in coal mining and hoped to entice the queen to visit him by creating a spectacular setting that she would enjoy. A royal visit was ruinously expensive, but did wonders for a man's prestige at court. Wollaton is one of several houses from the era that architectural historians refer to as "prodigy houses," because of their showiness. The exterior is busy with decoration, turrets, and towers. The most impressive interior room is the great hall, three stories high. When I visited, it was hosting an exhibition of Chinese dinosaur skeletons, and this central room was big enough for a full-size *Brontosaurus*. The house, standing on a hilltop, dominates the surrounding parkland, in striking contrast to the suburban landscape beyond the gates. It's slightly disappointing to learn that Elizabeth never actually visited Wollaton, confining herself throughout her reign to places in the south of England. A prodigy house that the queen did visit is Longleat, now famous as the site of a safari park, where it's possible to watch lions and giraffes wandering about the grounds.

Another fine example of the Tudor country house is Hardwick Hall in Derbyshire, which might also have been designed by the Wollaton architect, Smythson. Built on a hilltop, close to the ruins of an earlier hall, it belonged to Bess of Hardwick, a larger-than-life red-headed businesswoman, who somehow managed to outlive four husbands, three of them rich, each of whom bequeathed to her another fortune. Last of the four was the Earl of Shrewsbury, one of the richest and most politically important men in the kingdom. Their marriage was stormy, and they eventually separated, each with a vast fortune. She began to build the big house at Hardwick when she was already 63, just 100 yards from the old hall, which is now a ruin but was then inhabited by most of her retinue. The new hall's immense façade, dominated by expanses of window, was unprecedented. Glass was a luxury item, but she could afford it, having invested shrewdly in the glass and lead businesses that were developing in the area.

Visit Hardwick if you possibly can; it has some of the grandest staircases in the kingdom. There's just one fly in the ointment. Bess ordered a set of tapestries from the best Flemish workshops to decorate the High Great Chamber, the big public room on the top floor of the house. By all accounts they were brilliantly colorful and superbly well made. The National Trust, which now owns the house, has decided to leave nearly all of them hanging where she put them. Four centuries of deterioration from light, from damp, from insects, and from sheer age, have transformed them into dull, lifeless, deeply unattractive objects. I am one of many visitors to have pleaded with the National Trust to get rid of them and to put in their place replicas, of the same brightness as the originals were when new. Only by doing so can we get a sense of what the house felt like when she lived there. It might be a good idea to leave just one of the threadbare old tapestries for the sake of comparison, but to have the whole lot on display is madness, replacing what should be an exuberant scene with a feeling of fusty dullness. Bess herself would certainly not have put up with it.

Melford Hall in Suffolk is a striking example of a Tudor house built on formerly monastic lands. In fact, its cellars were part of the monastery and the current house was built right on top of them. It is a red brick structure with six impressive towers, topped by onion-shaped domes. They are echoed in its imposing gatehouse. Queen Elizabeth I visited in 1578 as a sign of favor to the Cordell Family, the owners and builders. She is memorialized in a fine stained-glass window. The house was smashed and looted during the Civil War of the 1640s but rebuilt. It was bought in the 1780s by the Hyde Parker family, the most famous member of which, Admiral Sir Hyde Parker, was Horatio Nelson's commander at the Battle of Copenhagen in 1801. It was he who signaled Nelson to disengage, an order that Nelson ignored. Legend has it that Nelson lifted the telescope to his blind eye in order not to be able to see the flag signal, then went on to win a smashing victory. A portrait of Admiral Hyde Parker has pride of place in one of the early 19th-century additions.

Melford House was partially redesigned in almost every generation—a grand staircase seems out of place ascending from the 16th-century great hall, though it's a fine thing in itself, with classical pillars on each side as it rises. The gardens are mainly Edwardian, from the early 20th century, and there's a "ha-ha" in good condition. A ha-ha is a walled ditch surrounding the house. It prevents farm animals from coming into the gardens, but has the added advantage of being invisible from the house, so that the family, as they gaze through their windows, have an unimpeded view into the distance. Beatrix Potter was a friend of the family and often went to stay, in the late 19th and early 20th centuries. Her bedroom is preserved, and an exhibit in the superb garden house includes many of the drawings she made at Melford. Ironically, she and Jemima Puddleduck are almost certainly better known today than the admiral.

Just over a mile from Melford stands Kentwell, another fine house from the same era, built in the same style. The parish church of Long Melford, Holy Trinity, lies between the two houses, and it is among the most spectacular churches in the whole kingdom. Built by prosperous wool merchants in the perpendicular style just before the Reformation, Holy Trinity could easily pass as a cathedral. Simon Jenkins, author of *England's Thousand Best Churches*, includes it in his top 20 for the whole country. Three wonderful buildings within a short walk of each other make this part of Suffolk particularly engaging.

Some late 16th and early-17th century builders created puns or lessons in stone. Sir Thomas Tresham, for example, took the considerable risk of converting to Catholicism in 1580, after which he suffered recurrent phases of persecution. He built a triangular lodge on his estate at Rushton, in Northamptonshire, designed as a three-dimensional tribute to the Holy Trinity. Each of its three sides has three roof gables, and three decorative motifs on each of three levels. Triangular buildings are of course impractical to live in and don't contain much space, but he was making his point in the boldest possible way. The poet Henry Oxinden built a round lodge on a hilltop in 1631 and explained his reasoning in a poem:

> Tell me how, Henry, in thy mind it came,
> Upon the hill thy house so round to frame?

I imitated the great architector, Lo
Both Earth and Heaven he hath fram-ed so!

Unfortunately, that house no longer exists.

A smaller-scale Tudor house is Sulgrave Manor in Northamptonshire, which has a special significance for American visitors. The land, part of a monastic estate, was bought in 1539 by Lawrence Washington, formerly mayor of Northampton. He was a well-to-do wool merchant, and over the next 20 years he built his home there, finishing it off with the coat of arms of Queen Elizabeth I over the main doorway. The house stayed in his family for the next century, until in 1656, John Washington emigrated to the colony of Virginia, after which his English relatives sold the house. This John, the emigrant, was the great-grandfather of George Washington, planter, soldier, revolutionary, and first president of the United States.

The house, which is far more modest than Hardwick, Wollaton, or Melford, but comfortable and distinguished, was bought in 1914 by a consortium of British and American antiquarians, in celebration of the fact that for the preceding 100 years Britain and the United States had never gone to war. The stars and stripes, as well as the Union Jack, fly in the garden, and there's a stern bust of George himself in the front yard. Volunteers in period costume strive to recreate the 16th-century mood of the house when it was new.

When Elizabeth I died in 1603, the Tudor dynasty came to an end. King James VI of Scotland became King James I of England. After centuries of border warfare, the kingdoms were finally linked by a common ruler, though another 104 years would pass before they were politically integrated. James, nicknamed "the wisest fool in Christendom," was the son of Mary Queen of Scots. She had died a martyr to the Catholic faith, which led England's Catholic minority to hope that he would look favorably on their plight, and begin to roll back the Reformation. But James was a Protestant, and understood the folly of repeating Queen Mary's mistakes.

When the English Catholics realized that the king was not going to help them, some of them decided to assassinate him, along with the leading men of the kingdom, by blowing up the Houses of Parliament when the king was present for the state opening. This was in 1605. Guy Fawkes led the conspirators, who began to cram barrels of gunpowder into a small storeroom underneath the House of Lords. The plot was discovered on November 5th, and the villains were arrested before they could carry out the plot. Fawkes and his friends suffered the horrifyingly cruel execution that befell all traitors in that barbarous era: they were hanged, drawn, and quartered.

Ever since then, November 5th has been England's national fireworks day. When I was a child, it was still common to uphold the tradition of making a human dummy from old clothes stuffed with straw or newspaper, and to roll it around the streets in a baby stroller, calling out "Penny for the Guy." Passersby gave us coins to use in buying fireworks. By that time, the anti-Catholic nature of the celebration had largely disappeared. English Catholic kids enjoyed the fireworks just as much as the Anglicans. Incidentally, I was surprised on coming to live in America to discover that July 4th is the comparable day here. The problem with July 4 is that it doesn't get dark until late, so the poor children have to wait and wait for the light to fade. England in November, on the other hand, is completely dark by 5:00 pm, so the festivities don't have to wait. On the other hand, rain often gets in the way, forcing a postponement, and it's nearly always bitterly cold.

In this lecture, we have visited several sites that illustrate the transition out of the Wars of the Roses and into an era of relative political stability, which made a new style of building possible and prompted competition and ostentation. The 17th century bore witness to a conflict between the monarchy and Parliament which eventually led to four years of civil war. The historical sites associated with that political crisis, and its resolution, will be the topic of the next lecture.

8

MAGNA CARTA AND CIVIL WAR

O ne of the inspiring aspects of British history is the way its kings were gradually forced to share power, to accept the rule of law, and eventually to submit to parliamentary domination. Today, Britain is a constitutional monarchy in which the monarch has a few residual shreds of influence, but is now comfortably constrained by representative institutions. Kings rarely gave up their powers without a fight. This lecture gives a guide to many of the places in which such fights happened and where many of the era's important figures resided and visited, including:

- Runnymede, signing place of the Magna Carta.

- Battlefields of the English Civil War.

- The locations of the trial, execution, and burial of King Charles I.

- Locations relevant to military and political figure Oliver Cromwell.

Runnymede

Runnymede and the Magna Carta

In England at Runnymede in 1215, King John signed the Magna Carta. The site is a broad open meadow in the valley of the River Thames, not far from Heathrow. It is delightfully rural, in view of its proximity to millions of people. If you're politically minded, it's the ideal first thing to see in Britain after you get off the plane, as it is only about a 20-minute drive from the airport. It was already historically significant by King John's time, being the place where the Anglo-Saxon kings had sometimes met their Witan, or council of advisors.

The meadow was donated to the nation in 1929 by Cara Rogers Broughton, a wealthy American's daughter who had married a British engineer and knew about the area's history. The architect Edwin Lutyens built a pair of memorials and two lodges in their honor, where you can park to begin your visit. A footpath takes you across the meadow to attractions in the area.

There is a copy of the Magna Carta on display at the British Library and one each at the Salisbury and Lincoln cathedrals. It was written as an attempt to mediate between King John and his rebellious barons, affording various legal rights and protections to them. It certainly didn't hold out much to the common people and was quickly repudiated by King John, then annulled by the pope.

When subsequent kings wanted to raise revenue, they sometimes reissued milder versions of it to mollify their subjects. In the early 1600s, however, when James I and Charles I came into conflict with Parliament over where ultimate sovereignty lay, the Magna Carta became an important precedent.

Sites from the 17th Century

The lecture now moves forward in time from King John at Runnymede to the early 17th century—a time when a combination of religious and political disagreements created a crisis in Britain. The religious differences divided the Church of England between those who emphasized its closeness to Catholicism in all but church governance and those who insisted it was a thoroughly Protestant church that rejected all vestiges of the Catholic past. This latter party was named the Puritans because they wanted to purify the church.

As for politics, the main disagreement of the 1620s and 1630s hinged on whether the king enjoyed absolute power as God's agent on earth or whether he was subject to the law and held sovereignty jointly with Parliament. In the decades after 1603, when James I came to the throne, he and his son Charles I summoned Parliament irregularly, usually because they needed to raise money for military expeditions. Parliament presented lists of grievances, saying it would grant money to the king once he had redressed them.

A series of bitter standoffs finally led Charles I to attempt government without parliamentary help through most of the 1630s. It worked until a Scottish invasion of northern England forced his hand. Rather than admit the principle of Parliament's right to a permanent place in power, Charles raised an army and declared war against Parliament. It raised an army of its own and fought back. This was the English Civil War.

So much time has passed since the English Civil War that most of its battlefields are now indistinct, often indicated just by stone markers. The two decisive battles of the war took place at Marston Moor, Yorkshire, in 1644, and Naseby in Northamptonshire in 1645. Marston Moor was, in terms of numbers, the biggest battle ever fought in England. It was also the place where Prince Rupert, the king's nephew, lost his reputation for

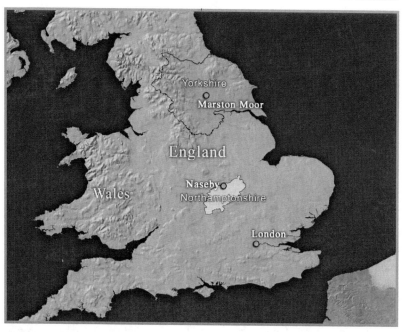

Naseby battlefield

invincibility as a cavalry commander. By contrast, Parliament's cavalry leader, Oliver Cromwell, distinguished himself as a first-rate battlefield commander.

At Naseby in 1645, Parliament's well-trained New Model Army, 22,000 strong, led by General Thomas Fairfax and Cromwell, routed a smaller Royalist army, killed or captured most of the king's veteran officers, and ended his ability to field a viable force. A few months later, the war ended in victory for Parliament. The Naseby battlefield, like Marston Moor, now comprises several working farms. A stone marker, a battlefield trail, a series of elevated platforms, and several historical plaques explain the main events of the battle to visitors.

The best way to get a feel for the English Civil War is by watching reenactments by two groups of enthusiasts, the Sealed Knot society and the English Civil War Society. They assemble at Marston Moor, Naseby, and other sites, such as Edge Hill in Warwickshire, usually on the anniversaries of the actual battles. They also reenact several major castle sieges from the conflict.

After the English Civil War

When the Civil War ended, the king and Parliament negotiated uneasily about the future balance of power. Charles I, however, took the view that God had appointed him and that Parliament had no rights except through his grace. He was imprisoned at Carisbrooke Castle on the Isle of Wight, a beautiful medieval castle that is now open to visitors.

He provoked a royalist revival, supported by a Scottish invasion into northern England. The New Model Army, outnumbered two-to-one but with Cromwell now in sole command, crushed this Royalist revival at the Battle of Preston in the summer of 1648.

Many of the Puritan soldiers were politicized by the war and began to speak out on behalf of radical changes to England's government. In the autumn of 1647, a group called the Levellers published *The Case of the Armie Truly Stated*, which led to a series of discussions on political first principles. These discussions, the Putney Debates, were held in the Church of St. Mary the Virgin in Putney, which people can still visit.

Some of the soldiers spoke eloquently on behalf of a one-man, one-vote democracy. Henry Ireton, Cromwell's son-in-law, a senior army officer, countered that only property owners should be permitted to vote, because only they had a permanent stake in the nation.

Cromwell, like Ireton, was skeptical about the Levellers, but he had now lost all patience with the king and was determined to get rid of him once and for all. He and his supporters purged Parliament of moderates who still wanted a reformed monarchy.

The remaining members in the so-called Rump Parliament put the king on trial for treason. The trial was held in Westminster Hall. This magnificent medieval building is one of the few parts of Parliament to have survived down to the present. This extraordinary roof has seen many spectacular moments over the last millennium, but probably none more dramatic than the trial of Charles I.

He stuck to his original point, that Parliament had no right to try him, but the Rump Parliament found him guilty and sentence him to death. The sentence was carried out by beheading in Whitehall, in front of the Banqueting House, on a cold January day in 1649.

St. George's Chapel

The body, with the head crudely stitched back on, was buried at St. George's Chapel at Windsor Castle, adjacent to the bodies of King Henry VIII and most beloved wife, Jane Seymour. This chapel is one of the highlights of Windsor. The Banqueting House, site of Charles's execution, is also worth a visit. Built by order of Charles's father, King James I, it is the handiwork of Inigo Jones, one of the great luminaries of 17th-century English architecture.

The Importance of Cromwell

The execution of Charles I made Oliver Cromwell the most important man in Britain, the leading regicide who had the confidence of the army and Parliament. He tried to maintain rule through the Rump Parliament until

Oliver Cromwell's house

1653, with it acting as legislature and executive. This was the English Commonwealth. Then, impatient at the Commonwealth's inability to get things done, he abolished it, had himself declared the lord protector of England, and he ruled as a military dictator until his death in 1658.

Cromwell had been born in 1599 in Huntingdon, East Anglia, to a family of prosperous gentlemen. He studied at the local grammar school, then went to Sidney Sussex College, Cambridge. He married the daughter of a wealthy London merchant, went through a religious conversion to become a committed Puritan, and lived in a fine timbered house in the town of Ely, which is open to visitors.

After Cromwell

After Cromwell's death, it was clear that no one else enjoyed the confidence of both the army and the Parliament, as he had done. His son Richard ruled as lord protector for less than a year. Then, for the sake of political stability, Parliament decided to invite the old king's son to return from exile in France.

He did so, being crowned King Charles II in 1660. Charles II never forgot what had happened to his father. Frequently at odds with Parliament, he was nevertheless careful not to antagonize it to the breaking point.

Charles II's successor, his brother James II, was hopelessly inept when it came to politics. He had become a Catholic during his long exile in France—which made him anathema to most Englishmen. Even so, he could have survived had he not antagonized all the influential groups whose help he needed.

After less than four years on the throne, he was forced to flee in 1688. Parliament then invited William of Orange, stadtholder of the Netherlands, who was married to James's Protestant daughter, Mary, to become king instead. They were equal monarchs: William III and Mary II. This sequence of events, in effect a bloodless coup, is remembered as The Glorious Revolution, important in British history and a source of inspiration to the American revolutionaries of the 1770s and 1780s.

Although William was a tireless soldier, he suffered from asthma and found life at Whitehall Palace unendurable because of the area's foggy humidity. Instead, he and Mary bought a big house at the western end of Hyde Park, a mile farther back from the river.

They hired the age's leading architect, Christopher Wren, to extend it and renamed it Kensington Palace. It has been a royal residence ever since and is an outstanding example of late 17th- and early 18th-century design and decoration.

Suggested Reading

Fraser, *Cromwell, Our Chief of Men*.

Starkey, *Magna Carta*.

Worden, *The English Civil Wars*.

Suggested Activities

1. Read 18th- or 19th-century accounts of Oliver Cromwell by Irish Catholics, to whom he is a devil figure, and then by English Protestants, to whom he is a hero. Reflect on bias among historians.

2. Visit Westminster Hall and the Banqueting House in London, the places where King Charles I was tried and then executed.

MAGNA CARTA AND CIVIL WAR

Winston Churchill once said that democracy is the worst political system, except for all the others. It's often undignified, often leads to slanging matches among candidates, has a long history of pettiness and corruption, and brings out the worst qualities in many politicians. Nevertheless, we cherish it, or we ought to. A glance at the dictatorships still thriving in the world around us, and a glance at the tyrannies that have dominated the world through most of its history, should make us very glad to live where and when we do. Britain is no exception. Its kings may seem colorful and fascinating from a safe distance, but at first hand they could be terrifying, arbitrary, and capricious.

One of the inspiring aspects of British history is the way its kings were gradually forced to share power, to accept the rule of law, and eventually to submit to parliamentary domination. Today, Britain is a constitutional monarchy in which the monarch has a few residual shreds of influence, but is now comfortably constrained by representative institutions, and survives only with their approval.

Kings rarely gave up their powers without a fight. Not only can we trace the history of these fights: we can visit many of the places in which they happened. In England, the place to start is Runnymede, where, in 1215, King John signed Magna Carta. It is a broad open meadow in the valley of the River Thames, not far from Heathrow Airport, and delightfully rural, in view of its proximity to millions of people. If you're politically minded, it's the ideal first thing to see in Britain after you get off the plane, only about 20 minutes' drive from the airport. It was already historically significant by King John's time, being the place where the Anglo-Saxon kings had sometimes met their Witan, or council of advisors.

The meadow was donated to the nation in 1929 by Cara Rogers Broughton, a wealthy American's daughter who had married a British engineer and knew about the area's history. The architect Edwin Lutyens built a pair of memorials and two lodges in their honor, where you can park to begin your visit. A footpath takes you across the meadow, first of all to *The Jurors*, a 2015 bronze sculpture in the form of 12 chairs, made by the English sculptor Hew Locke. Collectively, they represent the 12 chairs occupied by members of a jury, and they celebrate the principle of habeas corpus and the right to a trial by a jury of one's peers. Each one is illustrated by a scene or symbol of this process, as for example the scales of justice, or the imprisonment of Nelson Mandela in South Africa.

Further along the path, and through a gateway, you'll come to a small limestone rotunda at the edge of the valley, with eight columns. This is the Magna Carta Memorial, placed there by the American Bar Association in 1957, when it held its annual conference nearby. Its leaders were surprised to discover that the British themselves had left no marker. A standing granite pillar inside the rotunda carries the message: "To Commemorate Magna Carta, Symbol of Freedom under law." The American lawyers returned to the site on several subsequent visits, including 2015, the 800th anniversary of Magna Carta.

Leaving the meadow and climbing a wooded hillside path, you come to a grove where a great carved marker stone carries this message: "This acre of English ground was given to the United States of America by the people of Britain in Memory of John F. Kennedy." The dates of Kennedy's life are given, and then a passage from his inaugural address, declaring the intention to "pay any price, bear any burden . . . in order to assure the survival and success of liberty." The memorial's designer, Geoffrey Jellicoe, said he was inspired by *Pilgrim's Progress*, John Bunyan's allegory of Christian life as a journey through hardship and temptation. The 50 steps that lead up to the memorial stone correspond to the 50 states of the union. Two terraces, each with a stone seat, give you the chance to catch your breath after the climb. The leaves of an oak tree planted behind the memorial turn bright red in November, the month of Kennedy's assassination. The Queen, opening the memorial in 1965 in the presence of Jackie Kennedy and her two young children, noted that Magna Carta was "a part of the heritage which the people of the United States of America share with us," and that it was therefore "altogether fitting that Runnymede should be the site of Britain's memorial to the late President." You can watch the film of her speech online.

There is a copy of the Magna Carta on display at the British Library, and one each at Salisbury and Lincoln Cathedrals. It was written as an attempt to mediate between King John and his rebellious barons, affording various legal rights and protections to them. It certainly didn't hold out much to the common people, and was quickly repudiated by King John, then annulled by the Pope. When subsequent kings wanted to raise revenue, they sometimes reissued milder versions of it to mollify their subjects. In the early 1600s, however, when James I and Charles I came into conflict with Parliament over where ultimate sovereignty lay, the Magna Carta became an important precedent.

Now let's move forward in time from King John at Runnymede to the early 17th century—a time when a combination of religious and political disagreements created a crisis in Britain. The religious differences divided the Church of England between those, on the one hand, who emphasized its closeness to Catholicism in all but church governance, and those on the other who insisted it was a thoroughly Protestant church that rejected all vestiges of the Catholic past. This latter party were named Puritans because they wanted to purify the church.

As for politics, the main disagreement of the 1620s and 1630s hinged on whether the king enjoyed absolute power as God's agent on earth, or whether he was subject to the law and held sovereignty jointly with Parliament. In the decades after 1603, when James I came to the throne, he and his son Charles I called Parliaments irregularly, usually because they needed to raise money for military expeditions. Parliament presented lists of grievances, saying it would grant money to the king once he had redressed them. He answered that they must first grant the money and then he might give his attention to their petitions. A series of bitter standoffs finally led Charles I to attempt government without parliamentary help through most of the 1630s. It worked until a Scottish invasion of northern England forced his hand. Rather than admit the principle of Parliament's right to a permanent place in the constitution, Charles raised an army and declared war against Parliament. It raised an army of its own and fought back.

So much time has passed since the English Civil War that most of its battlefields are now indistinct, often indicated just by stone markers. The two decisive battles of the war took place at Marston Moor, Yorkshire, in 1644, and Naseby in Northamptonshire in 1645. Marston Moor was, in terms of numbers, the biggest battle ever fought in England. It was also the place where Prince Rupert, the king's dashing, hot-blooded young nephew, lost his reputation for invincibility as a cavalry commander. By contrast, the parliamentary cavalry leader, Oliver Cromwell, distinguished himself as first-rate battlefield commander. Justifying his appointment of officers who did not come from the gentry class, he wrote: "If you choose godly honest men to be captains of horse, honest men will follow them ... I would rather have a plain russet-coated captain who knows what he fights for and loves what he knows than that which you call a gentleman and is nothing else." Unfortunately, there is not a lot to see at Marston Moor except for a modest stone monument, raised in 1939 by the Cromwell Association.

At Naseby in 1645, Parliament's well-trained New Model Army, 22,000 strong, led by General Thomas Fairfax and Cromwell, routed a smaller Royalist army, killed or captured most of the king's veteran officers, and ended his ability to field a viable force. A few months later, the war ended in victory for Parliament. The Naseby battlefield, like Marston Moor, now comprises several working farms. A stone marker, a battlefield trail, a series of elevated platforms, and several historical plaques explain the main events of the battle to visitors, but their presence is, at least for now, low key. An organization called the Naseby Battlefield Project is working hard to restore the site, to make the events of the battle more obvious and more vivid for visitors. Let's hope they succeed.

The best way to get a feel for the English Civil War until the battlefields are improved is by watching reenactments by two groups of enthusiasts, the Sealed Knot society and the English Civil War Society. They assemble at

Marston Moor, Naseby, and other sites, such as Edge Hill in Warwickshire, usually on the anniversaries of the actual battles. They also replay several major castle sieges from the conflict. The Sealed Knot, founded in the late 1960s by a World War II veteran who had written a book about Edge Hill, emphasizes that it is a non-political organization, is dedicated to education, research, and enjoyment, not the glorification of war.

> Do you want to hear the roar of the cannon, the thunder of horses' hooves, see thousands of soldiers clashing in battle, watch the displays of battlefield standards, smell the smoke of the musketeers and hear the beating of the drums? Or do you even want to be a part of it?

Thousands of enthusiasts have answered this call, and the reenactments, carefully staged to avoid deaths and mutilations, bring out rival armies in splendid period dress. Participation has taught the members and the broader community a great deal about 17th-century weapons, dress, transportation, food, and organization. It is as valuable to the historical study of the Civil War as metal detectorists are to the recovery of Anglo-Saxon and Viking treasure hoards.

When the Civil War ended, King and Parliament negotiated uneasily about the future balance of power. Charles I, however, took the view that he had been appointed by God, and that Parliament had no rights, except through his grace. He was imprisoned at Carisbrooke Castle on the Isle of Wight, a beautiful medieval castle that is now open to visitors. The bed he slept in is on display, and the politics of the 14 months he spent there lucidly explained. Although he was a prisoner, he still had a great deal of influence and latitude of action. He provoked a royalist revival, supported by a Scottish invasion into northern England.

The New Model Army, outnumbered two-to-one but with Cromwell now in sole command, crushed this royalist revival at the Battle of Preston in the summer of 1648. It had shown itself to be a superb fighting organization, well-disciplined, well-trained, and driven by a high sense of purpose. Many of its Puritan soldiers were politicized by the war, and began to speak out on behalf of radical changes to England's government. In the autumn of 1647, a group called the Levellers published *The Case of the Army Truly Stated*, which led to a series of discussions on political first principles. These discussions, the Putney Debates, were held in the Church of St. Mary the Virgin in Putney, which you can still visit, just south of the River Thames.

Some of the soldiers spoke eloquently on behalf of a one-man-one-vote democracy, with the House of Commons supreme, annual Parliaments, equal constituencies, freedom of speech, religion, and the press, and no more censorship. The monarchy would be abolished. One soldier, Colonel Thomas Rainsborough, made the case for universal suffrage like this:

> I think that the poorest he that is in England hath a life to live, as the greatest he; and therefore truly, Sir, I think it clear, that every man that is to live under a government ought first by his own consent to put himself under that government; and I do think that the poorest man in England is not at all bound in a strict sense to that government that he hath not had a voice to put himself under.

Henry Ireton, Cromwell's son-in-law, a senior army officer, countered that only property owners should be permitted to vote, because only they had a permanent stake in the nation. Cromwell, like Ireton, was skeptical about the Levellers, but he had now lost all patience with the King, and was determined to get rid of him once and for all. He and his supporters purged Parliament of moderates who still wanted a reformed monarchy. The remaining MPs— Members of Parliament—in the so-called "Rump Parliament," put the king on trial for treason. The trial was held in Westminster Hall. This magnificent medieval building is one of the few parts of Parliament to have survived down to the present. It was spared from the disastrous parliamentary fire of 1834 and from the Nazi blitz of 1940. The beautiful hammer-beam roof measures 70 by 240 feet, providing a huge interior space, unobstructed by columns.

This extraordinary roof has seen many spectacular moments over the last millennium, but probably none more dramatic than the trial of Charles I. He stuck to his original point, that Parliament had no right to try him:

> This day's proceeding cannot be warranted by God's laws; for, on the contrary, the authority of obedience unto kings is clearly warranted,

and strictly commanded in both the Old and New Testament ... No learned lawyer will affirm that an impeachment can lie against the King: and one of their maxims is, that the king can do no wrong.

Unmoved, the Rump Parliament found Charles guilty and sentenced him to death. The sentence was carried out not at the usual execution site, the Tower of London, but in Whitehall, in front of the Banqueting House, on a cold January day in 1649. The king wore two shirts to keep warm, from fear that onlookers might otherwise mistake his shivering for fear. Soldiers separated the crowd of onlookers from the scaffold. After the headsman struck his blow, the crowd groaned—many pushed forward to dip their handkerchiefs in the blood.

The body, with the head crudely stitched back on, was buried at St. George's Chapel, Windsor Castle, adjacent to the bodies of King Henry VIII and most beloved wife, Jane Seymour. This chapel is one of the highlights of Windsor. Besides being the burial site of several monarchs and the wedding site of others, such as Edward VII, it is a fine example of late Gothic architecture, from just before the Reformation. When the mangled body of King Charles was laid to rest beneath its fan vaults, however, it was in poor repair after being vandalized and plundered by parliamentary soldiers. We see it today after extensive renovations in the late 1600s and again in the mid-1800s.

The Banqueting House, site of Charles's execution, is also worth a visit. Built by order of Charles's father, King James I, it is the handiwork of Inigo Jones, one of the great luminaries of 17th century English architecture. Jones was influenced by the Italian Renaissance and by the work of Michelangelo, which he had studied on a series of three visits to Italy. Charles himself, in quieter times, had commissioned Peter Paul Rubens, the era's greatest Flemish artist, to paint a set of murals for the ceiling: *The Union of the Crowns*, *The Peaceful Reign of James I*, and *The Apotheosis of James I*, which shows the old king being carried up to Heaven. Ironically, these paintings must have been some of the last things Charles ever saw, because he spent the morning of his final day in the Banqueting House, in prayer and in saying farewell to his children, before being led out through a specially created doorway onto the scaffold. Located right in the heart of London, the Banqueting House is a good place to meditate on the benefits of mixed government and political stability.

The execution of Charles I made Oliver Cromwell the most important man in Britain, the leading regicide who had the confidence of the army and Parliament. He tried to maintain rule through the Rump Parliament until 1653, with it acting as legislature and executive. This was the English Commonwealth. Then, impatient at the Commonwealth's inability to get things done, he abolished it, had himself declared the Lord Protector of England, and ruled as a military dictator until his death in 1658. He is one of the most controversial people in British history, a tyrant in the eyes of Royalists and Roman Catholics, but a hero of democracy and liberty to republicans and nonconformists. The complicated political circumstances of the 1640s and 1650s provide evidence in support of—and against—both views.

Cromwell had been born in 1599 in Huntingdon, East Anglia, to a family of prosperous gentlemen. He studied at the local grammar school, then went to Sidney Sussex College in Cambridge. He married the daughter of a wealthy London merchant, went through a religious conversion to become a committed Puritan, and lived in a fine timbered house in the town of Ely, which is open to visitors. Rooms in the house recreate 17th-century domestic life, and there's an informative exhibition on the Civil War and Cromwell's rise to power. The house also features an allegedly haunted bedroom.

Details of his early life are scanty. Cromwell might have studied law as a young man, and it is possible that he fought on the Protestant side in the Thirty Years' War, which would explain his military ability. A member of Parliament as the crisis of the early 1640s developed, he distinguished himself as an outstanding cavalry leader, then as a hard negotiator, willing to take the drastic step of sweeping away the monarchy. In 1657, Parliament offered him the crown—he could have become King Oliver I—but he was determined to avoid it.

The most famous employee of Cromwell's government was the poet John Milton. Son of a well to do London family, Milton had studied at Cambridge and made the grand tour of Europe. During the Civil War, he had written the *Aeropagitica*, an attack on censorship. A phenomenal polymath, he was the Commonwealth's foreign language specialist, the "Secretary for Foreign Tongues," who drafted Latin letters to other governments and maintained diplomatic correspondence with governments in France, Spain, Italy, and the Netherlands. He wrote a defense of the regicide, and a sonnet in praise of Cromwell, as a man of both peace and war. Here's how it begins. And "Darwen" is a reference to one of Cromwell's battle honors:

> Cromwell, our chief of men, who through a cloud
> Not of war only, but detractions rude,
> Guided by faith and matchless fortitude,
> To peace and truth thy glorious way hast ploughed,
> And on the neck of crowned Fortune proud
> Hast reared God's trophies, and his work pursued,
> While Darwen stream with blood of Scots imbrued.

By the end of the 1650s Milton had gone blind, but continued to work by dictation to his long-suffering daughter. He finished *Paradise Lost* in 1665 at a cottage in Chalfont St. Giles, Buckinghamshire, where he had taken his family to avoid the Great Plague that was devastating London. The cottage, his only surviving residence, is a small but lovely visit for anyone interested in writers' lives and homes. Operated as a museum, the cottage includes a collection of early editions of Milton's work—not only his poetry but also his numerous prose writings defending political and religious freedom. There's also a statue of Milton inside the London church where he is buried, St. Giles, Cripplegate.

After Cromwell's death, it was clear that no one else enjoyed the confidence of both the army and the Parliament as he had done. His son Richard ruled as lord protector for less than a year, then for the sake of political stability, Parliament decided to invite the old king's son to return from exile in France. He did so, being crowned King Charles II in 1660. Charles II never forgot what had happened to his father. Frequently at odds with Parliament, he was nevertheless careful not to antagonize it to the breaking point. By comparison with Cromwell, he was easy-going; he reopened the theaters and authorized the celebration of Christmas once more. Theaters and Christmas revels had been banned during the Commonwealth and Protectorate. Portraits from the time confirm the contrast. They show Charles in magnificent clothes and wigs, while Cromwell and his men are depicted in pared-down blacks and browns.

Charles II's successor, his brother James II, was hopelessly inept when it came to politics. He had become a Catholic during his long exile in France—which made him anathema to most Englishmen. Even so, he could have survived had he not antagonized all the influential groups whose help he needed. After less than four years on the throne, he was forced to flee in 1688. Parliament then invited William of Orange, stadtholder of the Netherlands, who was married to James's Protestant daughter, Mary, to become king instead. They were equal monarchs: William III and Mary II. This sequence of events, in effect a bloodless coup, is remembered as The Glorious Revolution, important in British history, and a source of inspiration to the American revolutionaries of the 1770s and 1780s. From then on, the two unarguable points in English political life were, first, that the monarch must be a Protestant, and second, that the monarch could not reign without the support of Parliament. Never again has Britain confronted "regime change" as it did twice in the 17th century. Instead, a gradual process of political evolution substituted for the revolutions that have been so common in the rest of the world.

Although William was a tireless soldier, scourge of Louis XIV, he suffered from asthma and found life at Whitehall Palace unendurable because of the area's foggy humidity, close to the evil-smelling River Thames. Instead, he and Mary bought a big house at the western end of Hyde Park, a mile further back from the river, on higher ground. They hired the age's leading architect, Christopher Wren, to extend it, and renamed it Kensington Palace. It has been a royal residence ever since and is an outstanding example of late 17th and early 18th-century design and decoration (with many of its showrooms now open to the public). It was one of the homes of Princess Diana, the first wife of Prince Charles. When she was killed in a Paris car crash in 1997, mourners left more than a million bouquets of flowers outside its gates.

The turbulence of the 17th century threw up many radical political groups, like the Levellers. It also generated new religious groups, of which the most enduring is the Quakers. George Fox, a shepherd and wool-trader from Leicestershire, began the group in the immediate aftermath of the Civil War. The intensity of his preaching convinced influential people to follow him, some from the higher reaches of society. His group, the Society of Friends, did not believe in original sin, were absolute pacifists, never swore oaths, never differentiated by social rank, accepted no rituals or hierarchies in their religion, and treated one another as brothers and sisters. These were revolutionary concepts for the era. When a Derby judge sentenced him to prison for blasphemy, Fox told him to "tremble at the word of the lord." The judge sneered that men who trembled were "quakers." The insult stuck, and was taken up as a badge of honor.

Quaker meeting houses were designed to make a sharp contrast with churches. Often square, unadorned, without altars or iconography, they were the embodiment of the society's commitment to fraternity and equality. One of the best and oldest examples is Briggflatts in Cumbria, on the Eastern edge of the Lake District, still in use but also open to visitors. Its plain wooden benches form a square; members often sit in silence for the hour of their meeting, or utter simple prayers without any liturgy, preaching, or hierarchy.

The most famous English Quaker of the era, after Fox himself, was William Penn. Ironically, he was the son of a warrior—William Penn, Senior being an admiral, first for Cromwell and then for the restored Charles II. It would be hard to exaggerate the father's horror at his son's decision to join what was then regarded as a freakishly radical sect. At one point, the old admiral tried to beat it out of his son with a stick, but to no avail. The rest is history. Penn went on to found the colony of Pennsylvania, and the Quakers went on to pioneer the idea that slavery is a moral affront to God and must be ended. This is one more way in which the radicalism of 17th-century England created a great and positive heritage for the future.

9

ENLIGHTENMENT BRITAIN

The Enlightenment refers to a historical period during the late 17th and 18th centuries when European thinkers emphasized scientific method and the power of reason to improve the human condition. The Enlightenment transformed intellectual life in France, Germany, England, and Scotland. This lecture looks at important sites and people from that time, including:

- St. Paul's Cathedral, the greatest achievement of architect Christopher Wren.

- The work of architect Andrea Palladio.

- Notable houses from the Enlightenment era.

- The homes and gathering places of intellectual figures.

The Work of Christopher Wren

Premonitions of the Enlightenment came in the work of Christopher Wren. He was a mathematician and astronomer, and one of the first members of the Royal Society, founded in 1660.

St. Paul's Cathedral

The multitalented Wren was also the architect who set about redesigning and rebuilding London after the catastrophic Great Fire of 1666, including many churches that still stand, London's monument to the fire, and the Royal Observatory and hospital at Greenwich. Wren's greatest achievement was St. Paul's Cathedral, which has been a London landmark for more than 300 years.

The Work of Andrea Palladio

The Enlightenment era in Britain witnessed a fashion for the Palladian style. Andrea Palladio was an Italian architect of the 16th century who aimed to

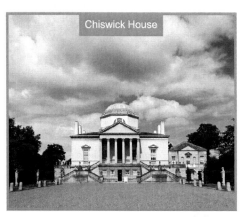
Chiswick House

revive building in the style of the Roman Empire. His *Four Books on Architecture*, first published in 1570, were influential throughout Europe and helped define British aristocratic taste in the 18th century. One of the first great Palladian buildings in Britain was Chiswick House in west London, recently restored and now in beautiful condition. Chiswick House is open to visitors regularly, while the grounds are open every day during daylight hours.

Homes of the Enlightenment

Hundreds of fine houses from the Enlightenment period survive. Many have become colleges, schools, or corporate headquarters, and some are now hotels. Luckily, dozens are open to the public as historic showplaces. Two notable sites are Kedleston Hall and Calke Abbey, both in Derbyshire. They are owned and cared for by the National Trust, but they tell very different stories.

Kedleston Hall

The estate of Kedleston belonged to the Curzon family before 1300. The current house was built by Robert Adam, a Scot who became one of the leading architects of the 18th century. Adam said his designs were not Palladian, but they certainly incorporated classical Roman themes.

From Kedleston, it's only about 20 miles to Calke Abbey, but Calke radiates a very different mood. Signs as visitors enter declare: "Welcome to Calke, the Un-Stately Home." Built in the first decade of the 1700s on the grand scale by an unknown architect, it was the property of the Harpur-Crewe family. The

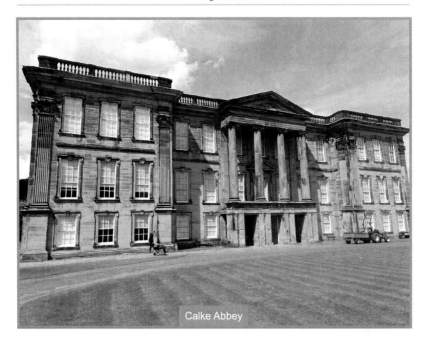
Calke Abbey

Harpur-Crewes became eccentric and reclusive, failed to keep up their great house, retreated into almost hermetic solitude, and let it go to ruin.

When the National Trust finally received the house in 1985, their first thought was to restore it to its days of splendor. On reflection, however, and in view of the terrifying expense that would have entailed, they decided on a different approach and put it on display as they had found it. Doing just enough work to prevent further deterioration, they offered visitors a glimpse of the other side of Britain's aristocracy.

The later generations of the Harpur-Crewes compulsively collected stuffed animals and stuffed birds, insects, and rocks and shells, and crammed the house with taxidermy, neglected areas of the house that began to leak, and retreated from one room after the next as it moldered. Calke acts as a reminder that old buildings of all kinds require constant work, that privileged people don't necessarily have good taste, and that the forces of order and entropy are constantly fighting it out.

Georgian Architecture

Members of the rising middle-class in the 18th century could not afford great stately homes, but the townhomes they favored were often sturdy enough to have survived in large numbers. The first four King Georges sat on the throne between 1714 and 1830, so buildings from this era are often called Georgian.

The place to see Georgian architecture at its best is Bath, in the county of Somerset. Robert Adam—earlier the architect at Kedleston—was also the architect of Pulteney Bridge, right in the heart of Bath. The town also features a circle of proud stone townhouses built in the 1750s and 1760s known as the Circus. The architects were a father-and-son team, both named John Wood.

Circus

Intellectual Figures

Britain's intellectual vitality continued to increase in those years, as new figures from the middle-classes began to affect national affairs. One place to trace their rising influence is in the modest Staffordshire town of Lichfield. It was home to three prominent Enlightenment-era figures: the writer Samuel Johnson, the actor David Garrick, and Erasmus Darwin, grandfather of Charles Darwin.

Johnson's birthplace and childhood home at the corner of the town square still stands; the square itself features a large statue of him. The house is now a museum and bookstore. One of Johnson's early ventures was to found a private school. It closed down after only one year for lack of business, but among the few pupils in attendance was Garrick. The Samuel Johnson birthplace includes plenty of pictures and busts of Garrick.

A few hundred yards from Johnson's house, best approached via Lichfield's wonderful medieval cathedral, is the home of Erasmus Darwin. He was a successful country doctor, inventor, poet, and polymath. He was also a

Erasmus Darwin's home

founding member of the Lunar Society, which included the innovative pottery entrepreneur Josiah Wedgwood, the scientist Joseph Priestley, the inventor James Watt, and Watt's business partner Matthew Boulton.

One of the rooms in the Lichfield house is an imaginative reconstruction of his medical office. His backyard is open to visitors, and this is where Mrs. Darwin kept her garden, where herbs for medicines were grown.

Suggested Reading

Foreman, *Georgiana, Duchess of Devonshire*.

Tinniswood, *His Invention So Fertile*.

Uglow, *The Lunar Men*.

Questions to Consider

1. Why should we, as tourists, be pleased by signs of the development of a vigorous middle class in the 18th century?

2. With which aspects of 18th-century aristocratic style is it easiest to be sympathetic, and with which the most difficult?

ENLIGHTENMENT BRITAIN

W̶e use the word "enlightenment" to mean a dawning realization, or an increased understanding of a complicated subject. If we capitalize the word and talk about "The Enlightenment," we're referring to a historical period, the late 17th and 18th centuries, when European thinkers emphasized scientific method and the power of reason to improve the human condition. The Enlightenment transformed intellectual life in France, Germany, England, and Scotland. To be enlightened was to reject arbitrary authority, to refute the tyranny of tradition, and to think logically.

Its supreme scientific representative in the English-speaking world was Isaac Newton. Its supreme representative in political theory was John Locke. Premonitions of the Enlightenment come in the work of Christopher Wren. He was a mathematician and astronomer, one of the first members of the Royal Society, founded 1660, along with Newton, Robert Hooke, Robert Boyle, and Edmund Halley, central figures of late 17th-century British scientific life. Other fellows of the Royal Society included Samuel Pepys and John Evelyn, two famous diarists, whose writing has left us with vivid descriptions of London's daily life in the era of King Charles II.

The multitalented Christopher Wren was also the architect who set about redesigning and rebuilding London after the catastrophic Great Fire of 1666, including many churches that still stand, the City of London's Monument to the fire, and the Royal Observatory and hospital at Greenwich. The Observatory, begun in 1675 and completed the next year, was Britain's first purpose-built scientific building. The Astronomer-Royal, John Flamsteed, labored there on accurate star charts as aids to navigation, and it became the site of the Prime Meridian, against which all the world's lines of longitude are measured.

Wren's greatest achievement was St. Paul's Cathedral, which has been a London landmark for more than 300 years, and became even more famous when it somehow escaped destruction during the intense German bombardment during World War II. Then it became yet more famous when Lady Diana Spencer married Prince Charles there in 1981. There's been a cathedral on the site for 1,400 years. The medieval gothic building lost in the fire was already in bad condition—Cromwell's army had stabled horses inside it during the interregnum. Wren, 34 years old at the time of the fire, had already proposed a radical makeover and the addition of a dome. When almost the whole medieval city burned to the ground, he proposed a new street plan with St. Paul's at its center. The plan was rejected as too ambitious and too costly. But the king, who admired Wren, did support his plans for a new Baroque cathedral. Intensive planning sessions followed and the landmark we know today was the outcome.

Building began in 1675. It wasn't finished until 1710 when Wren was 78, but that's relatively quick by comparison with most cathedrals. Wren was the first architect in European history to plan and begin building a cathedral, then have the satisfaction of seeing the job right through to completion. Its most prominent feature is the great dome. Part of the joy of visiting St. Paul's is climbing up to its "whispering gallery," whose acoustics are so good that whispers can be heard across its width, even when the place is humming with activity. Look down from the gallery, feel slightly queasy for a moment about what a long way down it is, then enjoy the view of the nave, and of the rich paintings on the spandrels and ceilings all around you.

Wren wanted this dome to be visible all across London, which meant it had to be high. For aesthetic reasons, however, it needed to be much shallower inside. He solved the problem by building a shallow dome inside a much steeper external one, with an empty space between them. Above the dome is the lantern, and finally the golden ball and cross, that make the top of St. Paul's so satisfying visually. Eighteenth-century views of London, such as the several painted by Canaletto, who made a long visit from Venice, show how brilliantly Wren succeeded in making St. Paul's dominate the city's skyline. The best of these paintings is *The River Thames With St. Paul's Cathedral on Lord Mayor's Day.* It's easy to imagine a performance of Handel's "Water Music" on the royal barges to complete the splendid scene.

Wren, son of an Anglican clergyman, did not want stained glass or the usual accoutrements of the many British cathedrals that had started out Catholic before the Reformation. St. Paul's was meant to be a distinctly Protestant place, an antithesis of the great domed Catholic cathedral of southern Europe, St. Peter's, in Rome. Only in the late 1700s, a century after its founding, did the first statues come in, slowly at first, but then more rapidly during the Napoleonic wars. The contrast with Catholic cathedrals is again instructive. There, the statues are always of saints. Here, they are of national heroes. By the 1770s, Westminster Abbey was already crammed with memorials, which made St. Paul's the logical next choice.

Britain's naval genius of the Napoleonic Wars, Horatio Nelson, is the subject of one of these statues. It was carved by John Flaxman to commemorate his victory and death at the Battle of Trafalgar in 1805. Nelson stands on a plinth, like a god, with a fur cape disguising the fact that his right arm is missing—it had been amputated after wounding in one of his many battles. Britannia, the spirit of the nation, guides two children to gaze at him and take inspiration from his example. This statue is in the main body of the cathedral. Underneath, in the crypt, is his tomb. The massive sarcophagus was not custom-built for the event, however. In fact, it was already nearly 300 years old, having been ordered originally by Cardinal Wolsey, Henry VIII's minister, back in the early 1500s. Wolsey fell from grace, Henry became too large to fit in it, and so the great object lay waiting for a hero sufficient unto its magnificence. Nelson was the man, and he is now lord of the crypt.

Britain's army genius of the Napoleonic Wars, the Duke of Wellington, is the subject of the biggest monument in the body of the cathedral itself. The Duke won, and survived, the Battle of Waterloo in 1815 and went on to a distinguished political career, including a stint as prime minister. His funeral in 1852 was one of the greatest state events of the century, for which 13,000 people crammed themselves into St. Paul's. A hole was cut in the floor so that his coffin could be lowered into the crypt, where it still lies in another massive marble sarcophagus. The memorial above, meanwhile, is a three-story monster, designed by Alfred Stevens, that took half a century to complete and features, on its highest level, an equestrian statue.

Dozens of other famous people from British life are buried at St. Paul's, including such artists as Anthony van Dyck, Joseph Mallord Turner, and Joshua Reynolds, writers like John Donne, and architects including Christopher Wren himself and Edwin Lutyens. On Wren's grave is a Latin inscription whose translation is: "If you seek my monument, look around you." They are joined by all the most important admirals and generals of the last two hundred years. The quality of the statues is extremely high, and you could spend hours admiring them and working out their iconography.

Perhaps the only drawback with St. Paul's was the temperature. One of the clergy, Sidney Smith, wrote to a friend who hoped to visit, in November 1833:

> To go to St. Paul's is certain death. The thermometer is several degrees below zero. My sentences are frozen as they come out of my mouth, and are thawed in the course of the summer, making strange noises and unexpected assertions in various parts of the church; but if you are tired of a world which is not tired of you, and are determined to go to St. Paul's, it becomes my duty to facilitate the desperate scheme.

The Enlightenment era in Britain witnessed a fashion for the Palladian style. Andrea Palladio was an Italian architect of the 16th century who aimed to revive building in the style of the Roman Empire. His *Four Books on Architecture*, first published in 1570, were influential throughout Europe and helped define British aristocratic taste in the 18th century. One of the first great Palladian buildings in Britain was Chiswick House in west London, recently restored and now in beautiful condition after some rocky years as a lunatic asylum and a fire station.

Chiswick House is open to visitors regularly, while the grounds are open every day during daylight. House and grounds are regarded by historians as equally important, because this was also a pioneer site of English landscape gardening. Richard Boyle, the third Earl of Burlington, a rich and learned man who had been on the Grand Tour to Italy, employed William Kent to design and build the house, less as a home than as a showpiece of the new style, and as a center for his extensive art collection. The house was finished in 1729.

In the late 1700s, Chiswick House passed into the hands of the Duke of Devonshire and his famous wife, Lady Georgiana Spencer. A biography by Amanda Foreman and a movie starring Keira Knightley have revived Georgiana's fame in recent years. It didn't hurt that she was an ancestor of Princess Diana, ran up immense gambling debts, was a fashion sensation in her time, and had a fascinating love life. She was a prominent political hostess for the Whig Party and held lavish receptions on behalf of the party at Chiswick House. She referred to the gardens there as her "Earthly paradise," and contributed a distinctive classical bridge, which is still there.

There's also a wonderful Ionic temple in the grounds, rather like a miniature version of the Pantheon in Rome. It's one of dozens of classically-influenced buildings and statues on the Chiswick estate that can be approached down hedged avenues and winding walkways. In 1813, a fine glass conservatory was added to the gardens for the cultivation of exotic plants, and it's still thriving. Every morning, dozens of local people walk their dogs in Chiswick Park, and on Sunday afternoons in summer there's usually a cricket match on one of the lawns. It's fun to see how this once-aristocratic milieu has been democratized.

Let's move from London to visit some provincial stately homes that were also built in the 18th century. Hundreds of fine houses from this period survive. Many have become colleges, schools, or corporate headquarters, and some are now hotels. Luckily, dozens are open to the public as historic showplaces. The two I have in mind—Kedleston Hall and Calke Abbey, both in Derbyshire—are owned and cared for by the National Trust, but they tell very different stories.

The estate of Kedleston already belonged to the Curzon family before 1300. The current house was built by Robert Adam, a Scot who became one of the leading architects of the 18th century. Adam said his designs were not Palladian, but they certainly incorporated classical Roman themes. Kedleston's South front, for example, emulates the Arch of Constantine in

Rome. The house overlooks artfully informal grounds, now grazed by sheep. Inside and out, it was designed to impress and to project the magnificence of its owners.

The great hall is immense, with high fluted pillars, marble, brown and cream, with life-size statues of gods, muses, and nymphs in niches. It's the perfect venue if you're holding a banquet with 60 guests, or a grand ball. Behind the hall, nearly as high but more livable, is the saloon—a circular room, domed, and with a skylight and superb acoustics. No one seeing a room like this today would describe it as a saloon, and no one hearing about a saloon would think of a room like this. But that's what it's called.

In the 1980s and 1990s, my father and his friends, enthusiasts for Renaissance-era music, played informal concerts there on crumhorns, racketts, recorders, and shawms, to charm or perplex the Sunday-afternoon visitors. I had the privilege of playing with them there several times.

The other state rooms at Kedleston are sumptuous and opulent. Experts have been restoring faded elements, notably the blue damask wall coverings and the gilding of couches and chairs. The plaster ceilings are wonderfully intricate, and the whole house is packed with family treasures from the ages. Countless members of the family led lives of public service, but the Curzons reached their zenith at the end of the 19th century with George Nathaniel, a haughty aristocrat and Conservative politician, who was Viceroy of India between 1898 and 1905.

The Viceroy's house in Calcutta, the Raj Bhavan, was itself modeled on Kedleston, with the result that George Curzon lived in a kind of home away from home. On the ground floor of Kedleston today is a collection of treasures that he brought back from India. One is a silver and brocade howdah, the elevated box in which you ride an elephant. Another is the spectacular peacock dress that Lady Curzon wore to a great Durbar in 1903, honoring the accession of King Edward VII.

The Kedleston church, right beside the great house, features a sundial, over which is written the two words "We shall." It's actually a pun, and an incitement to reflect on mortality. You look at the words, and then you look at the sundial, and then you say to yourself "We shall sundial." Slowing it down slightly, that becomes "We shall soon die all." Inside is the Curzons' family chapel, whose evidence confirms the message. Among the many memorials, each characteristic of its era, is one to William Curzon, a younger son of the family from the early 19th century, who fought with the Duke of Wellington's army and died in the Battle of Waterloo, at the age of 24.

From Kedleston, it's only about 20 miles to Calke Abbey, but Calke radiates a very different mood. Signs as you enter declare: "Welcome to Calke, the Un-Stately Home." Built in the first decade of the 1700s on the grand scale, but by an unknown architect, and at first comparable in magnificence to Kedleston, it was the property of the Harpur-Crewe family. But whereas the Curzons gained in social and political prominence, the Harpur-Crewes became eccentric and reclusive, failed to keep up their great house, retreated into almost hermetic solitude, and let it go to ruin.

When the National Trust finally received the house in 1985, their first thought was to restore it to its days of splendor, like most of the other stately homes they care for. On reflection, however, and in view of the terrifying expense that would have entailed, they decided on a different approach and put it on display as they had found it. Doing just enough work to prevent further deterioration, they offered visitors a glimpse of the other side of Britain's aristocracy. The later generations of the Harpur-Crewes had poor taste, compulsively collected stuffed animals and stuffed birds, insects and butterflies, rocks and shells, crammed the house with taxidermy, neglected areas of the house that began to leak, and retreated from one room after the next as it moldered. Houses of this size are hard to heat, hard to maintain, and very costly to run. Once the family loses the initiative to hire the right staff and keep on top of everything, decay soon sets in.

The rooms on the lower floors still show signs of the old magnificence, but as you ascend to the upper floors you find growing signs of neglect. In one bedroom, the wallpaper is coming off in strips, and flakes of paint sag from the ceiling. In another, the bed is covered with antlers and stuffed deer heads, along with bits of rock, old pictures, and cane chairs that have broken through. Ominous cracks across the greyish ceiling bespeak leaks. Heaps of antiquated newspapers are scattered over every surface in a third room, carefully left in place as they were found. And everywhere there are the display cases with hundreds of stuffed birds, insects, rock collections, and fossils. Peek around the door into a cupboard that contains dozens of ancient oil lamps, no two of them matching, which reflect the fact that electricity came late to Calke. Very late in fact; not until 1962. One of the first showers in world history is stuck in a moldy bathroom; in the old nursery is a clutter of mismatched children's chairs. The austere kitchen is in a bleakly fascinating state of decay. Calke acts as a reminder that old buildings of all kinds require constant work, that privileged people don't necessarily have good taste, and that the forces of order and entropy are constantly fighting it out.

Members of the rising middle-class in the 18th century could not afford great stately homes, but the town homes they favored were often sturdy enough, and graceful enough, to have survived in large numbers. The first four King Georges sat on the throne between 1714 and 1830, so buildings from this era are often called Georgian. The place to see Georgian architecture at its best is Bath, in the county of Somerset. I mentioned Robert Adam earlier—he was the architect at Kedleston. He was also the architect of Pulteney Bridge, right in the heart of Bath.

While you're in this lovely old city, with its Roman baths and its medieval abbey, go also to "the Circus," a circle of proud stone town houses built in the 1750s and 1760s in three ranges. The architects were a father-and-son team, John Wood the Elder and the Younger. They too incorporated classical elements, using Doric, Roman, and Corinthian pillars on each of the different levels, a decorated entablature, and a stone balustrade topped by big stone acorns. Their curved frontage is aesthetically satisfying, and these houses were popular right from the outset. Thomas Gainsborough, the leading portrait painter of his day, lived there in the 1760s and 70s. John Wood the Younger went on to build the Royal Crescent in Bath, an equally grand arc of neoclassical houses confronting a great lawn. It is 500 feet long with over a hundred Ionic columns. No film or TV version of a Jane Austen novel is complete without a scene or two showing the young ladies as they stroll in the circus or the Royal Crescent.

I don't mean to imply, with this lecture's choices, that great houses and great churches are the only legacy we have from the 18th century. Britain's intellectual vitality continued to increase in those years, as new figures from the middle-classes began to affect national affairs. One place to trace their rising influence is in the modest Staffordshire town of Lichfield. It was home to three prominent Enlightenment-era figures: Samuel Johnson, David Garrick, and Erasmus Darwin.

Johnson was a novelist, essayist, and journalist, and is best known for writing the first full-scale English dictionary. His birthplace and childhood home at the corner of the town square still stands; the square itself features a large statue of him. The house is now a museum but also a bookstore—go in, ramble up and down the five floors, buy a book, and give a contribution to the museum's upkeep if you feel like it. The top floor discloses the old timbered skeleton of the house; lower down is the room in which Johnson was born, and in the basement is the kitchen, where he got a terrible scare as a nine-year-old reading the ghost scene in *Hamlet*.

One of Johnson's early ventures was to found a private school. It closed down after only one year for lack of business, but among the few pupils in attendance was David Garrick. Johnson and Garrick left Lichfield together to try their luck in London, and both succeeded. Johnson became a literary celebrity, whose cult was amplified by his amanuensis and biographer, James Boswell. Garrick became the most famous actor of his era, excelling in tragic and comic roles, promoting Shakespeare to an 18th-century audience that had not yet learned to revere him as we do, and enjoying the patronage of major painters, who depicted him in some of his more famous roles. The Samuel Johnson birthplace includes plenty of pictures and busts of Garrick.

Pride of place at the Johnson house goes, as it should, to an original edition of Johnson's dictionary, which was published in 1755 after nine years' hard work. It wasn't the very first English dictionary but it was far more ambitious than its predecessors, and it contributed to the standardization of the language and of English spelling. What an amazing project for one man to undertake! It includes 40,000 entries, illustrated by 114,000 quotations and examples, most of which were provided by his six research assistants. As you browse the columns, you're struck by his phenomenal erudition and his stick-to-it-iveness. You're also likely to be struck by his dry humor. For "oats," he gives this definition: "A grain, which in England is generally given to horses, but in Scotland supports the people." That's a typical example of 18th-century English scorn for Scotland. His Scots friend Boswell retorted that the definition was true, but that it showed England had the better horses, and Scotland the better men.

A few hundred yards from Johnson's house, best approached via Lichfield's wonderful medieval cathedral, is the home of Erasmus Darwin. Grandfather of the evolutionary theorist Charles Darwin, he was himself an exemplar of the Enlightenment spirit. Interested in everything, he was a successful country doctor, inventor, poet, and polymath. He was also a founding member of the "Lunar Society," which included the innovative pottery entrepreneur Josiah Wedgwood, the scientist Joseph Priestley, the inventor James Watt, and Watt's business partner Matthew Boulton. Among other notable members was William Small, a physician and professor recently returned from the American colonies, where his best student had been young Thomas Jefferson. Benjamin Franklin, on his frequent visits to England, used to attend meetings too.

The Lunar Society met on Sunday evenings when the moon was full so that members could safely make their way home by moonlight afterwards. They prided themselves on practical usefulness and clear thinking. They were also early advocates of the abolition of slavery. At least one meeting of the Lunar Society took place in the Darwin house, where Erasmus's invention of a horizontal windmill was the topic for discussion. A drawing of the windmill, and others among his many inventions, are on display.

Erasmus Darwin's day job was as a doctor, and one of the rooms in the Lichfield house is an imaginative reconstruction of his medical office. His backyard, open to visitors, is Mrs. Darwin's "physic garden," where herbs for medicines were grown. A lucky early success in saving the life of a seemingly incurable patient gave him a valuable reputation in and around Lichfield, where he practiced for most of his adult life. So great was his renown that King George III invited him to become royal physician, an extremely well paid post, but he declined. Surprisingly, to me at least, he was also regarded in his lifetime as one of the great poets. His observations of nature gave him a premonition of the idea of evolution, which he outlined in a long poetic work, *The Botanic Garden*. But whatever its theoretical foreshadowings, you'll find it almost unreadable. It's packed with elaborate anthropomorphization, evocations of nymphs and satyrs, very long-winded, and soon tedious.

One more thing about Erasmus Darwin: he fathered 14 children. Two of them were illegitimate, daughters of his servant. He loved them both and, later in life, founded a girls' academy in the town of Ashbourne, Derbyshire, so that they could have work as its resident teachers. He intended them to put into practice his belief that girls as well as boys should learn science. The building, which had been a pub before they arrived, and later became the home of a respected doctor, is still there today, now known as "Madge House."

Here's one final 18th-century practice to look out for as you travel around Britain: bricked-up windows. A revenue-hungry government placed a tax on windows in 1696. The owners of houses with fewer than 10 windows paid a flat rate of two shillings, after which more windows meant a higher charge. Frugal homeowners responded by bricking up some of their windows, even though their homes' interiors must have been pretty dim already. In many cases, their descendants never got around to unbricking them when the tax was abolished in 1851, which is why they're still quite a common sight even today. What a satisfying irony, that the era of Enlightenment should witness people all over Britain diminishing the light in their homes.

There is much to admire in the Enlightenment spirit and in the extensive architectural heritage it has bequeathed to us. Military considerations are no longer significant. Where medieval Britain had been dominated by castles and cathedrals, Enlightenment-era Britain was indulging a taste for comfort, opulence, and the intelligent use of resources. It was also on the verge of a great economic and technological adventure: the Industrial Revolution.

10

INDUSTRIAL BRITAIN

T he Industrial Revolution began in the mid-1700s, picked up speed in the early 1800s, and transformed Great Britain more than any other process before or since. Several generations of inventors and entrepreneurs looked for new and better ways of solving old problems. The machines, factories, canals, railways, and cities they built transformed Britain and taught the rest of the world that industrialization could mitigate the age-old problems of mass poverty and privation. This lecture looks at sites that remain from the time of the Industrial Revolution. Topics discussed include:

- Textiles.

- Iron.

- Coal.

- Canals.

- Railways.

Textiles

Textiles were the first commodities to be factory produced in large quantities. Derbyshire in the North Midlands is the place where the industry started, and it is now a UNESCO-designated World Heritage Site of early industrialization. The fast-flowing River Derwent was adapted to turn water wheels that powered early spinning machines.

In the small town of Belper, more of this heritage is preserved at the North Mill. It is the oldest part of a textile-making complex that kept growing until the early 20th century, under the supervision of the Strutt family. Guides will show visitors examples of the old machines.

Belper Mill

A third old textile mill stands in the much bigger town of Derby, a bit farther south. This is the old Silk Mill, which is widely regarded as the first factory in Britain. It was built in 1721 by two brothers, John and Thomas Lombe, but still looks more or less as it has for three centuries.

The single best place in Britain to study the history of the textile trade is at Quarry Bank Mill in Cheshire, just south of Manchester. When Britain made the switch from water to steam power in the late 1700s and early 1800s, much of the textile business moved to big lowland towns near the coast, the most famous of which was Manchester. At Quarry Bank Mill, every generation of textile machinery is represented.

Iron

If textiles were the first boom commodities in the Industrial Revolution, iron was the next. The place to see vestiges of England's early iron industry is in the Coalbrookdale valley in Shropshire, near the Welsh border. Like the Derwent Valley, this is a hilly area with fast-flowing water that was, at first, the all-important source of energy. Many generations of the Darby family lived there and ran successful iron works.

Ironbridge

The most distinguished object in the valley was built in 1779 by Abraham Darby III. It is the world's first bridge made of iron. The local people were

Coalbrookdale

so proud of it that they changed the name of their town from Madeley to Ironbridge. It is elegant, elaborately decorated, and still strong enough to bear the weight of the thousands of pedestrians who come to visit every year.

Coalbrookdale, the section of the River Severn that flows through the Ironbridge Gorge, was designated a World Heritage Site by UNESCO in 1986. It features dozens of interesting places to visit, including the fine home of the Darby family itself. Best of all is the Blists Hill Victorian Town, which features dozens of historical reenactors.

Coal

As coal-powered steam engines displaced water wheels, British coal mining grew by leaps and bounds. Once the world's leading coal-producing nation, entire areas of the country were dominated by the mines.

However, after World War II, the whole industry was nationalized and gradually became uncompetitive. Margaret Thatcher broke the power of Britain's coal-mining unions in the 1980s and accelerated the closing of mines that had become inefficient and unprofitable. Only a handful of coal miners still work in Britain today. In one sense, that's a positive because mining was always an extremely dangerous job. In another sense, it's a negative because entire areas, once thriving with coal, are now blighted by high levels of unemployment.

To learn what the life was like for coal miners, go to the Big Pit in the South Wales village of Blaenafon, from which coal was dug between the 1880s and the 1980s. It stands on a bleak hillside that looks utterly miserable in the frequent rainstorms that sweep across it, but it has a gaunt beauty when the sun shines. The underground tour of the mine, led by retired miners, is a revelation for visitors.

Canals

Among the biggest problems confronting the producers of textiles, iron, and coal was how to move these heavy, bulky commodities from site to market and how to bring in the raw materials. Transportation in Britain during the 1700s was slow and costly, mostly by wagon or packhorse overland, or by sailing freighters along the coast.

That situation began to change with the creation of canals, the first of which to have a major economic effect was built by James Brindley for a Lancashire coal-mine owner, the duke of Bridgwater, in 1761. Between the 1770s and the 1820s, there followed a spate of canal building that linked up all the major towns of England, including many of the new ones that were springing up as industrial centers. The innovation of locks further improved canals.

A few spectacular canal-related sites are particularly deserving of a visit. The first is the Boat Lift in the village of Anderton, Cheshire, on the Trent and Mersey Canal. Designed and built in the 1870s, it carries boats from the high level of the canal down to the low level of the River Weaver.

Another great sight is long flights of locks, where the lower gate of one lock doubles as the upper gate of the next. The best example in the north of England is the Bingley Five Rise, near Bradford in Yorkshire.

A third great sight is the Pontcysyllte Aqueduct on the Llangollen Canal, in North East Wales. Built by the master bridge builder Thomas Telford, it took 10 years before its grand opening in 1805. It is the highest aqueduct in the world, standing 126 feet above the valley.

Railways

No sooner had a comprehensive canal system been finished than it was upstaged by railways. This is another world-changing technology that was pioneered in Britain and then spread everywhere else. Britain was seized by railway mania in the 1830s and 1840s, building hundreds then thousands of miles of lines. Journeys that had taken weeks shrank to hours.

Some ill-considered lines were destined never to make a profit. Others closed at various points in the 20th century, and they now comprise an important part of the Sustrans bicycle network and pedestrian-friendly paths. An example is the scenic High Peak Trail through the center of the Peak District National Park and the Tissington Trail to which it is linked.

In 1968 British Railways, the government-run organization that had controlled the whole system since nationalization in 1948, withdrew its last steam locomotives from service. Howls of anguish arose from steam train lovers throughout the nation.

They at once began buying up locomotives to prevent them from being scrapped. They also bought up lengths of disused railway and turned them back into working lines, lovingly restoring old equipment and putting it back into use every weekend.

There are more than a hundred of these heritage railways, with more than 400 steam-powered locomotives still in operation. Some are just a mile or two in length, but the best of them, such as the Great Central Railway in Leicestershire, the Severn Valley Railway in Worcestershire, the North

Yorkshire Moors Railway, and the Bluebell Railway in Sussex, are long enough to let the locomotives pick up speed and emulate their original performance. They have become a major tourist attraction in their own right, with tens of thousands of annual visitors.

Suggested Reading

Hannavy, *Britain's Industrial Heritage*.

Smiles, *Lives of the Engineers*.

Weightman, *The Industrial Revolutionaries*.

Suggested Activities

1. When you are in any of Britain's cities, look at the way the landscape has been modified by canal and railway builders.

2. Travel by train at least once. It's likely that you'll be following the exact course laid down by Victorian engineers nearly two centuries ago.

10

INDUSTRIAL BRITAIN

The Industrial Revolution began in the middle 1700s, picked up speed in the early 1800s, and transformed Great Britain more than any other process before or since. It was based on the insight that the future can be different from, and better than, the present, and that the traditional way of making things is not always the best way. From the mid-18th to the mid-19th centuries, several generations of inventors and entrepreneurs looked for new and better ways of solving old problems, such as how to make clothes and metal goods, and how to move heavy loads from one place to another. The machines, factories, canals, railways, and cities they built transformed Britain, and taught the rest of the world that industrialization could mitigate the age-old problems of mass poverty and privation.

It was a funny kind of revolution, however, not at all like the French or Russian Revolutions. It happened much more gradually, and didn't even get its name, "Industrial Revolution," until well after the fact. To most people it was almost imperceptible, even though its long-term effects have been profound. Only gradually, over the course of several generations, did large numbers of families give up farming or cottage industry and move to factories, foundries, coal mines, and the cities that grew up around them. Britain today is full of wonderfully interesting vestiges of its industrial past. Luckily, it is also full of men and women devoted to preserving it.

Textiles were the first thing to be factory-produced in large quantities. Derbyshire in the north Midlands is the place where it started, and is now a UNESCO-designated World Heritage Site of early industrialization. The fast-flowing River Derwent was adapted to turn water wheels that powered early spinning machines. Many of the most effective machines were designed and built by Richard Arkwright, originally a wig-maker from Preston in Lancashire. In the 1760s and 1770s, he built a factory in the village of Cromford which still stands, now serving as a museum of early industry. You can still see the mill race, the channel that brings fast-flowing water to the great pit in which immense water wheels were sited. Also, you can visit the worker's cottages that he built to house the workers he coaxed in from the surrounding countryside. It wasn't easy; rural English workers, mostly illiterate, were used to working according to the seasons, not the clock, and were reluctant to conform to Arkwright's ideas of punctuality, sobriety, and obedience. He, like all early industrialists, had to fight against the workers' tendency to keep chaotic hours and devote Mondays, nicknamed "Saint Monday," to carousing or sleeping off hangovers. Hard and monotonous work was one of the many unwelcome innovations of industrial life.

A few miles down the scenic Derwent Valley, along the A6, in the small town of Belper, more of this heritage is preserved at the old North Mill. It is the oldest part of a textile-making complex that kept growing, until the early 20th century, under the supervision of the Strutt family. Guides will show you examples of the old machines, such as Arkwright's "water frame" and its predecessor, the Hargreaves "spinning jenny," now hand-cranked to demonstrate how they converted raw wool or cotton into thread ready for weaving. In the cobbled back streets of Belper that climb up the steep valley sides, you can see superb surviving examples of purpose-built workers' cottages from the 1790s, the "Long Row," one range of which has a continuous sloping roof covering a long line of the houses. Also there stands the Unitarian Chapel built by the Strutt family. His and many of the earliest industrial families did not belong to the established Church of England.

The Strutts became philanthropists and tried to avoid the reputation of being hard-driving bosses who ground their workers' faces. The pleasure gardens they built behind the North Mill are still delightful; you can row a boat on an artificially widened part of the Derwent River and listen to brass bands play in the bandstand on summer days.

A third fine old textile mill stands in the much bigger town of Derby, a little bit further south. This is the old Silk Mill, which is widely regarded as the first factory in Britain. It was built in 1721 by two brothers, John and Thomas Lombe, and extended later, but still looks more or less as it has for three centuries. Legends surround the brothers' work, including one that they had stolen the secret of silk spinning from Italy, and that John's premature death in 1722 was caused by an Italian assassin who got his revenge by poisoning. A factory of any sort was a curiosity in the 1700s—among those who went to see it was Dr. Johnson's friend and biographer, Boswell. Like so many early factories it was insanitary, deafeningly noisy, and employed dozens of wretched pauper children. In recent decades, by contrast, it has been the city of Derby's industrial museum. It now stands in a fine open landscaped area between the River Derwent, Derby Cathedral, and a statue of Bonnie Prince Charlie.

Loyal as I am to my home town of Derby, however, I have to admit that the single best place in Britain to study the history of the textile trade is at Quarry Bank Mill in Cheshire, just south of Manchester. When Britain made the switch from water to steam power in the late 1700s and early 1800s, much of the textile business moved to big lowland towns near the coast, the most famous of which was Manchester. At Quarry Bank Mill, every generation of textile machinery is represented, including wonderful working examples of the Crompton mule, a sophisticated third-generation spinning machine, along with superb high speed looms, or weaving machines, harnessed to a massive, still-revolving water wheel whose power is transmitted throughout by an intricate series of shafts, gears, pulleys, and belts. It's deafening when all the machines are working, but well-trained curators turn them off frequently to explain what's going on.

If textiles were the first boom commodity in the Industrial Revolution, iron was the next. The place to see vestiges of England's early iron industry is in the Coalbrookdale valley in Shropshire, near the Welsh border. Like the Derwent Valley, this too is a hilly area with fast-flowing water that was, at first, the all-important source of energy. Many generations of the Darby family lived there and ran successful ironworks. Abraham Darby I discovered in the early 1700s that iron could be smelted out of the ore by using coke, a form of bituminous coal that has been baked to drive out sulfur impurities. This was important because until then charcoal had been used, and Britain was so widely deforested that charcoal had become costly and difficult to obtain. Coal, by contrast, was plentiful, especially in that area, such that Darby's discovery assured the future of the iron business. It didn't crush so easily as charcoal, with the result that bigger blast furnaces could be built, the remains of which are still visible up and down the valley.

The most distinguished object in the valley was built in 1779 by Abraham Darby III, grandson of the earlier iron master. It is the world's first bridge made of iron. The local people were so proud of it that they changed the name of their town from Madeley to Ironbridge. Far from being an ugly, utilitarian thing as you might expect of the first iron bridge, it is elegant, elaborately decorated, and still strong enough to bear the weight of the thousands of pedestrians who come to visit every year.

Coalbrookdale, the section of the River Severn that flows through the Ironbridge Gorge, was designated a world heritage site by UNESCO in 1986, and there are dozens of interesting places to visit, including the fine home of the Darby family itself. Best of all is the Blists Hill Victorian Town, which features dozens of historical reenactors running steam engines, making iron castings, shoeing horses, making paper by hand, and running shops and businesses as they were run in the mid-1800s. It is extensive and gives you a lively sense of what life in a pre-motor vehicle industrial town must have been like. The acrid smell of burning coal is also a reminder of what an extraordinarily clean atmosphere we enjoy by comparison.

Among the fascinating exhibits nearby is a set of immense bottle-shaped pottery kilns and the Coalbrookdale tar tunnel, originally built to carry a canal to the bottom levels of a hillside coalmine. When tar, or bitumen, began to ooze from the walls, it was collected in barrels and marketed as a naval waterproofing substance. Ropes covered in bitumen rotted more slowly than those left untreated, and the tar could be used to caulk the planking of ships. Tar even doubled as a patent medicine, sometimes mixed with opium. Altogether there are 10 museum areas up and down the valley, immensely interesting, well-curated, and informative. I cannot recommend it too strongly.

As coal-powered steam engines displaced waterwheels, British coal mining grew by leaps and bounds. Once the world's leading coal-producing nation, entire areas of the country were dominated by the mines, including parts of Yorkshire and Lancashire, County Durham, the Scottish Lowlands, parts of Nottinghamshire, and much of south Wales. D. H. Lawrence, a coal miner's son from Nottinghamshire, draws a harsh and vivid picture of life for mining families in his 1913 novel *Sons and Lovers*. His mother was determined that he would not follow his father into the mines.

After World War II the whole industry was nationalized and gradually became uncompetitive. Margaret Thatcher broke the power of Britain's coal-mining unions in the 1980s and accelerated the closing of mines that had become inefficient and unprofitable. Only a handful of coal miners still work in Britain today. In one sense that's a good thing, because mining was always an extremely dangerous job, exposing the miners to cave-ins, floods, poisonous gases, explosions, and lung disease. In another sense, it's a bad thing because entire areas, once thriving with coal, are now blighted by high levels of unemployment.

To learn what the life was like, go to the "Big Pit" in the south Wales village of Blaenafon, from which coal was dug between the 1880s and the 1980s. It stands on a bleak hillside that looks utterly miserable in the frequent rainstorms that sweep across it, but has a kind of gaunt beauty when the sun shines. The buildings are mainly of rusting corrugated iron, and the whole thing is grimly utilitarian. But the underground tour of the mine workings is a revelation. Old retired miners with beautiful Welsh accents guide you around, explaining how the mine was ventilated, how the miners' safety lamp works, how canaries could give early warning of asphyxiation, how young children often had to sit in total darkness guarding doors to the workings, how horses to pull coal wagons were stabled underground for years at a time, how rats came down along with the horses' feed, and how gradually machinery and safety devices made the miners' lives slightly safer.

Wearing overalls, helmets and headlamps you plunge down the shaft that carried working men to their daily tasks for a century, and tramp through corridors that have been twisted and distorted by geological forces, as streams of subterranean water run past in drainage channels. You feel grateful for the extensive shoring of pit props above your head that keep the roof up, and grateful for having to go into such environments so rarely that it's a treat rather than an ordeal.

Above ground, the Big Pit's museum of south Wales mining is exemplary, bringing the story right into the mid and late-twentieth century and revealing, perhaps inadvertently, just how much British mining didn't keep up with its overseas rivals. All around the mine itself, the hillside is disfigured by great lumpy slag heaps, now half-grown over with grass. Incidentally, the nearby village of Aberfan was the site of a terrible mining disaster in 1966 when 150,000 tons of slag slid down the hillside and smothered the local school and a row of houses, killing 116 children and 28 adults. I was 10 at the time and have a vivid memory of hearing the news. The Aberfan disaster rocked Britain, and led to a great outpouring of public grief and sympathy, along with a stern political review of the National Coal Board's negligent disposal practices. A row of white arches in Aberfan cemetery commemorates the lost children.

Among the biggest problems confronting the manufacturers of textiles and iron, and the miners of coal, was how to move these heavy, bulky commodities from site to market, and how to bring in the raw materials. Transportation in Britain during the 1700s was slow and costly, mostly by wagon or packhorse overland, or by sailing freighters along the coast. That situation began to change with the creation of canals, the first of which to have a major economic effect was built by James Brindley for a Lancashire coalmine owner, the Duke of Bridgwater, in 1761. The idea of building an artificial waterway was bold enough—what made it really extraordinary was Brindley's decision at one point to carry the canal over a river, using a bridge called the Barton Aqueduct. To see boats sailing overhead caused a sensation, but the success of the canal convinced early skeptics that this was a technology that really worked. A horse trudging along the adjacent towpath could pull a loaded canal barge 50 times its own weight. Coal went on sale in nearby Manchester for a much lower price than ever before, and handsomely rewarded the Duke of Bridgwater for the risk he had taken.

What followed between the 1770s and the 1820s was a spate of canal building that linked up all the major towns of England, including many of the new ones that were springing up as industrial centers. Canal travel was much safer than travel on coastal ships because there was no risk of storm or shipwreck. Canals also meant that entrepreneurs whose factories were inland, such as the china manufacturer Josiah Wedgwood, could bring in raw materials and export finished goods much more economically than before. Wedgwood acted as unpaid treasurer for the Trent and Mersey Canal, one of Brindley's biggest projects, and was able to persuade dozens of businessmen up and down the course of the canal that it would profit them to invest. It still runs beside the Wedgwood factories in Stoke-on-Trent, linking it to Liverpool on the west coast and Hull on the east.

By the 1770s, the technology of locks had been perfected, enabling canals in effect to climb hills. So long as a reliable supply of water flowed into the canal at the highest point, arranging for it to flow in a controlled way through the lock gates enabled barges to rise and fall to different levels. Much of the canal system fell into disuse in the early 20th century, but starting in the 1960s, a popular movement to restore them drew in thousands of enthusiastic citizens. By now, virtually the whole system is once more up and running, supervised by a government agency. On more than 2,000 miles of canals it is possible to sail in lovingly built and beautifully decorated long boats. Some families actually live on them, in marinas scattered all over the country. Many more people rent them for leisurely vacations, and the whole system is alive with these slow-moving beauties every day, and especially every weekend every summer.

At the locks, which are the system's bottlenecks, tolls used to be paid. Now the toll-keepers' cottages have been restored and are often festooned with summer flowers. Country pubs cluster nearby and do a thriving trade. The general air of peacefulness that pervades the canals makes it difficult to recall that these were integral parts of an industrial system. To remind yourself that these were commercial waterways, visit the Gas Street Basin in Birmingham where several canals came together around a series of wharves and warehouses. This too is an area now given over to restaurants and bars rather than bulk commodity shipping, but enough of the old buildings remain to create the mood of bustling trade.

Alongside every canal runs the towpath, on which horses once trudged, roped to the barges. Now these are parts of a vast nationwide system of footpaths, and in places are also elements of the national cycle network, "Sustrans." Dog walkers and joggers make extensive use of them, and so should you—it's the perfect place to get away from traffic and to enjoy the canal-side flora and fauna.

A few spectacular canal-related sites are particularly deserving of a visit. The first is the Boat Lift in the village of Anderton, Cheshire, on the Trent and Mersey Canal. Designed and built in the 1870s, it carries boats from the high level of the canal down to the low level of the River Weaver. It's based on a simple concept—that the weight of water plus a boat in one compartment will cause it to sink while the slightly lower weight of boat and water in the other compartment will cause it to rise. They are hydraulically linked. In this way, goods no longer had to be offloaded from one boat, dragged up an inclined plane, and loaded onto another. Instead, the same boat, fully laden, could sail on both waterways.

Another great sight is long flights of locks, where the lower gate of one lock doubles as the upper gate of the next. The best example in the north of England is the Bingley Five Rise, near Bradford in Yorkshire. It is part of the Leeds and Liverpool Canal, which crossed the Pennine Hills of central England, and was opened in 1774. Thirty thousand people turned out to see what was in its day, a sensational achievement, and if you're like me you'll agree that it's still very much worth watching even today. The best example in the south of England is the Caen Hill Locks on the Kennet and Avon Canal, in Wiltshire. Here there are 29 locks in three groups. The whole series rises nearly 240 feet and makes an astonishingly elegant display. Opened in 1810, they were the key to a waterway that linked Bristol and Bath in the southwest, to London and the Thames Valley in the east.

A third great sight is the Pontcysyllte Aqueduct on the Llangollen Canal, in northeast Wales. Built by the master bridge builder Thomas Telford, it took 10 years before its grand opening in 1805, and is the highest aqueduct in the world, standing 126 feet above the valley. Telford built a series of stone piers across the valley of the River Dee, then installed a cast-iron trough on top of them to carry the waterway itself, an approach which cost far less than an all-stone construction. It's possible today to take a boat across the aqueduct, and it's a thrill. On one side of your boat is the towpath, where anxious pedestrians grip the handrail and look a long, long way down into the valley. But on the canal side there is no fence—you just look straight out from the boat to the precipice. Incidentally, from Llangollen, it's possible to take a canal-boat ride old-style, pulled by a horse rather than powered by diesel.

No sooner had a comprehensive canal system been finished than it was upstaged by railways. This is another world-changing technology that was pioneered in Britain and then spread everywhere else. Horse-drawn tramways preceded steam railways by a century. The first steam-locomotive-powered train ran as a curiosity at a London show in 1808, built by a Cornish mining engineer named Richard Trevithick. Rapid improvements in the basic technology were made by George Stephenson, also a mining engineer. He was chief engineer for the Stockton and Darlington Railway which opened in 1825, and then for the Liverpool and Manchester Railway, that opened in 1830. On both projects, he overcame formidable construction difficulties and, with the help of his equally talented son Robert Stephenson, built the world's finest and fastest locomotives. Their engine, the *Rocket*, traveled at 30 miles per hour and caused a sensation on opening day. The original *Rocket* still exists, by now a rather grim black object in the Kensington Science Museum. To get a sense of how it looked in its glory days, however, see instead (or as well!) the bright-yellow working replica at the National Railway Museum in York.

Britain was seized by "railway mania" in the 1830s and 1840s, building hundreds, then thousands of miles of lines, eclipsing the canals, and further linking together every part of the kingdom. Journeys that had taken weeks shrank to hours. By 1850 it was possible to travel from London to Edinburgh, about 400 miles, on the same day—a previously unimaginable feat. Some ill-considered lines were destined never to make a profit, others closed at various points in the 20th century, and they now comprise an important part of the Sustrans bicycle network and as pedestrian-friendly paths. One of my favorites is the scenic High Peak Trail through the center of the Peak District National Park, and the Tissington Trail to which it is linked.

In 1968, British Railways, the government-run organization that had controlled the whole system since nationalization in 1948, withdrew its last steam locomotives from service. Howls of anguish arose from steam train lovers throughout the nation. Rather than just take it on the chin, however, they at once began buying up locomotives to prevent them from being scrapped. They also bought up lengths of disused railway, and turned them back into working lines, lovingly restoring old equipment and putting it back into use every weekend. There are more than a hundred of what are now called "heritage railways," with more than 400 steam-powered locomotives still in operation. Some are just a mile or two in length, but the best of them, such as the Great Central Railway in Leicestershire, the Severn Valley Railway in Worcestershire, the North Yorkshire Moors Railway, and the Bluebell Railway in Sussex, are long enough to let the locomotives pick up speed and emulate their original performance. Surviving on enthusiasts' donations, on government grants, and on fees from television and film crews, they have become a major tourist attraction in their own right, with tens of thousands of annual visitors.

Men and consortiums who had bought mainline locomotives weren't content to see their toys trundling along at a mere 20 miles per hour, however, and began to negotiate with the national system for access to the main lines. Interest in steam trains was so widespread, and steam train tours so lucrative, that the bureaucrats consented. Twenty or 30 of the greatest British locomotives now make frequent mainline tours, pulling trains packed with enthusiasts, watched, filmed, and cheered by thousands along the route. The most famous of all is the *Flying Scotsman*, a locomotive built in 1923, retired from regular service in 1963, and bought by an early steam preservation enthusiast named Alan Pegler. Pegler ran it on British lines, then did tours of the United States until he was forced to declare bankruptcy in 1972. Other enthusiasts stepped in, and today the *Flying Scotsman* is still going strong, almost certainly the most famous steam train in the world.

There can't be many hobbies more expensive than owning and running a steam locomotive, but cost didn't deter an even more dedicated group of enthusiasts who paid for the building of a new locomotive, the next one British Railways would have built before deciding to discontinue steam traction altogether. This one, the *Tornado*, number 60163, was begun in 1994 and finished in 2008 at an estimated cost of over £3 million. Because it's new, unlike all the other preserved locomotives, it's in superb condition, and on April 12, 2017 ran at 100 mph, the first steam train to do so since 1968. It's mad, but it's also wonderful.

In several other lectures in this series I will be discussing railway-related architecture, including the magnificent bridges and stations that the Victorians built, many of which remain highly functional. And if you would like to know more about how Britain pioneered most of the world's leading industrial processes, I encourage you to watch or listen to my Great Courses series on the history of the Industrial Revolution. Meanwhile, I hope you've enjoyed this tour of just a few of the many highlights that await visitors who would like to travel back to an era that changed the face, not just of Britain, but of the world.

11

VICTORIAN BRITAIN

Q ueen Victoria is a monumental figure in British history. She reigned from 1837 to 1901. During her reign, Britain consolidated its worldwide empire and continued its transformation into an industrial giant. This lecture highlights some important Victorian places that belong on the itinerary of every traveler to Britain, including:

- Examples of Victorian architecture.

- Sites related to intellectual figures Karl Marx and Charles Darwin.

- Sites related to Florence Nightingale, health care, and workhouses.

- Two sites related to Victoria's love, Prince Albert.

- Important town halls.

Architecture

Different groups of prosperous Victorians favored different styles of building. Many were revivals of older forms, Greek, Roman, Gothic, Renaissance, Baroque, Italianate, and French Chateau style.

From the Victorian era, the Gothic revival style is particularly notable. It is a confident, playful form. Gothic revival accelerated with the writings and buildings of Augustus Welby Pugin. A masterpiece among Pugin's surviving buildings is St. Giles Catholic Church in Cheadle, Staffordshire.

Pugin's achievement was widely admired by many Protestants. Three of the leading Protestant gothic revivalists were George Gilbert Scott, Alfred Waterhouse, and William Butterfield. The place to see Gilbert Scott's work at its best is St. Pancras Station on Euston Road, London

Alfred Waterhouse's greatest works are the Manchester Town Hall and the Kensington Museum of Natural History. At Balliol College, Oxford, on a smaller scale, Waterhouse managed to convey the impression of everything

St. Pancras Station

Manchester Town Hall

Balliol College

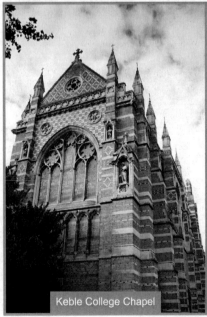

Keble College Chapel

soaring upward. When you visit Oxford, stop to admire the handsome Broad Street frontage that Waterhouse designed.

Oxford was also the site of several projects by William Butterfield, notably Keble College, half a mile outside the city's center. His use of brightly patterned and strongly contrasted polychromatic brick, especially in Keble College Chapel, was loved by some and deplored by others right from the beginning.

Another Victorian Gothic structure in north Oxford is the museum of natural history, designed by

Oxford University Museum of Natural History

Thomas Deane and Benjamin Woodward, with advice from the art historian John Ruskin. Deane and Woodward made good use of iron and glass.

Intellectual Figures

Several intellectual giants were active during the Victorian era, and visitors can still see sites related to them today. One example is Charles Darwin's dwelling, Down House in Kent. The house is now open to the public and run by English Heritage. The furnishings and decorations have been restored, including his wheeled armchair, while the gardens and greenhouses have been set up to duplicate some of his many experiments.

Another figure from the time is Karl Marx, who labored away in the great circular reading room of the British Museum in London. Marx lived for

Karl Marx

many years at 28 Dean Street in Soho. Although the rooms he occupied have long since been converted to other uses, visitors can sign up for a guided walk around Marx's London, led by scholarly enthusiasts.

Yet another of the era's intellectual giants was John Stuart Mill. *The Autobiography of John Stuart Mill* is one of the best books about childhood in British history. Mill's house in Kensington Square is marked with one of the distinctive blue plaques that mark historically important buildings throughout the country.

Florence Nightingale, Health Care, and Workhouses

Florence Nightingale

During his time serving in Parliament, Mill was the first to introduce draft legislation that would give women the vote. There were certainly plenty of distinguished and strong-minded women in Britain for Mill to admire. One was the nurse and social reformer Florence Nightingale, who lived from 1820 to 1910.

A museum dedicated to her life and work is located at St. Thomas's Hospital, just across the Thames from the Houses of Parliament. This was the hospital in which she founded a training school for nurses. Its original buildings have long since disappeared, but she continues to be honored for her work there. At the museum, visitors see her medicine chest; the clothes she and other nurses wore; her pet owl, Athena; her journals and letters; and some of the era's surgical instruments. There are also exhibits showing how Victorian gender ideas made it difficult for women to be taken seriously as organizers of large-scale health-care initiatives.

Nightingale was also important for improving medical care at England's workhouses. The workhouses, which destitute people were forced to enter for aid, and which they hated, were severe. One of the best surviving workhouses can be seen at Southwell in Nottinghamshire, a big, highly functional brick building with extensive grounds.

Southwell Workhouse

Another workhouse building at Lambeth in southern London, built in the 1870s to house 820 inmates, has been converted into a cinema museum. Charlie Chaplin, in his autobiography, describes his miserable life at the workhouse in the 1890s, when he was six and seven years old. There is also a circular tower that was designed and built in the 1890s as a workhouse infirmary at Camberwell in South London.

Prince Albert

The great tragedy of Queen Victoria's life was the premature death of her husband, Prince Albert, in 1861. The queen grieved the loss deeply. An area of Kensington in London was given over to commemorating him; it is nicknamed Albertopolis. The two most striking buildings there are the Royal Albert Hall and the Albert Memorial in Kensington Gardens.

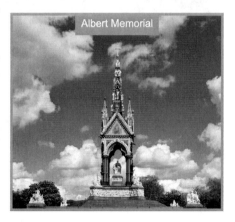
Albert Memorial

The hall was another innovative polychromatic brick building, designed by two officers from the Royal Engineers and featuring an immense iron dome, unsupported by interior pillars. The memorial, a few yards from the hall, is a ciborium—that is, a canopy covering a statue. It was designed by George Gilbert Scott and dedicated by the queen in 1872. The gilded statue of Albert himself was finished and added three years later.

Town Halls

In the years of Queen Victoria's reign, between 1837 and 1901, nearly all the big cities that had prospered with industrialization treated themselves to big new civic buildings, competing with each other for the grandest structure and boldest design. Early on, the favored style was classical. Birmingham, for example, built a town hall in the 1830s that was modeled on the Temple of Castor and Pollux in the Roman Forum. It was meant to project the idea of Birmingham as a place devoted to republican principles.

Birmingham Town Hall

St. George's Hall in Liverpool, built a few years later, was a combination concert venue and law court complex. The interior concert hall, extravagantly decorated from floor to ceiling, is adorned with statues of local dignitaries in its niches, and elaborate bronze doors. The open space in front of the building, St. George's Plateau, is a space for civic celebrations and protests.

The town hall in Wolverhampton, which opened in 1871, was designed in the style of a French chateau. The town hall at Leicester was built in the Queen Anne style a few years later, while civic planners in Glasgow used elements of the Italian Renaissance.

Suggested Reading

Clarke, *Gothic Revival*.

Mill, *Autobiography*.

Paterson, *Life in Victorian Britain*.

Wilson, *Charles Darwin*.

Suggested Activities

1. Compare medieval Gothic buildings with Victorian Gothic buildings to see how the Victorian architects used, but also deviated from, the originals.

2. In each town you visit, find how many buildings, streets, and parks are named for Prince Albert. You will find that they all date from the period 1840–1870 and that most date from the years immediately after his premature death in 1861.

11

VICTORIAN BRITAIN

Queen Victoria is a monumental figure in British history. She ascended the throne as an 18-year-old and reigned from 1837 to 1901, marrying Prince Albert in 1840, bearing nine children, and grieving his death in 1861 and for the rest of her life. During her reign, Britain consolidated its world-wide empire and its transformation into an industrial giant. It became richer than ever before. Thousands of the best buildings in Britain were constructed during Victoria's reign, and many of them survive. Fascinating original thinkers in Britain transformed human understanding, among them Charles Darwin, Karl Marx, and John Stuart Mill. If you're interested in a detailed history of the Victorian era, I encourage you to view or listen to my 36-lecture Great Courses series, *Victorian Britain*. Today, I'd simply like to highlight some important Victorian places that belong on the itinerary of every traveler to Britain.

Architecturally, the Victorian era was diverse and exciting. New materials made new designs possible. Iron girders and plate glass created superb possibilities; buildings that were lighter and brighter than ever before. For example, the Palm House at Kew Gardens, designed by Decimus Burton and built by iron-founder Richard Turner in the 1840s, used iron and glass to create a tropical environment. The much larger Crystal Palace, built by Joseph Paxton to house the Great Exhibition of 1851, amazed visitors from all over the world. Prefabricated off-site, it was later moved to South London, where it survived until 1936, and its memory lives on in the name of the local soccer team. Iron frames were also used in factories, to make them lighter and more fire resistant. They could be integrated in traditional designs, as with the new royal palaces of Balmoral in Scotland, and Osborne House on the Isle of Wight. It was at Osborne House, now open to the public, that Queen Victoria died in 1901.

Different groups of prosperous Victorians favored different styles of building. Many were revivals of older forms: Greek, Roman, Gothic, Renaissance, Baroque, Italianate, and French Chateau style. Others again were hybrids, blending elements from different styles, as with the approach known as "Jacobethan," taking elements from the 16th century Elizabethan and the 17th century Jacobean. Wildest of all the Victorian buildings I know of, incorporating five or six different major styles, is the Russell Hotel on Russell Square, London, built in 1898. It is now known as "The Principal: London." Every inch of its façade is decorated, right down to the details—the overall effect is thrilling and just a tiny bit comical. Neither is the interior an anticlimax. Everything that can possibly done with marble, gilding, pillars and chandeliers has been done, and the designers didn't feel any constraint about drawing on the best of half a dozen older traditions

My own favorite style from the Victorian era is Gothic Revival. It's so confident, so playful with design, decoration, and materials, and so satisfying to see and to occupy. Scattered 18th and early 19th century buildings had used Gothic themes like pointed arches and battlements. One was Strawberry Hill House in Twickenham, the home of Horace Walpole, prime minister's son, writer, gossip, and art historian.

Gothic Revival accelerated with the writings and buildings of Augustus Welby Pugin. Pugin converted to Roman Catholicism as a young man, and convinced himself that everything good about Britain came from its Catholic past, while everything debased and degraded about Britain came from its more recent Protestant and industrial years. His 1836 book *Contrasts* made the point with a series of illustrations of beautiful pre-Reformation churches and cathedrals juxtaposed against harshly utilitarian modern factories, workhouses, and prisons. He drew sympathetic attention, especially among Britain's Catholic minority. John Talbot, the 16th Earl of Shrewsbury, was the most prominent of his patrons, from whom he won a series of commissions.

Perhaps the masterpiece among Pugin's surviving buildings is St. Giles Catholic Church in Cheadle, Staffordshire. Carefully researched, skillfully built, and incorporating imitations of many pre-Reformation Gothic churches, its interior decoration is enchanting, with red and gold predominating. Every pillar is painted, bright tiles cover walls and floors, while intricate designs on the doors, the altar, and the rood screen make it a joy to visit. Pugin also worked hard on the Earl's own house, Alton Towers, nearby, whose estate is now the hub of an amusement park. For a while, the Earls of Shrewsbury lived there, but encroaching poverty and neglect led the house to fall gradually into ruin after the 1890s—today only fragments remain, and serve as the amusement park's gift shop and tearoom. Pugin's best-known work is Big Ben, the great clock tower of the Houses of Parliament, about which I'll have more to say in another lecture.

Pugin's achievement was widely admired by many Protestants, and they were not going to let this new style be the preserve solely of England's Catholic minority. Three of the leading Protestant Gothic Revivalists were George Gilbert Scott, Alfred Waterhouse, and William Butterfield. The place to see Gilbert Scott's work at its best is St. Pancras Station on Euston Road, London. The station is important for two reasons. First is the delightfully elaborate and playful façade in polychromatic brick. Having won the design award for this new station in 1865, Gilbert Scott ramped up many of the features he had tried, on a smaller scale, at Kelham Hall in Nottinghamshire, which he had completed in 1863. Kelham itself is a gem, which prepared the way for the masterpiece to come.

The second reason for St. Pancras's historic importance is the great iron and glass arch to shelter the trains and passengers on the station. It was designed and built by William Henry Barlow in 1868, and in its day, was the single greatest span ever achieved with those materials. It is 245 and a half feet across, 689 feet long, and has 24 main arches. Even today, more than 150 years later, it provides a fitting arrival and departure point for Eurostar trains going to and from the Channel Tunnel and continental Europe. It has the welcome effect of making you feel more important than you actually are! In the 1960s, there were serious plans to knock the whole place down. Luckily, the Victorian Society stepped in to campaign for its preservation. So did the widely-loved poet laureate, John Betjeman, a great admirer of Victoriana. Demolition was prevented and London is a better place for St. Pancras's survival. Extensively restored and cleaned between 1995 and 2010, it has never looked better.

Alfred Waterhouse's greatest works are the Manchester Town Hall and the Kensington Museum of Natural History. Both are treasures, and I'll have more to say about them in future lectures. At Balliol College, Oxford, on a smaller scale, Waterhouse managed to convey the impression of everything soaring upward. When you visit Oxford, stop to admire the handsome Broad Street frontage that Waterhouse designed.

Oxford was also the site of several projects by William Butterfield, notably Keble College, half a mile outside the city's center. Butterfield aimed not merely to duplicate medieval Gothic effects but to carry on developing the style from the point where it had broken off in England with the Reformation. His use of brightly patterned and strongly contrasted polychromatic brick, especially in Keble College Chapel, was loved by some and deplored by others right from the beginning. Keble is recognizably an Oxford college and yet the mood and feeling are very different from that of the stone colleges that dominate the city's center.

Another Victorian Gothic structure in north Oxford is the Museum of Natural History, designed by Thomas Deane and Benjamin Woodward, with advice from the art historian John Ruskin. Before 1850, Oxford offered virtually no teaching in the sciences—it's been trying to catch up ever since. Professor of Medicine Henry Acland proposed the museum, and it was built between 1855 and 1860. The museum was originally conceived as a building in which all the natural sciences would be taught—the expansion of the science curriculum forced most of them in later decades to leave, for premises of their own in the surrounding streets of north Oxford.

Deane and Woodward made good use of iron and glass. The large central court is made of iron gothic arches, holding up a glass ceiling. The stone building that surrounds it on three levels features cloisters and columns, every one of which is made of a different British stone—their labels are integral with the design. Different patterns of foliage from the various regions decorate these columns. Statues of eminent scientists fill niches around the building, which is an object of immense fascination even before you turn to its world-class collections in geology, entomology, ornithology, and paleontology. Among the exhibits is the skeleton of a dodo and a full-scale model of this extinct bird.

In one of the rooms on the middle level, shortly after the museum opened, a debate in 1860 showcased the growing dispute between evolution and the Bible. Charles Darwin had just published his book *On the Origin of Species by Means of Natural Selection*. It dismayed traditional Christians because it contradicted chapter 1 of Genesis, which states that God created all the species distinct, right from the beginning. Darwin was not present—he was shy and reclusive—but his champions Thomas Huxley and Joseph Hooker spoke up for the new theory. Other scientists were not convinced by Darwin's evidence, which was less complete than later studies have made it. The Bishop of Oxford, Samuel Wilberforce, is supposed to have asked Huxley, facetiously, whether he was descended from a monkey on his father's side, or his mother's. Huxley's alleged answer was that he had "no need to be ashamed of having an ape for his grandfather, but that he would be ashamed of having for an ancestor a man of restless and versatile intelligence who distracts the attention of his hearers from the real point at issue by eloquent digression and skilled appeals to religious prejudice." It's probably an apocryphal exchange, but it's good to be able to visit the room in which the long debate started, one that's not finished even today.

Many of you will know the story of Darwin's voyage to South America aboard a Royal Navy survey ship, the *Beagle*. Visits to Brazil, Argentina, Patagonia, Chile, and above all the Galapagos Islands off Ecuador, introduced him to hundreds of new species and profound puzzles about variations among them and the habitats in which they lived. The detailed journals and letters that Darwin sent back to Britain's leading scientists, along with hundreds of specimens, made him a celebrity, and he was feted on his return to Britain. He married his cousin Emma and settled with her, first in London, but then at Down House in Kent. The house, where he lived for the rest of his life, is now open to the public and run by English Heritage. The furnishings and decorations have been restored, including his wheeled armchair, while the gardens and greenhouses have been set up to duplicate some of his many experiments. The whole place is a time capsule of his life and work.

A voracious worker, Darwin spent over 20 years between his return from the *Beagle* and his publication of *On the Origin of Species*. He was finally provoked into publishing it because another outstanding naturalist, Alfred Russell Wallace, was coming to the same conclusions. Neither man's friends wanted the other to get sole credit for the idea, so the two scientists produced a joint paper on evolution in 1858. The publication of *On the Origin of Species* followed on November 22, 1859.

While Darwin labored away at Down House, Karl Marx was laboring away back in London, in the great circular reading room of the British Museum. He too had a theory of constant transformation and constant predation, of a world in flux and conflict. Species were the key for Darwin; social classes were the key for Marx. Marx had been born in 1818 and raised in Germany, but had fled after the failed German revolution of 1848. His friend Friedrich Engels had influenced young Marx's thinking with *The Condition of the Working Class in England*, an indictment of the harsh, alienating conditions and widespread suffering of industrial workers. Engels depicts Victorian England at its worst and bleakest.

Marx and Engels collaborated for the rest of their lifetimes, working out a theory of revolution in which the workers, achieving class consciousness and class solidarity, would overthrow the factory owners and share the benefits of industry among all the people, instead of just the privileged class. When I was a graduate student, working on my doctoral dissertation in the rotunda of the British Museum during the early 1980s, delegations of Russian and Chinese communists would sometimes come to visit the desk at which Marx had written *Das Kapital*. Marx wrote an admiring letter to Darwin and sent him a copy of the book in 1873; Darwin's reply was gracious but non-committal. His biographers doubt that he actually read it.

Marx lived for many years at 28 Dean Street in Soho. He was desperately poor, surviving on handouts from Engels and irregular work for German and

American newspapers. Although the rooms he occupied have long since been converted to other uses, you can sign up for a guided walk around Marx's London, led by scholarly enthusiasts. They will show you the places where he met with the many other European revolutionaries in exile who had congregated in London. Marx's grave in Highgate Cemetery was also, for decades, a pilgrimage site to all communists. A large granite block bearing the legend "Workers of all lands, unite!" it is topped by a large bust of his head with full beard and flowing locks, looking every inch the revolutionary.

Another of the era's intellectual giants was John Stuart Mill. Mill's house in Kensington Square is marked with one of the distinctive blue plaques that mark historically important buildings throughout the country. Mill's *Autobiography* is one of the best books about childhood in British history. It describes how his father, the philosopher James Mill, tried to raise and educate him without wasting a second. Young John had no toys and no contact with other children, except his own younger siblings, to whom he had to pass along everything he learned. As a result, he was fluent in Greek by the age of seven, knew all the major classics by the time he was 10, then got down to learning political theory and economics. Yes, he had a nervous breakdown and a phase of existential despair, but he dragged himself out of it and went on to write an immensely influential study of capitalist economics, *Principles of Political Economy*, and an immensely influential study of freedom, *On Liberty*. He scandalized his social circle by falling in love with the woman next door, Harriet Taylor, and sharing her with her husband until Mr. Taylor finally died and they could belatedly marry. As a Member of Parliament, Mill was the first to introduce draft legislation that would give women the vote.

There were certainly plenty of distinguished and strong-minded women in Britain for Mill to admire. One was Florence Nightingale, who lived from 1820 to 1910. Daughter of an upper-class family, she was born in Italy and raised partly in Derbyshire and partly in Hampshire. She was determined not to marry, despite several ardent suitors, but to serve as a nurse. Her horrified parents regarded nurses as scarcely better than prostitutes—the drunken Mrs. Gamp, from Charles Dickens's *Martin Chuzzlewit* was the era's best-known fictional nurse. Iron-willed Nightingale was undeterred, and trained in Germany. Lytton Strachey, writing about her later in *Eminent Victorians* joked that Nightingale's parents had expected their daughter to be a young swan, but discovered that they had hatched an eagle!

She contacted influential political friends when Britain went to war against Russia in the Crimea in 1854, and led a deputation of nurses to the British military hospital at Scutari, Turkey. There, she greatly improved conditions of care, supply, convalescence, and hygiene, all of which the army had mismanaged, and created the legendary reputation for which she is still remembered. There is a statue of her in Waterloo Place, just off the Mall in London, adjacent to the Crimean War Memorial, and another in the midlands town of Derby, on the site of the Derby Royal Infirmary.

Florence Nightingale devoted the rest of her life to establishing nursing as a respectable profession for middle-class women, and to improving hospital conditions. As a woman, she was barred from speaking before parliamentary committees but she recruited prominent politicians to work on her behalf, of whom the best known was Sidney Herbert. His statue stands close to hers in Waterloo Place, London. A museum dedicated to her life and work is located at St. Thomas's Hospital, just across the Thames from the Houses of Parliament. This was the hospital in which she founded a training school for nurses. Its original buildings have long since disappeared, but she continues to be honored for her work there. At the museum you can see her medicine chest, the clothes she and other nurses wore, her pet owl, Athena, her journals and letters, and some of the era's surgical instruments. There are also exhibits showing how Victorian gender ideas made it difficult for women to be taken seriously as organizers of large-scale health care initiatives.

Nightingale was also important for improving medical care at England's workhouses. The workhouses, which destitute people were forced to enter for aid, and which they hated, were severe. Dickens again gives us a memorable picture of workhouse life in *Oliver Twist*. Infectious diseases were rife, and death rates high. Nightingale trained nurses to serve in workhouses, so that at least the poor would have some elementary health care. One of the best surviving workhouses can be seen at Southwell in Nottinghamshire, a big, highly-functional brick building with extensive grounds, in which the inmates grew their own food. Sparsely decorated today, it has a satisfying minimalist feel, but must have been awfully oppressive when packed with 200 broken-down paupers, many of them old and disabled. It may sound odd to recommend a visit to the workhouse as part of your vacation, but you won't regret it. Southwell Workhouse will give you valuable insight into the realities of Victorian life, acting as a kind of antidote to *Downton Abbey* nostalgia.

Another workhouse building at Lambeth in South London, built in the 1870s to house 820 inmates, has been converted into a cinema museum. Charlie Chaplin, in his autobiography, describes his miserable life at the Lambeth Workhouse in the 1890s, when he was six and seven years old, and the brutal corporal punishment meted out to the children for minor offenses.

One of Florence Nightingale's friends and admirers was Angela Burdett-Coutts, an heiress who also declined numerous offers of marriage. Her motive was suspicion that her suitors were really after her money. She made an offer of marriage to the Duke of Wellington, even though he was 45 years her senior, but he declined. She then devoted herself to philanthropy, often using another friend, Charles Dickens, as her intermediary, because she preferred to give money anonymously. Burdett-Coutts was probably Britain's foremost philanthropist of the Victorian era, and played a role in founding important societies, such as the Royal Society for the Prevention of Cruelty to Animals, and the National Society for the Prevention of Cruelty to Children. She funded schools and infirmaries for poor children, churches, and an elaborate park sundial and memorial in St. Pancras Churchyard, London. She lived in Holly Lodge, in Highgate, in north London. It no longer exists, but on the adjacent land stands Holly Village, a set of neo-gothic houses that she planned with the architect Henry Darbishire. Unfortunately, Holly Village is not open to the public, but you'll walk right past it on your way to see Karl Marx's grave in the adjacent Highgate Cemetery.

Angela Burdett-Coutts also provides us with a link back to Queen Victoria, who gave the philanthropist a noble title, and wrote her affectionate letters. So let's return to Victoria, and specifically to the great tragedy of her life—the premature death of her husband, Prince Albert, in 1861. As I've noted, the queen grieved the loss deeply. She wore mourning for all of the 40 years she outlived him, and had his clothes laid out every morning and his shaving kit made ready. An area of Kensington in London was given over to commemorating him—it is nicknamed "Albertopolis." The two most striking buildings there are the Royal Albert Hall and the Albert Memorial in Kensington Gardens.

The Hall was another innovative polychromatic brick building, designed by two officers from the Royal Engineers, and featuring an immense iron dome, unsupported by interior pillars. Anxiety about whether the dome would collapse when its temporary supports were removed, in 1870, led all but a handful of the workmen to leave the building. The design proved itself, however, and the roof stayed on. Queen Victoria and her son Prince Edward opened Albert Hall early the next year.

At first, it had a reputation for excessive echo, which made it difficult for audiences to get a clear sense of the music they were hearing. For a century and a half, experiments with acoustic baffles have aimed to improve it. It is now the setting for the annual Promenade Concerts, or "Proms," 60 or 70 of which take place over eight weeks each summer. Founded by Henry Wood in 1895, they began as an attempt to educate a wider public to the joys of classical music. On your visit to Britain, you can pay a high price for a seat beforehand, or stand in line on the day of your chosen concert for a low-priced ticket which gives you a place on the concert hall floor, where you stand to enjoy the music. I did it often as an undergraduate—most of the other "Prommers" were also in their late teens and early 20s in those days, but now the floor attracts enthusiasts of all ages. The last night of the Proms, each year, is an opportunity for Britain's music lovers to wallow in nostalgia, with patriotic favorites like "Rule Britannia," "Land of Hope and Glory," "Auld Lang Syne," and "Jerusalem." It is broadcast not just on the BBC, but throughout the English-speaking world.

The Albert Memorial, a few yards from the Albert Hall, is a gothic tower or ciborium, a kind of canopy covering a statue. It was designed by George Gilbert Scott, the architect of St. Pancras Station, and dedicated by the queen in 1872. The gilded statue of Albert himself was finished and added three years later. It has recently been re-gilded and now glitters magnificently, as if touched by King Midas. All around the base of the memorial are statues and friezes representing the different parts of the world, the different arts, crafts, sciences, and virtues. It is one of those lovely public objects that you can enjoy looking at time after time, constantly coming upon new elements that you had missed on your previous visit, or which suddenly come back to life after cleaning and restoration. Don't miss the elephant and its attendants that represent Asia, or the camel that represents Africa. This is the greatest of the Prince Albert memorials, but by no means the only one. There's another, similar in design, in the aptly named Albert Square, Manchester, and equestrian statues of him in Liverpool, Edinburgh, and Wolverhampton.

Earlier in this lecture I mentioned Manchester Town Hall, one of the great Victorian civic buildings. In the years of Victoria's reign, between 1837 and 1901, nearly all the big cities that had prospered with industrialization treated themselves to big new civic buildings, competing with each other for the grandest structure and boldest design. Early on, the favored style was classical. Birmingham, for example, built a town hall in the 1830s that was modelled on the Temple of Castor and Pollux in the Roman Forum. It was meant to project the idea of Birmingham as a place devoted to republican principles.

St. George's Hall, Liverpool, built a few years later, was a combination concert venue and law court complex. The design competition was won by Harvey Lonsdale Elmes, a prodigy then aged only 25 who beat out all the more experienced architects of his era. A classical structure on the grandest scale, it took 15 years to complete, but has been a proud centerpiece for the city ever since. The interior concert hall, extravagantly decorated from floor to ceiling, is adorned with statues of local dignitaries in its niches, and elaborate bronze doors. The open space in front of the building, St. George's Plateau, is a space for civic celebrations and protests. Thousands of mourners gathered there when news came in 1980 of the death of local hero John Lennon.

The town hall in Wolverhampton, which opened in 1871, was designed in the style of a French chateau. The town hall at Leicester was built in the Queen Anne Style a few years later, while civic planners in Glasgow decided on the Beaux Arts style, with elements of the Italian Renaissance. All these buildings are self-indulgent, designed to make a statement about the cities they represent. They embody the confidence and pride of an imperial nation at its height. All are worth a visit, and nearly all look a lot better now than they did 30 years ago, before a great round of cleaning and restoration took place.

The word "Victorian" is sometimes used to suggest whatever is old-fashioned, frumpy, and prudish. Victorian moralists certainly could exhibit those characteristics, but there's so much more to the Victorian era than that. These were bold, confident, forward-looking people, exhilarated to discover new technologies, new styles, and new ideas about the proper ordering of society. We still live in the world they helped shape, and we owe them a great debt of gratitude, that we should remember much more often.

12

20TH-CENTURY BRITAIN

A nyone who visits Britain is going to see far more buildings from the 20th century than from any other century, but they are the glum background against which the many magnificent old structures stand out so proudly. However, there are some sites and topics from the time that are worth noting, including the contents of this lecture, which are:

- Notable works by the architect Edwin Luytens.

- Government buildings.

- Buildings constructed in the interwar years between the World Wars.

- Housing from the 1920s and 1930s.

- Motorways and office buildings.

Edwin Luytens

Edwin Lutyens, one of the most inventive and talented architects in British history, built impressive houses for wealthy clients, such as Tigbourne Court in Surrey, a fine country home. Another exemplary country house is Lutyens's Castle Drogo in Devonshire. Everything inside is gratuitously oversized; it is austere and opulent at the same time. The adjacent formal gardens make Castle Drogo a good place for a day out, despite its remoteness down tiny rural lanes.

Castle Drogo

Lutyens also carried out commissions for major public and corporate buildings, such as a headquarters for the Midland Bank in London and for the same company in Manchester.

Castle Drogo Gardens

Government Buildings

In the first 20 years of the 20th century, builders constructed most of the monumental buildings in which the British government now works, which are referred to collectively as Whitehall. Most of them stand on, or adjacent to, the street named Whitehall. For example, the Government Offices stand on Great George Street, just off Parliament Square. Designed by John Brydon, the impressive complex was begun in 1898 and finished in 1917.

Equally imposing is the Admiralty Arch. The arch was commissioned by King Edward VII in memory of his mother, Queen Victoria, and was designed by Aston Webb. Webb was also responsible for the superb Royal School of Mines at Imperial College, London.

Interwar Buildings

Even after World War I, some superb buildings were raised in Britain. One example is the Hoover Building, which is visible while approaching London on the M40 motorway, coming in from Oxford and the west. The firm of Wallis, Gilbert, and Partners was renowned for its Art Deco designs. The Hoover Building, in which vacuum cleaners were made, carried the distinctive big windows, curved walls, and bright colors that make Art Deco distinctive.

The same company also built Wallis House, a 12-story tower that strikes the eye as one approaches London on the long, overhead section of the M4 motorway. After years as a factory, it too has been restored and turned into a combination of offices and expensive apartments.

A third Art Deco building, the Carreras Cigarette Factory, built in Camden Town, London, illustrates the 1920s craze for Egyptian-themed objects. Great black cat statues guard the entrance, and a black cat motif recurs along the façade.

Another gem of the interwar years is Battersea Power Station. Its designer, Giles Gilbert Scott, responded to concerns about a power station being huge and ugly by coming up with an imaginative design, creating the impression that its chimneys are classical columns. It is recognizable on the cover of Pink Floyd's album *Animals*.

Housing

The 1920s and 1930s were an era of suburbanization. Respectable and decent housing spread throughout the land, greatly improving the quality of domestic life for the growing middle class. Probably the most representative style of house from this era was the suburban, semi-detached, three-bedroom, one-bathroom home. England possesses hundreds of thousands of examples; no city is without them.

As the interwar, semi-detached houses approach their centenary, they're still sought after and well maintained. The means of their owners have gradually increased with improvements in the standard of living.

Motorways and Office Buildings

In the 1960s and 1970s, new motorways arrived, designed to make it easier to get around the overcrowded country. The first to be built, the M1 from London to the north and the M6 from Birmingham to Scotland, display many of the modernist features of their age. They feature concrete bridges and flyovers, along with the convenient motorway service centers that were heralded as triumphs of modern functionalism when new. Another familiar element of postwar building was modern schools and office buildings, which also emphasized function, not style.

Suggested Reading

Amery, *Lutyens*.

Lodge, *Changing Places*.

Nairn, *Nairn's London*.

Prince Charles, *A Vision of Britain*.

Questions to Consider

1. Why did the tastes of architects differ so greatly from those of ordinary Britons in the decades after World War II?

2. As you travel around Britain, try to estimate the year of construction of the many undistinguished houses you'll see. With a little practice, you can learn to be accurate to within the decade.

20TH-CENTURY BRITAIN

Some of the greatest buildings in the United States have been built since World War II. On the other hand, most of the worst buildings in Britain come from the same period. A combination of lack of money, the need to recover from wartime bomb damage, a chronic housing shortage, and a fashion for raw concrete, made for a vicious spiral and a race to the bottom. It was worsened by a generation of domineering architects and city planners dedicated to the unforgiving International Style and to Brutalism.

As a result, for 30 years, joyless gray concrete and a grim functionality imparted a sorrowful quality to the British built environment. Occasional diamonds have been seen in this wilderness but they are few and far between. Anyone who visits Britain is going to see far more buildings from the 20th than from any other century, but only masochists would visit Britain in order to see them. They're the glum background against which the many magnificent old structures stand out so proudly.

The 20th century started out with great promise. The confident days before World War I bore witness to beautiful buildings of all sorts, residential, official, and ecclesiastical. Edwin Lutyens, one of the most inventive and talented architects in British history, built impressive houses for wealthy clients, such as Tigbourne Court in Surrey, a fine country home that embodies the virtues of the Arts and Crafts movement. Another exemplary country house is Lutyens' Castle Drogo in Devonshire. Built for a retail-store millionaire, Castle Drogo was begun in 1911 and not finished until 1931. At first glance, you could mistake it for a building 800 years older, but it took advantage of modern materials and electricity right from the outset. Everything inside is gratuitously oversized, austere and opulent at the same time. The adjacent formal gardens make Castle Drogo a good place for a day out, despite its remoteness down tiny rural lanes.

Lutyens also carried out commissions for major public and corporate buildings, such as a headquarters for the Midland Bank in London, on a short street named "Poultry," and for the same company in Manchester. The Manchester bank, on King Street, is a Neo-Classical structure of white Portland stone, standing out strongly against the mainly gothic style of central Manchester. Lutyens also designed the Cenotaph, Britain's principal World War I monument, and many other war memorials, about which I'll say more in another lecture.

Also in the first 20 years of the century were built most of the monumental buildings in which the British government now works, which are referred to collectively as "Whitehall." Most of them stand on, or adjacent to, the street named Whitehall. Look, for example, at the Government Offices on Great George Street, just off Parliament Square. Designed by John Brydon, it was begun in 1898 and finished in 1917. If it was anywhere else in the world, it would be regarded as a wonder. It's just that in this location it is overshadowed by Westminster Abbey and the Houses of Parliament. Most visitors regard it simply as part of the blurry background, which is less than it deserves. Equally imposing is the Admiralty Arch, under which runs the Mall as it leads from Trafalgar Square to Buckingham Palace. The arch was commissioned by King Edward VII in memory of his mother, Queen Victoria, and was designed by Aston Webb. Webb was also responsible for the superb Royal School of Mines at Imperial College, London. With such works, the 20th century was off to a promising start.

Even after World War I some superb buildings were raised in Britain. One of my favorites is the Hoover Building, which you'll see if you approach London on the M-40 motorway, coming in from Oxford and the west. After miles of dreary suburbia, you'll feel your spirits lift as you see it. The firm of Wallis, Gilbert, and Partners was renowned for its Art Deco designs. And the Hoover Factory, in which vacuum cleaners were made, carried the distinctive big windows, curved walls, and bright colors that make Art-Deco such fun. A great flaring glass light over the central door, and wonderful corner stair towers, along with angular wrought iron gates, all contribute to the spectacle. It has been restored, and converted into luxury apartments.

The same company also built Wallis House, a 12-story tower that strikes your eye as you approach London on the long, overhead section of the M-4 motorway. You'll know it by the word "Barratt" which stretches across its top floor. After years as a factory, it too has been restored and turned into a combination of offices and expensive apartments. A third Art Deco building, the Carreras Cigarette Factory, built in Camden Town, London, illustrates the 1920s craze for Egyptian-themed objects. Great black cat statues guard the entrance, and a black cat motif recurs along the façade, above the red, blue, and green-painted pillars.

Another gem of the interwar years is Battersea Power Station. Its designer, Giles Gilbert Scott, was the son of a leading Victorian architect and was already famous in his own right as architect of Liverpool's Anglican Cathedral. Responding to citizens' concern about a power station being huge and ugly, he came up with an imaginative design, creating the impression that its chimneys are classical columns. If you ever saw the cover for Pink Floyd's album *Animals*, this is a building you'll recognize. It also appeared briefly in the Beatles film *Help!* When it went out of service in 1983, being inefficient, a major pollution source, and structurally decayed, Battersea Power Station was already a London icon. It was therefore listed for preservation and, after many failed plans and delays, is finally undergoing transformation into high-priced housing. Another power station by the same architect, further along the River Thames, has been converted successfully into the Tate Modern art gallery.

For every medieval or baroque building in Britain there are today thousands from the 1920s and 1930s. This was an era of suburbanization, when respectable and decent housing spread throughout the land, greatly improving the quality of domestic life for the growing middle class. Probably the most representative style of house from this era was the suburban, semi-detached, three-bedroom, one-bathroom home. England possesses hundreds of thousands of examples—no city is without them. I'm one of the millions of Britons alive today who grew up in them. The most famous one of all is probably 251 Menlove Avenue in Liverpool, the house in which John

Lennon grew up. It's a museum now, with furniture and decorations from the 1950s when the young Beatle lived there. To British eyes it's just stunningly ordinary! But it's a distinct cut above 10 Admiral Grove where Ringo Starr grew up, a dingy little Victorian row house in a now-largely-abandoned street.

The semi-detached house in which I grew up, in Mickleover, an ancient village that had been absorbed into the expanding suburbs of Derby, was heated by coal fires well into the 1960s. Once a month, brawny men covered from head to foot in coal dust, the "coal-men," heaved sacks of shiny black coal into the shed adjoining the house. The house was cold inside until you had cleaned the ashes out of the grate and made a new fire—every house in the street belched coal smoke from its chimneys. But the high-ceilinged rooms, solid doors, decorative stained glass in the front windows, and a mood of solidity, all imparted the feeling to us, and to millions like us, that we were living well.

Incidentally, for about 30 years the Holy Grail of suburbanites in these houses was to replace the coal fires with central heating. As a child, I heard countless conversations on the topic, in which adults yearned for the money to be able to install it, only to find it still just beyond their reach. In David Lodge's satirical novel *Changing Places*, about British and American professors crossing the Atlantic to teach at each other's campuses, the American can hardly believe the primitive state of his counterpart's house, and the intense winter cold inside. When the British professor has an extramarital affair, his wife avenges herself not by leaving him or suing for divorce but by installing central heating and forcing him to accept the cost. It's a wonderful plot device, accurately capturing one of the era's great obsessions.

As the interwar, semi-detached houses approach their centenary, they're still sought-after, well-looked-after, and much extended by owners whose means have gradually increased with improvements in the standard of living. Everywhere you look attic conversions and glassy conservatories distort the original lines, while giving residents more space to stretch out. The downside is that there are so many of them, and they're monotonous. Just before World War II, the poet John Betjeman wrote a wicked but amusing poem about the drabness of English suburbs, and the drabness of their residents, epitomized for him in the town of Slough, just West of London. It begins like this: "Come friendly bombs and fall on Slough/ It isn't fit for humans now."

Betjeman was a divisive figure. His poetry is accessible, entertaining, and metrical, which made him far more popular than most 20th-century poets among the middlebrow public. Devotees of high modernism despised him, just as they despised his taste for Victoriana and his sentimental nostalgia for the old social classes. Betjeman loved the architecture of Oxford but had been a hopeless student there in the 1920s, failing his exams and never getting a degree. His professor of English, C. S. Lewis, described him as an "idle prig" and they had a lifelong mutual dislike. Betjeman stood for the proposition that Victorian building was better than anything that had come since. He led an unsuccessful campaign to preserve the great entrance arch at Euston Station, London, which was tragically demolished in 1962, but he energized the ultimately successful campaign to preserve St. Pancras Station, in whose precincts, fittingly, a statue of him now stands. I'm one of many who think of him as a national treasure.

Not every Briton in the interwar years was able to afford a suburban semi-detached house. For those further down the social and economic scale the great innovation was "council housing." The British welfare state began around 1910 and grew in the hands of Liberal and Labour governments from then on. Council houses—rented from local government by their tenants—were supposed to be the superior alternative to the ghastly industrial slums condemned by Engels, Dickens, and many others in the 19th century. They were better in a way—more sanitary, more likely to have indoor running water, proper bathrooms, and proper kitchens. But they were also ugly, regimented, joyless, and cold. George Orwell's 1937 book *The Road to Wigan Pier* contains a bravura passage on northern working-class people who were being steered toward such houses, but who went to them only with sinking hearts.

> I found that the people in corporation houses don't really like them. They are glad to get out of the stink of the slum. They know that it is better for their children to have space to play about in, but they don't really feel at home … Certainly, most corporation estates are pretty bleak in winter. Some I have been through, perched on treeless

clayey hillsides and swept by icy winds, would be horrible places to live in … There is an uncomfortable, almost prison-like atmosphere, and the people who live there are perfectly well aware of it.

My grandmother lived in one, on Capilano Road in Birmingham. Almost every weekend throughout the year we would drive over to see her on Sunday afternoons. When you're five or six you don't think in terms of aesthetics, but I remember even then the contrast between her welcoming warmth and the pinched, gloomy chill of the street itself.

One of Margaret Thatcher's schemes in the 1980s was to sell council houses to their tenants, on relatively favorable terms. Of her many experiments, this is one that nearly everyone thinks turned out well. As owners, the occupants felt a pride in the houses that they'd previously lacked, when they were mere renters whose tenure might not last. Almost at once exteriors that had been drab and grey started to get painted in bright colors. Extensions were added to create bathrooms and bedrooms, along with bigger kitchens and conservatories at the back. The result is a great improvement in every way— the automatic heart-sinking that used to attend arrival on a council estate is no longer a matter of course.

After the long misery of the Great Depression, with its widespread unemployment and dreary housing, came the catastrophic Second World War. Fear of enemy bombardment, and fear that the bombs would carry poison gas as well as explosives, led to the mass evacuation of children from the major industrial cities, and their relocation in safer rural settings. Sure enough, the bombing soon began—it was worst for Britain in the nine months beginning around September 1940. It slackened in mid-1941 when Hitler turned his attention to the mad project of invading Russia. Industrial cities were the worst afflicted, notably the East End of London, much of Birmingham, Glasgow, Coventry, Portsmouth, Southampton, Leeds, Manchester and Liverpool. A famous photograph shows St. Paul's Cathedral standing proud amid the blazing wreckage of the neighborhoods all around it.

In addition to industrial targets, much housing was destroyed. Government attempted to rehouse the survivors in what were known as "prefabs." These structures, prefabricated off site, largely from corrugated iron and asbestos, were meant to be short-term stop-gaps, adequate for the war years, after which they would be replaced. Bluntly unimaginative, they were nevertheless sturdy and serviceable. On our way to see my grandmother in her council house we drove through street after street of prefabs—by then approaching their 30th birthdays. Nearly all have gone, by now, though enthusiasts ensured that at least a few houses on one representative estate would remain. It is the grandly named Excalibur Estate in Catford, South-East London, whose street names are all drawn from the Arthurian legends. But don't expect medieval grandeur if you go to visit. Sadly, all but six of the houses are slated for demolition and replacement.

Giant concrete tower blocks replaced most of the prefabs in the 50s, 60s, and 70s. They quickly became a byword for ugliness, alienation, crime, depression, drugs, and misery, yet 384 of them were built in London alone, and hundreds more around the country. Historian Roy Porter referred to them as "slums in the sky [that] … killed traditional street-life, atomized communities, and produced disaffection, delinquency, and crime."

Just as most visitors won't seek out the suburban villas, so most won't care to devote their vacation time to the tower blocks. But since they're tall and not easy to avoid, they'll be there in your peripheral vision whenever you're in urban Britain. One of them, Ronan Point, collapsed in 1968 and began a long period of questioning as to their desirability. Another, Grenfell Tower, built in the "brutalist" style during the 1970s, caught fire in 2017 and killed 71 of its residents, due to inadequate fireproofing.

Still standing, and widely disliked, is Trellick Tower in Kensal Town, London, begun in 1966 and finished in 1972. It is 31 floors high, made of raw gray concrete that even bright sunshine cannot mitigate, and includes slit-windows that radiate a mood of "prison" rather than "home." The architect was a Hungarian immigrant, Erno Goldfinger. Among the people who hated the building was Ian Fleming, who named one of his most famous villains "Goldfinger" as a kind of anti-tribute to the architect.

The American writer Jane Jacobs had published *The Death and Life of Great American Cities* in 1961. Deploring urban clearance and high-rise public housing, she had argued that what gives life and warmth to cities was street life, short city blocks, diverse types of people and activity in the same area, and a modest scale to the buildings themselves. Regarded as a maverick at the time, and widely denounced by the Anglo-American architectural mainstream, her ideas were picking up steam by the 1970s.

Then, in the 1980s and 1990s, many public housing high-rise blocks were demolished by city councils that recognized how badly they had failed as alternatives to the old slums. It can't have been entirely coincidence that they were often demolished by dynamite, a method known as "blowdown," rather than by piecemeal dismantling. The explosion and sudden fall gave a cathartic moment of pleasure to all the people who had detested them. The writer Joe Kerr noted that blowdowns were "widely advertised … in recognition of the enormous publicity value to be derived from these acts of architectural cleansing." He went on to say that they drew "large crowds in the manner of public executions of centuries past." Ironically, some cities recognized, after demolishing half of their public-housing high-rises, that an alternative might be to sell off the remainder to private developers, for transformation into luxury apartments. This approach has worked well, especially in London, where property prices rose vertically after the year 2000. In the 1950s and 1960s, poor people lived high in the air. Now rich people live there.

More justifiable than the tower blocks, in the 60s and 70s, were the new motorways, designed to make it easier to get around the overcrowded country. The first to be built, the M1 from London to the north, and the M6 from Birmingham to Scotland, display many of the modernist features of their age. As you zip along them, or, more accurately, as you stand still on them in the frequent traffic jams, you'll have a chance to inspect the concrete bridges and flyovers, along with the convenient motorway service centers that were heralded as triumphs of modern functionalism when new. Those that have not been renovated look forlorn by now, but they were never meant to be more than functional, and the system they're a part of is certainly a huge improvement over the ramshackle road system it replaced.

Another familiar element of postwar building was modern schools and office buildings, which also emphasized function, not style. The school I went to, John Port School, in Etwall, Derbyshire, was similar to thousands like it. Concrete frames, glass and plastic fill, and boxy shapes made them entirely adequate but devoid of grace. When I was a student at John Port, in the late 60s and early 70s, the buildings were named, as if in parody of their forthright lack of charm: A Block, B Block, and C Block. Since then someone with a glimmering of imagination has renamed them Ashbourne, Bakewell, and Chatsworth.

The post war style was not lacking for critics. One was Ian Nairn, whose 1956 book *Outrage* was a slashing attack on the horrible style in which Britain was being rebuilt after the war. He coined the term "subtopia" to describe the suburban uniformity of vast areas around the edge of every city, deploring "the annihilation of the site, the steamrollering of all individuality of place to one uniform and mediocre pattern." Published when he was only 25, it made him famous, and before long he was appearing on TV as an architectural critic, and even addressing parliamentary inquiries into the condition of the cities. In his view, Britain should cherish the fact that its different places were indeed different from one-another. He showed a more upbeat mood in a later book, *Nairn's London*, in which he singled out some of the city's most famous buildings, and some of its most obscure ones, for their distinctive qualities.

In Nairn's footsteps came Prince Charles, Queen Elizabeth II's oldest son and long-time heir to the throne. He also deplored the ugliness of the buildings going up all around Britain, and his position gave him instant credibility, at least among some audiences. About the brutalist Birmingham Central Library, he memorably wrote that it looked more like the kind of building in which books were incinerated than one in which they were protected. In opposing a new development next to St. Paul's Cathedral, he remarked: "You have to give this much to the Luftwaffe; when it knocked down our buildings, it didn't replace them with anything more offensive than rubble." He described plans for the new British Library as looking like the "secret police's assembly hall." Its architect retorted that the Prince's architectural views were as backward-looking as Hitler's.

Even so, on several occasions, Charles' criticisms led to plans being abandoned. In 1984, for example, he described a planned extension to the National Gallery in Trafalgar Square as "a monstrous carbuncle on the face of a much-loved and elegant friend." His intervention enraged the modernist architectural establishment but drew thousands of positive letters. The plan was abandoned and a more conciliatory style adopted for the extension.

Prince Charles went on to publish his ideas on the topic in a TV documentary from 1988, *A Vision of Britain: A Personal View of Architecture*, which he also published in book form the following year. The Victoria and Albert Museum mounted an exhibition to coincide with its publication, which proved highly popular. His next move was to build a model village according to the principles he favored, on land belonging to the Duchy of Cornwall. It was Poundbury, in Dorset, near Thomas Hardy's old home of Dorchester. Working with the designer Leon Krier, Charles aimed to take what was best in British vernacular design from the preceding centuries, ensure variety in street views, high-density housing, and more consideration for pedestrians than cars. It is now more than 20 years old, loved by some architectural critics, hated by others.

Prince Charles was implacable in his opposition to skyscrapers. To him they seemed inhuman in scale, dwarfing the individuals who had to live and work around them. He was dismissive about Canary Wharf, the great East London development of the late 20th century that gave a new lease on life to an abandoned former dockyard area. Dominated by immense glass towers, Canary Wharf has actually turned out rather well. Bustling with life during the week, as one of the centers of the financial industry, it's also busy at weekends because of the shops, parks, cafes, restaurants, and museums along its waterfront.

In the spirit of Ian Nairn and Prince Charles, the editors of *Building Design* magazine award the Carbuncle Cup each year to "the ugliest building completed in the UK in the last 12 months." Since it first singled out the Drake Circus Shopping Centre in 2006, the Carbuncle Cup has led to a lot of amusing controversies and heated exchanges between the partisans of different styles. Inevitably, the judges' decisions are second guessed, but the existence of the Carbuncle Cup is a blessing, making it at least slightly more likely that architects will aim to avoid the crowning dishonor. One building that took the cup—rightly in my view—was the immense high-rise office building at 20 Fenchurch Street in the City of London, designed by Rafael Viñoly and finished in 2014. Nicknamed the "Walkie Talkie," it's a horrible blockish affair, grotesquely out of proportion with everything around it, overbearing and insensitive, and lacking even the straight lines that would blend it slightly with its surroundings. A spokesman for the Royal Town Planning Institute described it as "a daily reminder never to let such a planning disaster ever happen again."

At the other end of the spectrum from the Carbuncle Cup is the Stirling Prize—an award given by the Royal Institute of British Architects to what its members consider each year's best new building. The prize is named after James Stirling, a post-modernist British architect, whose work in the later years of his life creates the hope that better things are coming. At the beginning of this lecture I mentioned Edwin Lutyens's Midland Bank building on Poultry Street. Let me finish with James Stirling's building on the same street, completed in 1997. It's a delightfully playful, cheering, colorful place in striped pink and yellow brick, with lots of interesting angles and curves plus a roof-garden, built on a wedge-shaped site and topped by a circular clock tower. Best of all, it fits in its surroundings and doesn't ignore or overawe them in the manner of the Walkie Talkie.

Stirling himself, who lived from 1926 to 1992, had the courage to break away from the orthodoxy of his early life and to offer something better. His example, and that of many other late 20th and early 21st century architects, is encouraging. It's hard to imagine visitors coming to Britain to seek out 20th or 21st-century buildings the way they now seek out the castles and country estates of earlier eras. Still, after the appalling architecture of the post-war decades, it is heartening to see some new projects that deserve a place alongside Britain's best architectural achievements.

13

EDINBURGH AND GLASGOW

E ngland and Scotland have had the same monarch since 1603 and have been politically united since 1707. Scotland covers 30,000 square miles and has a population of 5.2 million. This lecture looks at notable sites in Scotland's capital, Edinburgh, and another important city, Glasow. Sites discussed include:

- Edinburgh's Royal Mile.

- High points in the city of Edinburgh.

- Edinburgh's museums and galleries.

- General sites and museums in Glasgow.

Edinburgh's Royal Mile

Edinburgh is a magnificent city, and the obvious place to start a visit there is with the city's main axis, the Royal Mile. As you begin to climb the Royal Mile, you'll come first to the Scottish Parliament building, a structure famous for its architectural daring and for its breathtaking delays and cost overruns. It was begun in 1999 and completed in 2004, three years late.

David Hume

Continuing up the Royal Mile from Parliament, tenement buildings on either side rise sharply from the street. On your right, you'll see the graveyard of Canongate church. Go inside, turn left, and you'll at once come upon the grave of Adam Smith, the moral philosopher and pioneering economist.

A bit farther up the Royal Mile is a statue of Smith in front of St. Giles's Cathedral. Just across the road from Adam Smith is a statue of his near contemporary, the philosopher and historian David Hume.

Royal Mile

A famous house on the Royal Mile is the John Knox house, built in the 15th century. Knox was one of the firebrand leaders of the Scottish Reformation and the founder of Presbyterianism.

The farther up the Royal Mile you go, the higher and grander the buildings become. Eventually, you will emerge onto a great, gently sloping plaza in front of the entrance to Edinburgh Castle. Here each August, at the height of the Edinburgh Festival, bleachers are set up for audiences to watch the Royal Edinburgh Military Tattoo, featuring marvels of precision marching by the best military and civilian squads from all over the world.

Edinburgh's High Points

Edinburgh Castle is one of the city's three great high points, all worth the effort of climbing for the great views they afford. The other two are Calton Hill and Arthur's Seat. The top of Calton Hill is covered in monuments, mainly from the late 18th and early 19th centuries. If the weather is good, you can

Edinburgh Castle

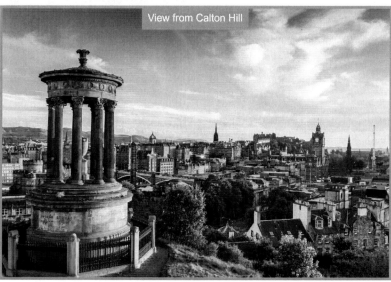

View from Calton Hill

see the whole city from this point, including the dozen or more towers and spires that contribute to Edinburgh's wonderful vertical feeling.

The third high point for views of the city is Arthur's Seat, an extinct volcano that used to be part of the royal estates but is now open to everyone. It's wild country, yet it's right next to the capital.

Edinburgh's Museums and Galleries

There are many fine museums and galleries in Edinburgh. In the National Museum of Scotland, visitors are drawn to an early version of the guillotine called the Maiden. Used between 1564 and 1710, the Maiden claimed over 150 victims, mostly in public executions. Another, very different, attraction at the National Museum is Dolly, a sheep (now stuffed) that played a vital role in the development of genetics. She was the first mammal to be cloned from an adult cell and lived from 1996 to 2003.

This course particularly encourages you to visit the Scottish National Gallery, centrally located on Princes Street Gardens. It was opened in 1859 and occupies a beautiful building, reminiscent of a Greek temple. Highlights of the gallery's collection include paintings by Rembrandt, El Greco, Goya, Botticelli, Vermeer, Reynolds, Turner, Cézanne, and many others.

Glasgow

West of Edinburgh stands Glasgow, Scotland's other great city. Through the long era of the British Empire, it was the shipbuilding capital of Britain. The banks of the River Clyde still bear evidence of this shipbuilding history, especially a series of immense but no longer active marine cranes.

The University of Glasgow is an attractive hilltop structure, with an iconic tower visible from all across the city. Though the university was founded in the 15th century, the main building of the current campus was designed by George Gilbert Scott in the 1870s, and is the second largest neo-Gothic building in Britain, after the Houses of Parliament.

University of Glasgow

Kelvingrove Art Gallery and Museum

Another Victorian edifice, almost too big and too decorative to be believed, is the Kelvingrove Art Gallery and Museum that stands nearby. Its curators obviously know that museum going is supposed to be fun, but also that most visitors have short attention spans. They cater to these realities by having different exhibits on display in close proximity.

A second superb museum in Glasgow is the Riverside Museum, located on the banks of the Clyde in a dramatic new building by Zaha Hadid. Made of glass and stainless steel, it shimmers and seems to draw a zigzag line across the landscape. It opened in 2011 and now draws over 1 million visitors per year. On land that was once dedicated to shipbuilding, it has a tall ship right outside the front door, the only Glasgow-built sailing ship still afloat.

Suggested Reading

Fry, *Edinburgh*.

Taylor, *Glasgow*.

Wilson, *A Life of Walter Scott*.

Suggested Activities

1. Climb Arthur's Seat, one of the three hills that give great views over the whole of Edinburgh.

2. Ask one of the custodians at the Scottish Parliament building why it cost so much.

3. Before a summer visit to Scotland, buy tickets online for events in the Edinburgh Festival and the Royal Edinburgh Military Tattoo.

13

EDINBURGH AND GLASGOW

E ngland and Scotland have had the same monarch since 1603 and have been politically united since 1707. Scottish history until 1700 was a tale of brutality, bloodshed, and poverty. Since then, it's been a story of stability, peace, and plenty, which is why English people, including me, are surprised by the strength of Scottish nationalism. Still, national self-love is one of the most powerful forces in the world. The English themselves proved this point in 2016 by voting to leave the European Union, whereas the Scots voted to stay in.

Scotland covers 30,000 square miles and has a population of 5.2 million. The land area of England, 50,000 square miles, contains 10 times as many people, just over 55 million, a much greater density. Scotland not only has fewer people; it's also famous for exporting them. Some Scottish expatriates are famous, including Andrew Carnegie, Alexander Graham Bell, and David Livingstone. Others are obscure, including the thousands of clansmen who came to America in the late 1700s and the thousands who settled large areas of Canada and Australia in the 1800s. A 2001 book, *How the Scots Invented the Modern World* may be a trifle exaggerated but there's no doubt about the immense Scottish contribution to our civilization.

Let me hand over at this point to Paul Meier so that he can give you a taste of the distinctive Scottish accent, and tell you how to begin your tour.

[Paul] Thanks Patrick. The obvious place to start a visit to Scotland is in the capital, Edinburgh. What a magnificent city it is, a dramatic site unrivalled anywhere, except possibly by Quebec in Canada and Lhasa in Tibet. The Royal Mile is old Edinburgh's main axis, a mile-long road that climbs from

Holyrood Palace at the bottom to Edinburgh Castle at the top. Holyrood, the Queen's official Scottish residence, is built on the grounds of an old monastery, whose ruins still peek out from behind the palace. There, Mary Queen of Scots witnessed her Italian secretary, David Rizzio, being stabbed 50 or 60 times by her jealous rogue of a husband, Lord Darnley, in 1566.

Thanks, Paul.

As you begin to climb the royal mile, you'll come first to the Scottish Parliament building, a structure famous for its architectural daring and for its breathtaking delays and cost overruns. It was begun in 1999 and completed in 2004, three years late. Originally estimated to cost around £20 million, it finally cost £414 million, which prompted more than a few questions from irritable taxpayers, plus an official inquiry. The cold grey exterior is unremarkable except for some irregularly shaped sections, which look a little like boats when viewed from above. But go inside and things improve. The theme is pale wood, raw concrete, and exposed metal. Unusual angles keep you slightly off-balance—oblique diagonal patterns on the doors are intriguing. The big debating chamber is dramatic, steeply angled down toward the speaker's chair at the front, and with plenty of seats for interested observers. The committee rooms are irregularly shaped, with bowed ceilings, daring approaches to lighting, and a sense of austere opulence.

Continuing up the Royal Mile from Parliament, tenement buildings on either side rise sharply from the street. The prevailing sensation is vertical. Behind the high frontages lie "the wynds," networks of alleys, courts, and staircases that historically housed a dense population, living cheek by jowl and susceptible to epidemics.

On your right, you'll see the graveyard of Canongate church. Go inside, turn left, and you'll at once come upon the grave of Adam Smith, the moral philosopher and pioneering economist who, in 1776, published *An Inquiry into the Nature and Causes of the Wealth of Nations*. It's a book just bursting with shrewd insights into human nature. When the industrial revolution was just starting, Smith could already foresee many of its most important elements. He radiates common sense, raised to the highest level of acuteness. It's a pleasure, after seeing his final resting place, to go a little further up the royal mile to find a statue of him, seemingly alive and well, in front of St. Giles's Cathedral.

Just across the road from Adam Smith is a statue of his near contemporary, the philosopher and historian David Hume. Hume is dressed in a toga despite the whipping wind that keeps temperatures low on most days of the year. Remember those winds when you visit, by the way: even in July and August the average high temperature in Edinburgh is only 66-degrees Fahrenheit. In any case, Smith, Hume, and many other 18th-century writers led the Scottish Enlightenment, a philosophical movement that argued for many of the principles we still live by today. It had effects on city planning as well as academic life, as we'll see shortly.

Another famous house on the Royal Mile is the John Knox House, built in the 15th-century. John Knox was one of the firebrand leaders of the Scottish Reformation; the founder of Presbyterianism. His best-known book, published in 1558, is entitled *The First Blast of the Trumpet against the Monstrous Regiment of Women*. In his view, it was plain that the Bible prohibits women from ruling over men. That view fitted well with his antagonism to Mary Queen of Scots and Queen Mary I of England. I'll read a little passage and leave you to decide whether he's popular today among feminists:

> For who can deny but it is repugnant to nature that the blind shall be appointed to lead and conduct such as do see, that the weak, the sick and impotent persons shall nourish and keep the whole and strong; and, finally, that the foolish, mad, and frenetic shall govern the discreet and give counsel to such as be sober of mind? And such be all women, compared unto man in bearing of authority. For their sight in civil [affairs] is but blindness, their counsel, foolishness, and their judgment, frenzy.

You can also speculate about whether the first Protestant queen of England, Elizabeth I, regarded him as a dependable supporter. There's some doubt about whether Knox actually occupied the place now advertised as his house, though he certainly lived and preached nearby. Ironically, the house seems to have belonged to a prominent Catholic goldsmith who was on the opposite side of the religious divide in Knox's day. Among the pulpits that Knox occupied was that of St. Giles's Cathedral, which I mentioned a moment ago. Also known as the High Kirk of Edinburgh, St. Giles is distinguished by a crown steeple from the late 1400s.

The further up the Royal Mile you go, the higher and grander the buildings become. At last you emerge onto a great, gently sloping plaza in front of the entrance to Edinburgh Castle. Here each August, at the height of the Edinburgh Festival, bleachers are set up for audiences to watch the Royal Edinburgh Military Tattoo, featuring marvels of precision marching by the best military and civilian squads from all over the world. Often windswept, in the late summer evenings, and with the backdrop of the ancient castle, the Tattoo brings the festival season to a climax.

The castle itself has the perfect defensive location, unapproachable from most sides because of daunting cliffs, and towering over the more manageable access points. It's been a fortress since at least the 12th century. Twenty-six sieges over the centuries have made it one of the most fought-over points in Britain—its only rival might be the Anglo-Scottish border towns of Carlisle and Berwick-upon-Tweed. Edward I of England, nicknamed "Hammer of the Scots," seized it in 1296 but Robert the Bruce recovered it in 1314, shortly before the Battle of Bannockburn. Edward III of England seized it again in 1335 but William Douglas recaptured it for Scotland in 1341 and annihilated the defenders. It was an active military barracks well into the 20th century, and several proud Scottish regiments still have museums on the site. Every day at 1:00 pm a cannon is fired from the battlements. Audible throughout the city, it's an opportunity for everyone to set right their clocks and watches. No single site in the whole of Scotland is more magnetically attractive. One and a half million people visit every year.

Edinburgh Castle is one of the city's three great high points, all worth the effort of climbing for the great views they afford. The other two are Calton Hill and Arthur's Seat. The top of Calton Hill is covered in monuments, mainly from the late 18th and early 19th centuries. Dugald Stewart, a philosopher, mathematician, and friend of Adam Smith and David Hume, is the subject of one of them, though he's not actually depicted. A second monument is a tower shaped like an inverted telescope, commemorating Admiral Nelson's victory at the Battle of Trafalgar in 1805. There's also a partial replica of the Parthenon, begun in the 1820s to celebrate victory over Napoleon, but never completed, for lack of funds. It's variously known as "The Scottish National Monument" and "Scotland's Disgrace."

If the weather is good, you can see the whole city from this point, Calton Hill, including the dozen or more towers and spires that contribute to Edinburgh's wonderful vertical feeling. One of the towers belongs to a vast and imposing five-star hotel, the Balmoral, completed in 1902 at the very center of the city. This is the kind of hotel where you pay £350 for one night, feel important, but have to cope with the bagpipers who start early and finish late, and the rumble of trains passing almost straight underneath.

The third high point for views of the city is Arthur's Seat, an extinct volcano that used to be part of the royal estates but is now open to everyone. It's wild country, yet it's right next to the capital. Easy to climb from most directions, it's also adjacent to the jagged Salisbury Crags, a cliff face into which a track called "The Radical Road" was hewn by unemployed workmen in 1820. I've climbed Arthur's Seat many times, with groups of American students who are amazed to discover that even at 10 in the evening, in June and July, it's light enough to see far horizons in every direction.

I mentioned earlier that the Scottish Enlightenment had practical consequences for city planning. One was the decision, in the 1760s, to extend Edinburgh across the low-lying swamp that lay below the castle, to the high ground on the far side. Rational planning and better spacing would alleviate the housing shortage, the epidemics, and the overcrowding from which Edinburgh suffered. The upshot was the New Town, a set of elegant structures laid out on a grid. It was designed by a talented young architect named James Craig, who was only 26 when he submitted his design. It was extended several times through the next century and much of it survives intact, now forming the most expensive and sought-after property in the city. Moray Place, a circle of grand houses surrounding a private garden, is particularly impressive. Statues of kings and noblemen stand at several New Town intersections.

In St. Andrew Square, built in the 1770s and now center of the financial district, on a column more than 100 feet high, stands the carved figure of Henry Dundas, the first Viscount Melville. Your reaction is probably the same as mine: never heard of him! Last time I was there I asked several people in the square if they knew who he was. Most had no clue but one said "he was a Tory politician in the old days." A little research disclosed that he was one of the patrons of the Scottish Enlightenment, and one of the movers and shakers behind the building of the New Town. So far, so good.

On the other hand, he was impeached for embezzlement in 1806, and was an outspoken opponent of the abolition of slavery. A skilled political operator with great influence over Scottish affairs, he was nicknamed "the Great Tyrant" and "the uncrowned king of Scotland." It's very hard to imagine such a figure getting the royal treatment today. But it's also difficult to imagine that he's going to be removed. The monument is a Grade A listed building, Britain's highest ranking for an historical structure. The column has the added interest of having been constructed by Robert Stevenson, an expert lighthouse builder, who is known to us as the grandfather of the novelist Robert Louis Stevenson.

One of the finest buildings on St. Andrew's Square has been cleaned, restoring its reddish sandstone to glory after two centuries of accumulating soot. The saddest thing about Edinburgh is how dirty most of its grand buildings remain. Far behind London, Oxford, and Cambridge in this respect, the whole city needs the face lift that cleaning would bring. When the whole of Britain was coated in soot, Edinburgh looked just like all the rest. Now that the great cleaning has taken such strides, however, Edinburgh stands out, in the wrong way, as the dirty laggard. Sure, it's expensive, but Britain's high environmental standards mean that the soot would not return, and Edinburgh would achieve an unrivalled splendor far into the future. Meanwhile, every visitor comments that it's impressive but dirty.

Blackest of all the great sooty structures is the 200-high Walter Scott Monument. Scott was the most popular novelist in the English-speaking world in the early 19th century. Immensely influential, he was a key figure in literary romanticism, and helped make the idea of Scotland fashionable among the English (it had been in disgrace since the Bonnie Prince Charlie uprising of

1745-46). Scott's death occasioned a great outpouring of grief, along with a competition to design a suitable memorial. A self-taught architect named George Meikle Kemp won the contract with an elaborate gothic design, and construction began in 1841. The site chosen was central, on Princes Street, overlooking the valley that runs through the heart of Edinburgh. It's fun to climb the series of tight spiral staircases of the Scott Monument that lead up to a high lookout point. Every inch of the monument is covered with statues of characters from Scott's novels and of other poets and notables, including Lord Byron and Mary Queen of Scots. They were sculpted by a wide array of different artists, who clamored to be included. Sadly, Kemp, the architect, didn't live to see its completion in 1846—two years before, on a foggy evening, he had stumbled, fallen into the canal, and drowned. His achievement remains today the biggest monument to a writer anywhere in the world.

Among Scott's many works were the "Waverley" novels, published anonymously at first, but acknowledged by him in the mid-1820s, and including several of his best-known books, such as *Ivanhoe* and *Rob Roy*. When railways came to Scotland, the central station was named "Edinburgh Waverley" as a tribute to Scott. Waverley station sits in the valley between the Royal Mile and Princes Street, and could not be more central. Unlike the grand London terminals, none of which stand in the heart of the city, this one was able to do so because the land hitherto had been swampy and useless. The railway engineers themselves transformed it into usable ground.

There are many fine museums and galleries in Edinburgh. In the National Museum of Scotland, ghoulish visitors are drawn to an early version of the guillotine called "the Maiden." A slightly indignant placard explains that beheading machines were not first invented during the French Revolution. Used between 1564 and 1710, the Maiden claimed over 150 victims, mostly in public executions. Another, very different, attraction at the National Museum is "Dolly," a sheep (now stuffed) that played a vital role in the development of genetics. She was the first mammal to be cloned from an adult cell, and lived from 1996 to 2003.

Let me particularly encourage you to visit the Scottish National Gallery, centrally located on Princes Street Gardens. It was opened in 1859 and occupies a beautiful neo-classical building, reminiscent of a Greek temple. A source of great national pride, it's a major collection of Old Masters by any standard. The building itself is superb, its ground floor rooms all decorated in a sumptuous red. Highlights of the collection include paintings by Rembrandt, El Greco, Goya, Botticelli, Vermeer, Reynolds, Turner, Cezanne, and many of the other stars. Everyone's going to have favorites. Among the paintings I like best are *The Honourable Mrs. Graham* by Gainsborough, painted around 1776. She was a society beauty, recently married to a Scottish aristocrat, and for the painting she dressed in the style of the previous century, to evoke the world of Van Dyck. It is more than life-sized, the fabrics shimmer, and she looks exquisite yet vulnerable. The sad story behind the painting is that she died very young of tuberculosis, distressing her husband so much that he had the painting taken down and never looked at it again.

Alexander Nasmyth's 1825 painting of the Scottish Royal Institution on Princes Street is superb. First, it's local; the artist's easel was set up only a few yards from where the painting is now on display. Second, it shows Edinburgh in the early 1820s, when many of the principal buildings were already there, but with conspicuous exceptions (no Scott Monument, obviously, and no railway). A few weeks before seeing the painting, I had read the autobiography of the artist's son, James Nasmyth, an important figure in British industrial history. His affectionate description of his father made me feel I already knew the artist; the work itself confirms his skill.

Another irresistible painting, at least to me, is John Duncan's 1913 depiction of Saint Bride. Bride, or Bridget, was an Irish abbess and saint of the 5th century, but somehow she was also able, nearly 500 years earlier, to visit Bethlehem and witness the birth of Christ. The painting shows two angels carrying her across the sea, their robes embroidered with scenes from the later life of Christ. Seagulls and a seal accompany them. It's nutty but lovely, in just the right way.

When I'm in Scotland I always take a short train journey from Edinburgh to North Queensferry, nine miles Northwest of the city. It's a wonderful ride because you start out under the looming walls of the castle. But the highlight comes near the end with a crossing of the Forth Bridge. If I had to give my list of the five most interesting objects in Britain, the Forth Bridge would be on it. Immense, metallic, rust-red in color, comprised of three stupendous steel cantilevers, it dominates the Firth of Forth for miles in every direction. Begun in 1882 and opened in 1890, it was built in response to a recent tragedy.

A long iron bridge over the Firth of Tay, 40 miles further north, had collapsed in a night storm in 1879, only a year and a half after opening. It carried a train full of travelers to their deaths and occasioned a great scandal. The architect, recently knighted by Queen Victoria, died in disgrace the next year. When you go over the bridge that replaced it, you can still see the stumps of the old bridge's piers projecting from the water. Ominous! The engineers of the Forth Bridge, begun just three years after this disaster, wanted something that not only was strong but looked strong, to reassure passengers that they would be safe as they crossed the estuary. Engineers who subjected it to stress tests in the 20th century reported that it's overbuilt many times over. Never mind: the visual impact is stunning, from the shore, where it towers over you, from the stations at either end, and from boats in the firth itself.

There's a lovely boat trip available from South and North Queensferry, at the two ends of the Forth Bridge. It takes you out to Inchcolm Island. On the island stand the picturesque ruins of an ancient abbey. It's one of many in the Edinburgh area that remind you that, John Knox notwithstanding, Scotland was once a strongly Catholic country. The island was heavily fortified in both world wars, to protect the approaches to the naval yard of Rosyth and the docks at Leith. A complex of pillboxes, concrete bastions, and gun emplacements are partly off limits now, because the island doubles as a bird sanctuary. Thousands of seagulls and fulmars nest there every year, and become aggressive if you try to get too close. In fact, one of the distinctive noises of Edinburgh is the cry of gulls. In the city itself, you're rarely aware of being right next to the sea, but the gulls give you the necessary reminder.

West of Edinburgh stands Glasgow, Scotland's other great city. Through the long era of the British Empire it was the ship-building capital of Britain, and a seafaring city that made fortunes out of slavery, sugar, and tobacco.

Among the ships built there were the *Queen Mary*, *Queen Elizabeth*, and *Queen Elizabeth 2*. The banks of the River Clyde still bear evidence of this shipbuilding history, especially a series of immense but no longer active marine cranes. Glasgow has always been a hands-on, working city, so it's appropriate that its most famous native son is James Watt (1736-1819). He was the genius who turned steam engines from monstrous, clumsy, slow-moving mine-drainage devices into the smaller, faster, more powerful and more efficient devices that accelerated the entire industrial revolution. He came from Greenock on the River Clyde, worked as an instrument-maker and repairer at the University of Glasgow, impressed all his contemporaries, and went on to claim patents on several decisive technologies.

The University of Glasgow is itself an attractive hilltop structure, with an iconic tower visible from all across the city. Though the university was founded in the 15th century, the main building of the current campus was designed by George Gilbert Scott in the 1870s, and is the second largest neo-gothic building in Britain, after the Houses of Parliament. Another Victorian edifice, almost too big and too decorative to be believed, is the Kelvingrove Art Gallery and Museum that stands nearby. Its curators obviously know that museum-going is supposed to be fun, but also that most visitors have short attention spans. They cater to these realities by having different exhibits on display cheek by jowl. A World-War II Spitfire plane hangs from the ceiling of one exhibition hall, directly over a stuffed elephant and gazelle. In the adjacent galleries are Egyptian mummies, old master paintings, and artifacts from Glasgow's long manufacturing history. There's also a gallery devoted to the work of Charles Rennie Mackintosh, the famous late 19th-century architect and designer, who turned tables and chairs from functional objects into works of art.

Kelvingrove's most unexpected exhibit is the *La Faruk Madonna*. During World War II, the British army defeated an Italian force in what is now Somalia, and took many prisoners. One of the POWs, Giuseppe Baldan, painted three religious pictures on the back of flour sacks to go inside a little makeshift chapel made of mud bricks: one of the Virgin Mary, and two of kneeling angels, to flank her. Behind the angels, the camp huts are visible. When the war ended, the pictures were rescued from imminent destruction and given to the camp commander, Captain Alfred Hawksworth, who had treated the prisoners well.

He and the artist stayed in touch for the rest of their lives, while the paintings themselves came to rest in Kelvingrove. Maybe they're not great art, but the story more than makes up for their aesthetic limitations.

The second superb museum in Glasgow is the Riverside Museum, located on the banks of the Clyde in a dramatic new building by Zaha Hadid. Made of glass and stainless steel, it shimmers and seems to draw a zig-zag line across the landscape. It opened in 2011 and now draws over a million visitors per year. On land that was once dedicated to shipbuilding, it has a tall ship right outside the front door, the only Glasgow-built sailing ship still afloat.

A third outstanding Glasgow museum is the Burrell Collection, in Pollok Country Park, away from the city center. It closed down for a major upgrade in 2016 with the promise of reopening in 2020. Sir William Burrell was a shrewd businessman who built a shipping empire. He waited for slumps in the business cycle then ordered ships from the Glasgow yards at knockdown prices, enlarging his fleet and being well-placed to profit when the market revived. Amassing a fortune, he then devoted himself to spending it on art, specializing in works from medieval and Renaissance Europe, particularly tapestries, along with Chinese ceramics, Persian rugs and Indian textiles, but also in works by such modern painters as Whistler. He gave the whole lot, 9000 items, to the city of Glasgow, specifying that it should be housed outside the city and away from what was then a severely polluted environment.

There's a lot more to Scotland than the big cities of Edinburgh and Glasgow, of course, as we'll see in the next lecture, but if you have only limited time, that's where you should spend it. The drone of bagpipes will be in your ears nearly all the time, you'll meet men in kilts, and you'll understand Scottish pride, embodied in the diagonal white cross on a blue field of St. Andrew's flag. The Scottish accent, too, entirely unlike any from England, reminds you that this is a different country, and yet one whose history is central to that of Britain as a whole.

14

WILD SCOTLAND: BEYOND EDINBURGH AND GLASGOW

Scotland has a wild history and a wild landscape. Its highlands are the least densely populated part of Europe. Scotland has a complicated western coastline, indented with long inlets from the sea, along with dozens of islands. Most of it is poor farmland, where for centuries crofters eked out a bare existence, organized in clans and beholden to their local chieftains. Castles, most of them now in ruins, dot the landscape, bearing witness to centuries of strife, bloodshed, and chronic insecurity. This lecture covers some interesting travel topics regarding Scotland, including:

- Stirling Bridge and Bannockburn, which are sites commemorating Scottish victories over the English.

- Travel tips for Scotland.

- Glencoe.

- Fort William, Glenfinnan, and Loch Ness.

- Scotland's islands.

- Lockerbie.

Stirling Bridge and Bannockburn

King Edward I of England, in the late 1200s, conquered Wales and then set out to conquer Scotland too. He never managed it. Great English armies crossed the border but met fierce resistance. Two battlefields—Stirling Bridge and Bannockburn—commemorate English defeats and Scottish victories.

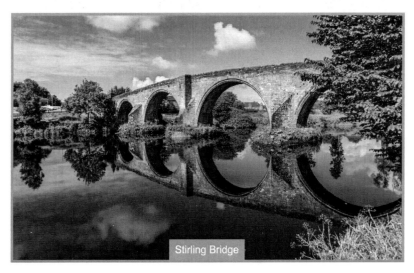

Stirling Bridge

249

Stirling Bridge is the place where, in 1297, Scottish fighter William Wallace defeated a much larger English army under the earl of Surrey. The medieval bridge over the River Forth has gone now, but there's a fine 15th-century stone bridge in its place, surrounded by meadows on which historical markers recall the event. A few miles from the battlefield, on a dramatic hilltop named Abbey Craig, stands the Wallace Monument, a great craggy tower in his honor.

Wallace Monument

Stirling Castle

Stirling Castle, on a great rocky outcrop, dominates the area. As with Edinburgh Castle, Stirling has an ideal defensive location, being unapproachable from most directions because of the near-vertical cliffs. This castle commands the best routeway from southern to northern Scotland, the Stirling Gap, so it's not surprising that armies should often have met there.

Only two or three miles from Stirling Bridge is Bannockburn, where, in 1314, Robert the Bruce defeated another English army. An ambitious interpretive center on the site describes the battle and the war of which it was a part, with plenty of interactive features for children.

Travel Tips for Scotland

Keep in mind that if you drive from the lowlands into Scotland's mountains, roads are scarce. Even those that do exist are narrow, winding, and slow. Don't expect to average more than about 30 miles per hour in northern Scotland.

One of the most scenically spectacular major roads is the A82, which leads north across the bleak ground of Rannoch Moor and, eventually, to the valley of Glencoe. Hike there if you possibly can. Note that the steepness of the hike can be challenging, and waterproof clothing is advised.

Glencoe

Glencoe

Glencoe, another site in Scotland, was the scene of a famous massacre in the year 1692, in the aftermath of the Glorious Revolution. King James II of England, who was also King James VII of Scotland, had fled to France after alienating nearly all the important people of his kingdom. Parliament invited William of Orange, a Dutch prince, to become King William III of England in his place. William secured the throne and ordered all his new subjects to swear oaths of allegiance. The Macdonald clan of Glencoe, however, had been allied with the cause of King James and were slow to sign the oath. As a result, soldiers in British service who belonged to the Campbell clan massacred 38 members of the MacDonald clan.

At the Glencoe visitor center, you'll learn that long before the massacre, the area already had a history of hard fighting. Eight centuries earlier, a fleet of Viking long ships had sailed up Loch Leven to seize the lands around Glencoe from their current owners.

Fort William, Glenfinnan, and Loch Ness

If you drive north from Glencoe, you'll reach the town of Fort William, named after King William III. Here you're standing in the shadow of Ben Nevis, the highest mountain in Britain.

Ben Nevis

The road west from Fort William to the town of Mallaig is called the Road to the Isles because from Mallaig, there's a ferry across to the Isle of Skye. A few miles down this road, you'll come to Glenfinnan, at the head of Loch Shiel. It's one of the most beautiful places in the whole of Scotland.

Glenfinnan Lake

Drive back to Fort William to see another marvel, Neptune's Staircase. It is a series of canal locks built in the early 1800s. They are part of the Caledonian Canal, a broad canal designed to carry seagoing ships across Scotland without exposing them to the stormy dangers of Cape Wrath and the Pentland Firth. The canal was designed by Thomas Telford, one of the leading engineers of the early Industrial Revolution. The most famous of the lochs along the

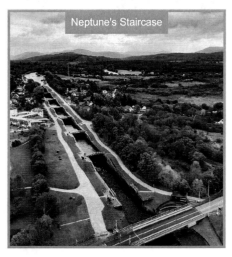
Neptune's Staircase

canal is Loch Ness. It's 800 feet deep in places and 23 miles long, and is notable for unconfirmed rumors of a monster living in its depths.

Scotland's Islands

A large part of Scotland's land area is made up of islands, most of which are accessible by ferry and a few by air. They can be bleak and barren in winter, and not always hospitable even in the summer, but they have a craggy charm along with some terrific historical lures.

North of the mainland are the Orkney Islands, comprising some of the richest archaeological sites in the whole of Britain. The Orkneys became famous as the headquarters in World War I of the British Grand Fleet.

The island of Skye, off the west coast of Scotland, is the haunt of hikers and climbers. A broken and narrow ridge, the Cuillin Ridge, is among its most

Skye

daunting challenges. It is one of the few places in Britain that looks as jagged as the Alps or Rockies.

Lockerbie

If you drive south out of Scotland at the end of your visit, think about going to the village of Lockerbie, just before you reach the English border. It's an old town whose medieval prosperity was based on the wool trade. An endearing statue in the main street depicts a line of lambs trotting along beside the shops.

Lockerbie became famous in a horrible and unexpected way in December 1988, when a jumbo jet blew up in the sky overhead and the debris rained down on the town. All 259 people on the plane were killed, and 11 more died in Lockerbie itself when a large section of the wing fell on a suburban street, Sherwood Crescent. An official of the Libyan government was convicted and jailed for the attack.

Sherwood Crescent today is a quiet suburban street again, but the line of single-story houses breaks off at one point, and a well-kept garden of high shrubs and flowers takes its place. Tucked away behind the greenery stands a marker in memory of the two families whose homes had stood there. A mile or two away is the town's cemetery, a special section of which has been set aside as a memorial garden to the victims. It's a windswept setting that is sobering to visit.

Suggested Reading

Prebble, *Glencoe*.

Traquair, *Freedom's Sword*.

Williams, *A Monstrous Commotion*.

Suggested Activities

1. At a fish and chip shop, ask for the local specialty, haggis and chips.

2. Find the family names of all the people who live on your street or everyone at your place of work. Then, check a map of the Scottish clans to see how many of those names you can find there.

WILD SCOTLAND: BEYOND EDINBURGH AND GLASGOW

Scotland has a wild history and a wild landscape. Once you go beyond the central Lowlands, and into the Highlands, you will be entering the least densely populated part of Europe. Look at the map and you'll see a complicated western coastline, indented with long inlets from the sea, along with dozens of islands. Most of it is poor farmland, where for centuries crofters eked out a bare existence, organized in clans and beholden to their local chieftains. Castles, most of them now in ruins, dot the landscape, bearing witness to centuries of strife, bloodshed, and chronic insecurity.

King Edward I of England, in the late 1200s, conquered Wales and then set out to conquer Scotland too. He found it a tougher nut to crack, and at one point, according to legend, swore an oath that he would never sleep two nights in the same place until he had succeeded. If true, he must have been on the move until his dying day, because he never managed it. Great English armies crossed the border but met fierce resistance. Two battlefields—Stirling Bridge and Bannockburn—commemorate English defeats and Scottish victories.

Stirling Bridge is the place where, in 1297, William Wallace defeated a much larger English army under the Earl of Surrey. The medieval bridge over the River Forth has gone now, but there's a fine 15th-century stone bridge in its place, surrounded by meadows on which historical markers recall the event.

Wallace, a nobleman in the service of Robert the Bruce, became one of the heroes of Scottish nationalism through this feat, even though Edward defeated him the following year at the Battle of Falkirk. A few miles from the battlefield, on a dramatic hilltop named Abbey Craig, stands the Wallace Monument, a great craggy tower in his honor. It's visible from Stirling Bridge, and is meant to look medieval. Actually, it's Victorian, built in 1869 at the height of the vogue for romantic nationalism.

Inside is a half-historical, half-legendary version of Wallace's story. The best part of the Wallace Monument, however, is the open-air platform at its summit, where you have to battle the wind to stay upright but can enjoy superb views in every direction. For a few years, back in the 1990s, a comically bad statue of Mel Gibson as William Wallace (derived from his role in the film *Braveheart*) stood at the base of the Monument. I'm happy to be able to tell you that it is no longer there.

Stirling Castle, on a great rocky outcrop, dominates the area. As with Edinburgh Castle, Stirling has an ideal defensive location, being unapproachable from most directions because of the near-vertical cliffs. An Italian alchemist who thought he could fly using artificial feathered wings, took advantage of its height in 1507 to launch himself into the air. He landed in a dunghill but survived.

Mary Queen of Scots was crowned in Stirling's Chapel Royal in 1543 when she was only nine months old. Her own son, King James VI, was baptized there in 1566, shortly before she was deposed and fled to England. For centuries after that, it served as a prison and as a garrison for Scottish regiments, before becoming a museum in the mid-20th century. Stirling's most striking feature is the Great Hall, built in the late Middle Ages in the style of a Renaissance Palace. Extensively renovated in the late-20th century, its lime-washed exterior, which is thought to be historically authentic, makes it lighter and brighter than all the surrounding structures.

This castle commands the best route-way from southern to northern Scotland, the "Stirling Gap," so it's not surprising that armies should often have met there. Only two or three miles from Stirling Bridge is Bannockburn, where, in 1314, Robert the Bruce defeated another English army. The best-remembered event of the two-day battle is the dramatic meeting of Bruce and the English leader Henry de Bohun, both on horseback. With one mighty stroke of his battle-axe, Bruce split the helmet and the head of de Bohun, killing him instantly and demoralizing the English army. An impressive equestrian statue of King Robert stands on the high ground of the field. Next to it is an open rotunda, engraved with a poem by Kathleen Jamie, "Here lies our land." Over the scene flies the St. Andrew flag of Scotland. An ambitious interpretive center, on-site, describes the battle, and the war of which it was a part, in detail, with plenty of interactive features for children.

Nearby, in the town of Dunfermline, once the royal capital, Bruce was buried after his death in 1329. His tomb stands inside the abbey church, and is visited by thousands of people each year. On the four sides of the tower parapet, visible from all around the town, are carved in stone the four words "King Robert The Bruce," to underline the point that this is his place. It's a robust and well-proportioned building, standing adjacent to the ruins of an abbey that fell into disuse during the Scottish Reformation.

Just down the hill from the Abbey stands the little cottage in which Andrew Carnegie was born in 1835. It's a modest little house, and would probably have been swept away long ago had not Carnegie's wife bought it for him as a gift in 1895. It is now attached to a visitor-center and museum, where you can learn a lot about a man who really did live out the rags-to-riches myth. In his *Autobiography*, Carnegie paid tribute to Dunfermline, and its lasting importance for him:

> Fortunate, indeed, the child who first sees the light in that romantic town. The child ... absorbs poetry and romance with the air he breathes, assimilates history and tradition as he gazes around. These become to him his real world in childhood—the ideal is the ever-present real ... No bright child of Dunfermline can escape the influence of the Abbey, Palace, and Glen. These touch him and set fire to the latent spark within, making him something different and beyond what, less happily born, he would have become.

Carnegie's father was a hand-loom weaver; and one of the exhibits in the cottage is a loom, with an operator who explains how to work it. But the rise of power looms in factories brought hard times to the hand-loom weavers. Carnegie's family responded by emigrating to Pittsburgh, Pennsylvania when he was 13. After making his fortune in America, his later life was devoted to philanthropy, much of it in England and Scotland, where Carnegie libraries are still a familiar sight. He also bought a castle, Skibo, in County Sutherland (unfortunately, not now open to the public). He spent £2 million to make it bigger and more comfortable, and hired a bagpiper to play outside its gates each morning whenever he was there.

As you drive north from the Lowland towns of Dunfermline and Stirling, into the mountains, you begin to realize that roads are few and far between. Even those that do exist are narrow, winding, and slow. Don't expect to average more than about 30 miles per hour in northern Scotland. One of the most scenically spectacular major roads is the A82, which leads you north across the bleak ground of Rannoch Moor and, eventually, to Glencoe. "Glen" is the word for valley, but few valleys can compete with this one for grandeur. Hike there if you possibly can. The valley, carved by glaciers into a characteristic U-shape, gets steeper the further up you climb, but the waterfalls all around you, and the exhilarating sense of altitude, make it worth the effort. Don't forget your waterproofs. Last time I was there, my brother and I climbed one of the mountain paths, lashed by almost horizontal rain.

This being Scotland, however, there's a tragic as well as a beautiful side to Glencoe. It's the scene of a famous massacre in the year 1692, in the aftermath of the Glorious Revolution. King James II of England, who was also King James VII of Scotland, had fled to France after alienating nearly all the important people of his kingdom. Parliament invited William of Orange, a Dutch prince, to become King William III of England in his place. William secured the throne and ordered all his new subjects to swear oaths of allegiance. The Macdonald clan of Glencoe, however, had been allied with the cause of King James and were slow to sign the oath. As a result, soldiers in British service who belonged to the Campbell clan massacred 38 members of the MacDonald clan.

Actually, old feuds and political subterfuges were mixed among the motives for this slaughter, which was particularly atrocious because the MacDonalds had hospitably welcomed the Campbells in the foregoing days. In addition to the 38 MacDonalds killed in the massacre itself, another 40, including women and children, died of exposure in the wintry mountains. Every aspect of the massacre has been studied exhaustively by historians; none are satisfied with the conclusions of a royal inquiry made at the time, whose main purpose seems to have been to clear King William of all responsibility.

At the Glencoe visitor center, incidentally, you'll learn that, long before the massacre, the area already had a long history of hard fighting. Eight centuries earlier, a fleet of Viking long ships had sailed up Loch Leven to seize the lands around Glencoe from their current owners. Let me now quote the visitor center's display board:

> They were led by the Norse King, Erragon of Lochlann, who suggested that the two sides should fight to the death, with the victor claiming the lands of Glencoe. On the field of Achnacon … each side put forward 140 of their best warriors. A long and bloody battle commenced. Hours later, much blood was shed and many men lay dead, including King Erragon himself. The Vikings retreated and the lands were kept by the people of Glencoe.

After Glencoe, keep driving north and you'll reach the town of Fort William, named after King William III. Here you're standing in the shadow of Ben Nevis, the highest mountain in Britain. At 4,400 feet, it can't be compared in altitude to the highest mountains of the Alps, the Rockies, or even the Appalachians. Nevertheless, it's a steep climb, and has to be done right from sea level. If you're in good shape it will take about four hours going up and three more coming down. Pray, when you set off, that the clouds won't come down to cover the top, as they so often do. The poet Keats climbed it in 1818, and had exactly this experience. He could see the stones at his feet but that was about all. It struck him that this was an analogue of the human condition, and prompted him to write the following sonnet:

> Read me a lesson, Muse, and speak it loud,
> Upon the top of Nevis, blind in mist!
> I look into the chasms, and a shroud
> Vaporous doth hide them,—just so much I wist
> Mankind do know of hell; I look o'erhead,
> And there is sullen mist, even so much

Mankind can tell of heaven; mist is spread
Before the earth, beneath me,—even such,
Even so vague is man's sight of himself!
Here are the craggy stones beneath my feet,—
Thus much I know that, a poor witless elf,
I tread on them,—that all my eye doth meet
Is mist and crag, not only on this height,
But in the world of thought and mental night!

Mrs. Allitt and I also climbed Ben Nevis one day in the 1980s, and also could see nothing in the mist, but I can't claim that the experience prompted an equally profound meditation.

The road west from Fort William to the town of Mallaig is called "The Road to the Isles," because from Mallaig there's a ferry across to the Isle of Skye. A few miles along this road you'll come to Glenfinnan, at the head of Loch Shiel. It's one of the most beautiful places in the whole of Scotland. Dominating the scene is a tower, placed there to commemorate the start of Bonnie Prince Charlie's uprising in 1745. He, Charles Edward Stuart, was the 25-year-old grandson of King James II. Claiming to be the rightful king of England and Scotland, he traveled from France to Scotland, raised his standard at Glenfinnan, and rallied many of the clans. At first, his army swept all before them, won a victory at Prestonpans, seized Edinburgh and the border town of Carlisle, then marched south into England.

The government of King George II faced the imminent danger of a Stuart restoration, and responded by raising an army under the leadership of the Duke of Cumberland. Londoners panicked as the Scottish army approached. In the midlands town of Derby, however, far from their Highland homes and discouraged by organized opposition, the Highlanders turned back toward Scotland. It was a fatal mistake. Cumberland pursued them relentlessly and eventually smashed their army at the Battle of Culloden Moor, near Inverness, in 1746. The young prince was spirited away by friends; a brave Hebridean girl, Flora MacDonald, rowed him to safety on the Isle of Skye, for which she later served a prison term in the Tower of London. He spent the rest of his life in exile, drinking heavily.

After Culloden, many of the clan chiefs were executed. Others were imprisoned or deported. Legislation banned the wearing of some tartans, and ordered all weapons to be handed over to government authorities. After that, a transformation in land-use began, with sheep being brought in to graze on lands that had previously supported villages. Crofters were forced to leave their traditional homes, either for the coast, for the Lowland towns, or for overseas colonies. This process, collectively known as the "Highland clearances," continued for much of the next century and contributed to a depopulation whose effects can still be seen today.

The Glenfinnan monument was built in 1815, by which time Napoleon had been defeated, Walter Scott had helped restore the idea of Scottish loyalty to Britain, and the Stuart threat had dwindled almost to nothing. Even so, the plaque on the monument has a slightly apologetic tone. "This column," it reads, "was erected by Alexander Macdonald, esquire, of Glenaladale, to commemorate the generous zeal, the undaunted bravery, and the inviolable fidelity of his forefathers, and the rest of those who fought and bled in that arduous and unfortunate enterprise." Use of the word "unfortunate" all but admits that the 1745 rising was actually a very poor idea. At the top of the monument stands a statue of a Highland soldier in full regalia—widely, though wrongly, believed to be Bonnie Prince Charlie himself.

Also at Glenfinnan is a superb 21-arched viaduct, which carries the railway line to Mallaig. Built in the 1890s, it became famous in 2002 when the "Hogwarts Express" was filmed crossing it in the first *Harry Potter* film. This scenic railway often runs special trains drawn by steam locomotives—it's one of the two or three most picturesque lines in the whole British railway system.

Drive back to Fort William to see another marvel, Neptune's Staircase. It is a series of canal locks built in the early 1800s. They are part of the Caledonian Canal, a broad canal designed to carry seagoing ships across Scotland without exposing them to the stormy dangers of Cape Wrath and the Pentland Firth. Look at the map and you'll see a strong diagonal across Scotland from Inverness in the Northeast to Fort William in the southwest, about 70-miles long. This is the "Great Glen," a geological fault line. The Caledonian Canal, which runs along this glen, was designed by Thomas Telford, one of the leading engineers of the early Industrial Revolution. His insight was that most of the distance was already covered by a succession of lochs. All he needed to do was link them together with about 20 miles of canal.

"All" makes it sound easy but it wasn't. He faced endless technical challenges. The canal took 12 years longer to complete than expected, ran over-budget by more than 100 percent, and was already too small for a new generation of ships by the time it was finished. The eight locks that comprise Neptune's Staircase raise the level of the canal 64 feet, and are the biggest "staircase lock" in the whole of Britain. It's possible to bike the length of the Caledonian Canal, to travel it by barge, or just to cross it by road. Some of the crossings are swing bridges, where you can enjoy the interruption of your drive by watching the entire deck of the bridge swing aside to let bigger boats sail through.

The most famous of the lochs along the canal is Loch Ness. It's 800 feet deep in places, and 23 miles long. Does a monster live in its depths? Saint Columba certainly thought so, back in the year 565, when he was trying to convert the Scots to Christianity. In fact, he saw it terrorizing the local population, ordered it in the name of God to stop, and had the satisfaction of seeing it retreat into the depths of the lake. Jump forward to the year 1933 when an Inverness newspaper reported a couple who had seen "an enormous animal rolling and plunging on the surface." London newspapers picked up the story and the quest resumed, not least because a circus offered a £20,000 reward to anyone who could take the monster alive. A 1934 photograph showed what looked like a long sinuous dinosaur. Although it was later revealed as a hoax, fascination with the idea of the monster has never abated. University expeditions with state-of-the-art sonar regularly try to confirm its existence.

Overlooking the loch on a short peninsula stand the romantic ruins of Urquhart Castle. It was fought over in the era of Stirling Bridge and Bannockburn, again in the early 1500s, and for the last time in the age of the Glorious Revolution. Forces loyal to the new king William resisted a siege in 1689. When it was over, they slighted the castle, which is to say: blew up most of the defensive features to make sure it could never subsequently become a military stronghold. Its location at a gentle curve in the loch made it a key defensive point in earlier centuries and now makes it one of the most popular visitor attractions in northern Scotland.

If you manage to escape the Loch Ness Monster, and keep going northeast, you'll reach the town of Inverness. Head east from there to the Spey Valley, home of the world's best single malt Scotch whiskey. The Spey is the river from whose water Glenlivet, Glenfiddich, and others are made. Single malt whiskey is made from malted barley and aged in oak barrels for at least three years and a day. Several of the distilleries offer tasting tours, in which you watch the various stages of manufacture and then drink a glass or two at the end. Think carefully about who's going to be the designated driver before you launch out on Speyside's Malt Whiskey Trail.

A large part of Scotland's land area is made up of islands, most of which are accessible by ferry and a few by air. They can be pretty bleak and barren in winter, and not always hospitable even in the summer. But they have a craggy charm along with some terrific historical lures. North of the mainland are the Orkney Islands, comprising some of the richest archaeological sites in the whole of Britain. Among the sites there are two stone circles from the Neolithic Age, The Standing Stones of Stenness, and the Ring of Brodgar. The latter is a henge, about 425 feet across, containing a circle of standing stones from more than 2,000 years ago. In this completely treeless area their narrow verticals are impressive and memorable. Meanwhile, the Ness of Brodgar, a huge Neolithic complex, was discovered in 2003. Annual excavations each summer since then have disclosed high levels of sophistication in the community that once lived, farmed, and worshipped there.

The Orkneys became famous as the headquarters, in World War I, of the British Grand Fleet. Only once, and only briefly, did the British and German fleets actually come to blows. This was the Battle of Jutland, that took place on May 31, 1916, when they met in the North Sea. The Germans sank three of Britain's fast but poorly armored battlecruisers. Once his big ships came under the withering fire of the British Dreadnought battleships, however, the German Admiral, Reinhard Scheer, realized he was outmatched, turned, and scurried back to base. Never again did his fleet challenge the Royal Navy.

Instead, when the fighting stopped, in November 1918, the German fleet was ordered to Scapa Flow. Rather than turn it over to the British, Scheer's successor gave the command that all the ships should be scuttled: deliberately sunk. The mass scuttling took place on June 21, 1919, with over 50 of the German ships lost, out of 74.

A few were later raised but seawater had ruined them and they were fit only for scrap. Others remain in the waters of Scapa Flow, attractive sites for scuba divers to explore. A British ship, the *Royal Oak*, also lies in these waters. It was torpedoed in the first month of World War II by a daring German submarine captain. More than 800 men were lost with the *Royal Oak*, and, as a war grave site, it is off limits to recreational divers. Even from shore, though, parts of the old hulks are still visible at low tide, as are some of the block-ships that the British sank deliberately to protect the base against U-boats. Old anti-aircraft guns and blockhouses make the area around Scapa Flow a magnet for military history enthusiasts.

The island of Skye, off the west coast of Scotland is the haunt of hikers and climbers. A broken and narrow ridge, the Cuillin Ridge, is among its most daunting challenges, and one of the few places in Britain that looks as jagged as the Alps or Rockies. I camped on Skye one summer, back in the 80s, near the little town of Portree. Pitiless rain came down all night. Waking up on days like that, you just want to hunker down in your sleeping bag. However, the campground owner warned us that if we didn't break camp quickly, a rapidly rising river would trap us on the wrong side, possibly for days. Complying, we were soaked to the skin and half frozen. Not that I mean to discourage you from visiting Skye, which can also be radiantly beautiful.

Also, radiantly beautiful—and highly photogenic—is Eilean Donan Castle, on the western coast not far from Skye. You've seen it on a hundred calendars and as the background for many a Scottish movie. Built by Clan Mackenzie in the 1200s, it was all but destroyed in 1719 after the clan took the wrong side in a Jacobite uprising. John MacRea-Gilstrap, a survivor of World War I, restored it in the 1920s, built a bridge from its island to the mainland, and set up a war memorial to lost members of his clan. It is now open to visitors and is pretty close to the platonic ideal of what a Scottish castle should look like.

If you drive south out of Scotland at the end of your visit, think about going to the village of Lockerbie, just before you reach the English border. It's an old town whose medieval prosperity was based on the wool trade. An endearing statue in the main street depicts a line of lambs trotting along beside the shops. But Lockerbie became famous in a horrible and unexpected way in December 1988, four days before Christmas, when a Pan Am jumbo jet blew up in the sky overhead, and the debris rained down on the town. Everyone on the plane was killed, 259 people, and 11 more in Lockerbie itself when a large section of the wing fell on a suburban street, Sherwood Crescent. An official of the Libyan government was convicted and jailed for the attack, and the Libyan dictator himself, Muamar Gaddafi, is widely assumed to have ordered the bombing.

I visited the site nearly 30 years after the disaster. Sherwood Crescent today is a quiet suburban street again, but the line of single-story houses breaks off at one point, and a well-kept garden of high shrubs and flowers takes its place. Tucked away behind the greenery stands a marker, in memory of the two families whose homes had stood there. A mile or two away is the town's cemetery, a special section of which has been set aside as a memorial garden to the victims. It's a windswept setting, sobering to visit—above all when you learn that a large group of students from Syracuse University was on board, in their late teens or barely 20. The memorials to them from bereaved parents are particularly affecting.

Lockerbie is tranquil now. So are Glencoe and Scapa Flow, Stirling Bridge and Bannockburn. The persistent paradox of tourism, very clear in Scotland, is that some of the most interesting and stimulating places to visit are also those in which people fought against each other to the death, or spent their lives preparing to do so.

15

NORTH WALES

Wales is a lovely place to visit: hospitable, charming, scenic, and full of places that vividly bring to mind its turbulent earlier history. North Wales is often wet and windy—you need to be prepared with bad-weather gear—but it's a worthwhile visit. This lecture looks at some notable sites that can be seen if you drive into North Wales from England, including:

- The walled town of Conwy and nearby Llandudno.

- Snowdon, the highest mountain in Wales.

- Sites related to the Wales's railways.

- Sites related to Wales's slate industry.

- Castles in the area.

- A prime ornithology area near the town of Holyhead.

- South Stack Lighthouse.

- Llanystumdwy, the home of David Lloyd George.

Conwy

Conwy and Llandudno

As you drive into North Wales from England, you'll come first to the walled town of Conwy, which stands on the north coast, fronting the Irish Sea. King Edward I designed and built it as an entirely English colony inside Wales. He deliberately placed it on the site of a venerated Welsh monastery, whose monks he displaced, sending them to a new site eight miles away.

Conwy was built between 1283 and 1289, in the form of a triangle. The site's castle forms one of the triangle's corners. An almost continuous set of high city walls, very well preserved and partly on dramatic sloping ground, make up its sides.

From the east wall of the castle, look out over the Conwy River, which is crossed here by three bridges. The middle one is the oldest. It was built by Thomas Telford between 1822 and 1826. His Conwy bridge is among the earliest suspension bridges in Britain.

Conwy Telford Bridge

The oldest dwelling in the town, probably from the early 1400s, is Aberconwy House. Occupied over the centuries by merchants, officers, sea captains, and a temperance hotel, it's been imaginatively restored by the National Trust and is open to visitors.

About four miles from Conwy is Llandudno, a beach resort town built on an elegant curving bay. The seafront hotels are dignified Victorian places, built on the grand scale, and still popular among British holidaymakers who want to stay in the British Isles. The most interesting part of Llandudno is a huge headland called the Great Orme, which is protected from urbanization. A tram climbs the hill using the same system as the San Francisco cable cars.

Llandudno Hill

Snowdon

From Llandudno, drive about 20 miles inland to Snowdon, the highest mountain in Wales. It is just over 3,500 feet high and can be climbed in three or four hours. According to legend, the pile of rocks on its summit is the burial place of a fearsome giant named Rhitta, who tried to kill King Arthur, failed, and paid the ultimate price. Three of the lakes on the mountain's lower slopes each claim to be the one into which Arthur's sword Excalibur was thrown as his life neared its end.

Snowdon

The easiest way to climb Snowdon is on the Snowdon Mountain Railway, a narrow-gauge line that snakes up the mountain using antique steam locomotives.

Railways

North Wales is honeycombed with narrow-gauge railways, which can negotiate steeper bends than standard-gauge lines and squeeze through tighter cuttings. Some have always been tourist-oriented: the Snowdon Mountain Railway is a case in point. Most of the others began life as commercial railways, linking stone quarries with the main lines or with ports from which stone could be shipped abroad. Two superb examples of quarry lines are the Talyllyn Railway and the Ffestiniog Railway, which have long since converted from carrying rocks to carrying visitors.

The Slate Industry

In North Wales, the slate industry was big business for two centuries. While you're in the Snowdonia region, visit the National Slate Museum in the town of Llanberis. It stands on a flat patch at the bottom of a steep mountain slope, and you can see that in its years as a working quarry, its quarrymen were steadily dismantling the mountain itself. The disused quarry is now a challenging arena for rock climbers.

At the museum, you'll see workshops and blacksmith's forges where all the quarry equipment was maintained and repaired. Skilled slate workers reproduce the work of their predecessors.

Castles

From Llanberis, go a few miles west to the coast. A narrow passage of water, the Menai Strait, separates the mainland from the island of Anglesey. At this location are two of Wales's more famous castles.

Menai Bridge

On the mainland side is Caernarvon. It's spectacular, even bigger than Conwy, and in better repair because of almost continuous habitation. By tradition, it is the site of the investiture of the prince of Wales, the male heir to the British throne.

Caernarvon

Beaumaris Castle

On the Anglesey side of the Menai Strait stands Beaumaris Castle. Beaumaris means "the beautiful marsh" in Norman French, and fittingly, it's built on low ground right by the sea. Its walls are so thick that there's a warren of staircases and passages inside them, which are fun to explore.

Ornithology

Across Anglesey Island from Beaumaris is Holyhead, the most northwesterly town in Wales and the ferry port for Ireland. Just beyond the town, the land rises into high moorland that breaks off in dramatic sea cliffs.

The area is honeycombed with the remains of ancient habitations. A series of stone rings on one of the hillsides are the remains of farmers' huts from the Roman era or even earlier.

The cliffs are the nesting grounds of puffins, seagulls, cormorants, and guillemots. One bird, the chough, a kind of crow with an orange beak, is rare throughout Britain but is breeding well there, carefully monitored. The

Anglesey cliffs

Chough

Royal Society for the Protection of Birds has organized the area as a sanctuary. Not surprisingly, this is a good place to see ornithologists in their natural habitat, with their powerful long-distance lenses and rugged bad-weather clothes.

South Stack Lighthouse

South Stack Lighthouse stands on an island just offshore. It's a lighthouse worthy of the best adventure stories, because to get to it you have to climb down 410 steep steps, zigzagging down the cliffside, and then cross a girder bridge that spans a high chasm where ocean waves crash against the rocks. The lighthouse has been there since 1809. It's all white and just over 90 feet tall.

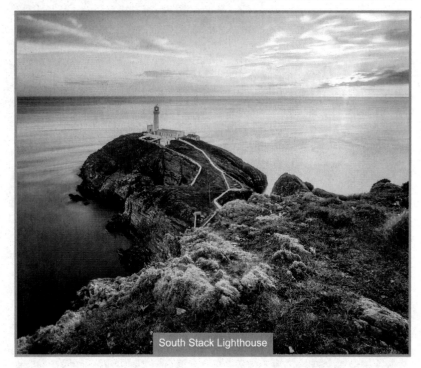

South Stack Lighthouse

Llanystumdwy

Heading south from Anglesey Island, you can drive across the Llŷn Peninsula to the village of Llanystumdwy. This is the home of David Lloyd George, the only British prime minister to come from Wales.

The house where Lloyd George grew up is a modest little place, but is open to visitors. His widowed mother brought him up there with the help of her brother, a shoemaker and Baptist minister. The home radiates lower-middle-class respectability and a sense of moral rectitude. A picture of Abraham Lincoln hangs in the parlor; he was a hero to many mid-century British artisans for his belief in free labor and his opposition to slavery. The museum attached to the house includes the shoemakers' workshop and the Victorian classroom where Lloyd George studied as a schoolboy.

Suggested Reading

Davies, *A History of Wales*.

Taylor, *The Welsh Castles of Edward I*.

Toye, *Lloyd George and Churchill*.

Wilson, *Narrow Gauge Railways of North Wales*.

Suggested Activities

1. Learn a few Welsh phrases before you visit, and then try out your accent at hotels, shops, restaurants, and petrol stations.

2. Stand on the battlements of Conwy, Beaumaris, Harlech, or Caernarvon. Try to imagine what it would be like when the castle was surrounded, besieged, and cut off from outside help.

NORTH WALES

The Welsh language is different from English, and much harder to learn than French, Spanish, or Italian. In the face of English attempts to suppress it over nearly eight centuries, it has survived as a living language, and is spoken by about a fifth of Wales's three million people. It's commonest in North Wales, where to enter a shop or any public space is to be surrounded by it, as much among children and teenagers as among older folk. Let me turn it over to Paul Meier here, and he can explain further.

[Paul] Road signs and public notices are given first in Welsh and only afterwards in English. Luckily for us monoglots, there's no-one who can't speak English too, and Welsh-accented English is lovely: musical, lilting and emotionally expressive. Welsh includes lots of double fs, double ls and double ds, and dense clots of consonants. The most famous Welsh word is the name of a railway station, 58 letters long, which has become a minor tourist attraction in its own right. The sign takes up the whole front of the station building, while on the station platform, another helpful sign gives a pronunciation guide. It goes something like this: "Lan-vire-pool-guin-gill-go-ger-u-queern-drob-ooll-llandus-ilio-gogogoch." It's usually abbreviated to "Llanfair PG," and it means: "St. Mary's Church in the Hollow of the White Hazel near the rapid whirlpool and the parish church of St. Tysilio with a red cave." How's that for a really specific set of directions?

Thanks, Paul.

By comparison with Scotland, where the Gaelic language is spoken by very few people but nationalism is a strong political force, Welsh nationalism is comparatively slight but the language is thriving. Wales itself, whatever your language, is a lovely place to visit; hospitable, charming, scenic, and full of places that vividly bring to mind its turbulent earlier history.

The Romans conquered Wales but the Anglo-Saxons didn't, and by 1066, the year of the Norman Conquest, two ethnically and linguistically distinct groups faced each other across the border. Offa's Dyke, built by one of the Anglo-Saxon kings of Mercia in the late 700s, is a long earthwork running from north to south, close to the current border. It consists of a wide ditch on the Welsh side, with the soil thrown up to create a raised embankment on the English side. The whole thing was once about 65 feet wide and eight feet high—enough to create a severe obstacle to raiders. Centuries of erosion have worn it down in some places, but in others it's still distinct. A 176-mile-long footpath now follows it from the Bristol Channel to Liverpool Bay.

Ruling two centuries after the Norman Conquest, King Edward I of England was a handsome, swaggering bully who loved to fight; a man who went into towering rages when he didn't get his own way. Unusually tall, he was nicknamed "Longshanks." He decided to conquer Wales in 1277, after years of conflict between Welsh princes and the English barons who owned the border lands, the so-called Marcher Lords. The fiercest resistance to Edward's army came from Welsh chieftains in the mountains of the northwest. Edward responded by building a ring of castles around the mountains to ensure his own command of the lowlands and the sea-ports. He had stamped out all resistance by 1294. Four of these castles have been designated as UNESCO World-Heritage sites: Conwy, Caernarvon, Beaumaris, and Harlech. Today, we'll stop at each of these castles and visit many other sites along the way.

As you drive into North Wales from England, you'll come first to the walled town of Conwy, which stands on the north coast, fronting the Irish Sea. Edward designed and built it as an entirely English colony inside Wales. He deliberately placed it on the site of a venerated Welsh monastery, whose monks he displaced, sending them to a new site eight miles away. Conwy was built between 1283 and 1289, in the form of a triangle. The castle forms one of the triangle's corners. An almost continuous set of high city walls, very well preserved and partly on dramatic sloping ground, make up its sides.

The castle was a state-of-the-art building in its day, designed to intimidate potential aggressors, featuring a strong series of towers that bulge out from the curtain wall to give defenders a complete field of fire against anyone approaching. Within the walls stands a second line of defense around the royal apartments. Even attackers who somehow broke through the first line of defense would be exposed to withering fire from secure positions. You're free, as a visitor, to roam around the battlements and to climb most of the turrets, up extremely steep and narrow spiral staircases, holding on tight to rope banisters. The parapet, or stone fence, protecting you at the top of some of these lofty towers is inadequate. If you suffer from vertigo, don't go up. Whoever you are, tread warily!

From the east wall of the castle, look out over the Conwy River, which is crossed here by three bridges. The middle one is the oldest. It was built by Thomas Telford between 1822 and 1826. Telford is a man I mention many times in this series: a great road, bridge, and canal builder, and one of the most honored men in the history of civil engineering. His Conwy bridge is among the earliest suspension bridges in Britain. What makes it such a charmer is the fact that he's mimicked the castle's towers, creating a 19th-century echo of the 13th-century building.

When the railway arrived at Conwy in 1848, another great engineer, Robert Stephenson, also took the hint. The body of his bridge, just to the right of Telford's when seen from the castle, is an enclosed iron-girder structure, but the towers at each end are also castellated, though not so elegantly. Stephenson was working right on the edge of the mainland, and at one point his route had to pierce the old city walls, leaving a graceful crenellated arch that railway photographers cherish.

Did anyone succeed in capturing Conwy Castle? Yes, but not by siege. Owen Glendower, the romantic hero of Welsh resistance, took it by a clever trick in the year 1401. When most of the garrison were at Sunday church, he dressed a group of his soldiers as carpenters, had them roll up to the castle in a wagon and talk their way in. The two sentries who had been left to guard the castle fell for the trick, only to discover they had lost the castle. Then they lost their lives. It's a reminder that no castle is better than the men who defend it.

There's more to see in Conwy than just the fortifications. The oldest dwelling in the town, probably from the early 1400s, is Aberconwy House. Occupied over the centuries by merchants, officers, sea captains, and a temperance hotel, it's been imaginatively restored by the National Trust and is open to visitors. It feels simultaneously ancient and solidly middle-class. Each of the different rooms is furnished from a different era of its history but the ancient timber beams are on display throughout, and floors are delightfully uneven. Plas Mawr, nearby, is an equally fascinating Tudor townhouse, now decorated in the style of the 1660s. Down on the waterfront where the seagulls call and there's a smell of salt, fish, and seaweed, you'll find a tiny red building that's billed as Britain's smallest house. Hard to disagree with that claim, as it's scarcely wider than two people standing right next to each other.

About four miles from Conwy is a beach resort town built on an elegant curving bay. English people pronounce its name "Llandudno." However, the two Ls at the beginning of the word should be pronounced "thl," so try to pronounce it "Thlandidno." The seafront hotels are dignified Victorian places, built on the grand scale, and still popular among British holidaymakers who want to stay in the British Isles. But the most interesting part of Llandudno is a huge headland called the Great Orme, which is protected from urbanization. A tram, climbs the hill using the same system as the San Francisco cable cars. Don't challenge yourself to walk up this hill unless you're in good shape—it's one of the steepest roadways in Britain, and had me gasping for breath.

Two thirds of the way up you come to a marvel: Great Orme's Bronze-Age copper mine. The Victorians knew there was malachite, a greenish copper ore, in the area, and they sank deep mine shafts to get at it. Along the way, they also encountered some older tunnels, many of them filled in with rubble, but thought little of it. Only in 1987, when the area was about to be paved over for a parking lot, did archaeologists discover that there was a labyrinth of tunnels, at nine different depths, bearing witness to large-scale ancient mining at the site. Radio carbon dating established that the mines had been active about 1500 BC. Until this discovery the conventional wisdom had been that there was no metal mining in England before the Romans' arrival in 43 AD. It's an exciting development in pushing back one of the markers of civilization in Britain.

If you share my experience there, you'll find highly-motivated archaeological workers on site willing to talk about their work. Spare a thought for the bronze age mine workers. They were trying to excavate a metal ore using primitive stone and bone tools, hundreds of which have been found there. Some of the tunnels are so small, twisting, and cramped that they must have required child laborers. Today's healthy adult archaeological workers literally cannot enter some of them at all. You'll emerge from your own subterranean tour through the contorted galleries feeling that your neck has been twisted, your elbows and knees bumped, and grateful that your head was protected by a hard hat.

From Llandudno, drive about 20 miles inland to Snowdon, the highest mountain in Wales. It is just over 3,500 feet high, and can be climbed in three or four hours. According to legend, the pile of rocks on its summit is the burial place of a fearsome giant named Rhitta, who tried to kill King Arthur, failed, and paid the ultimate price. Three of the lakes on the mountain's lower slopes each claim to be the one into which Arthur's sword Excalibur was thrown as his life neared its end. The 21-year-old Wordsworth climbed Snowdon at night back in 1791, with a friend and a local shepherd as guide. They began in heavy mist but had the good fortune to come out above the clouds, into brilliant moonlight. Or, as he put it in his long narrative poem *The Prelude*:

> [A] light upon the turf
> Fell like a flash, and lo! as I looked up,
> The Moon hung naked in a firmament
> Of azure without cloud, and at my feet
> Rested a silent sea of hoary mist.
> A hundred hills their dusky backs upheaved
> All over this still ocean; and beyond,
> Far, far beyond, the solid vapors stretched,
> In headlands, tongues, and promontory shapes.

As usual with Wordsworth, the experience led on to a meditation about the relationship between the natural world and his own imagination. To be above the clouds, hiking in Britain, is still a rare and exhilarating experience.

For climbers of Snowdon today, there's an easy way and a hard way of doing it. The easy way is on the Snowdon Mountain Railway, a narrow-gauge line that snakes up the mountain using antique steam locomotives. A Victorian scheme, it had to overcome the objections of landscape lovers who saw it as a desecration. It did overcome them, Parliament gave the nod, and the line was built in just over a year, opening in 1896. It ascends at a steady gradient of one in seven or 14 percent, something an ordinary train could not manage—hence its use of a rack and pinion system. The good thing about the Snowdon Mountain Railway is that it's wonderful, like all steam trains, and that it gives people who would never otherwise get to the summit a chance to do so, where they can admire the super views. Hikers and climbers sometimes grumble about it, even today, but it's now a venerable part of Welsh tradition. Besides, there are plenty of areas on Snowdon where ordinary visitors never stray, such as the strenuous rock climbs on which Edmund Hillary practiced before his first ascent of Everest in 1953.

North Wales is honeycombed with narrow-gauge railways, which can negotiate steeper bends than standard-gauge lines and squeeze through tighter cuttings. Some have always been tourist-oriented: the Snowdon Mountain Railway is a case in point. Most of the others began life as commercial railways, linking stone quarries with the main lines or with ports from which stone could be shipped abroad. Two superb examples of quarry lines are the Talyllyn Railway, and the Ffestiniog, which have long since converted from carrying rocks to carrying visitors. Enthusiastic preservation societies look after both, donating the necessary time and money to make up the shortfall in revenue that comes from visitors. I mention elsewhere in this series that maintaining old steam railways is a quasi-religious activity in England. The same is just as true in Wales.

Riding the Ffestiniog Railway recently charged up my spiritual battery. Starting in Porthmadog amid the distinctive smell of burning coal, our train rolled across "the Cob," a harbor-front wall, then chugged up into the mountains of

Snowdonia National Park. Clanking, groaning, and puffing, the engine poured out smoke and steam. On the sharp bends the wheels sang and shrieked while the coaches jolted. Maximum speed can't have been much more than 15 miles per hour. The train's destination, Blaenau Ffestiniog, is a grim, no-nonsense slate-quarry town surrounded by mountains and spoil tips, but the proud maroon engine cheered it up on arrival. Blaenau Ffestiniog's nickname is "the town that roofed the world."

In North Wales, the slate industry was big business for two centuries. So, while you're in the Snowdonia, the region, I encourage you to visit the National Slate Museum in the town of Llanberis. It stands on a flat patch at the bottom of a steep mountain slope, and you can see that in its years as a working quarry, its quarrymen were steadily dismantling the mountain itself. The disused quarry is now a challenging arena for rock climbers. Slate is a fascinating stone. Under a skilled workman's hands, it will shear into thinner and thinner sheets, depending on whether it's designed for use on walls, floors, or roofs. Extremely durable, slate became the favored material for building roofs throughout rainy Britain in the 19th century. Then demand began to rise throughout Europe. Slate from this quarry, Dinorwic, was eventually exported all over the continent. Three thousand men labored at the quarry in 1900, which was alive with cranes, gravity slides, steam engines, and the sound of hammering.

At the museum, you'll see the workshops and blacksmith's forges where all the quarry equipment was maintained and repaired. Skilled slate workers reproduce the work of their predecessors, creating the necessary shapes, and the necessary degrees of thinness, as you watch. One highlight is the museum's waterwheel, housed in a three-story building and providing what we would call sustainable energy to the whole complex. Also illuminating is a row of typical workers' cottages, of the kind occupied by Dinorwic's workers. They depict the possessions the miners' families would have lived with in 1860, 1901 (during an era of long and bitter strike in the district), and 1969 when the quarry era was coming to an end. They may not be as small as Conwy's Smallest House in Britain, but they certainly are awfully tight and cramped.

From Llanberis, go a few miles west, to the coast. A narrow passage of water, the Menai Strait, separates the mainland from the island of Anglesey. Here stand two more of the famous castles I mentioned earlier. On the mainland side is Caernarvon. It's spectacular, even bigger than Conwy, and in better repair because of almost continuous habitation. By tradition, it is the site of the investiture of the Prince of Wales, the male heir to the British throne. Edward I bestowed the title on his own son (later Edward II) at Caernarvon back in 1301 after completing the conquest of Wales. Queen Elizabeth II bestowed it on her son, Prince Charles, in 1969. He was 20. I was a 13-year-old schoolboy at the time, and was one of millions who watched it live on TV. He had to give a short speech in Welsh and another in English. He also had to swear this oath to his own mother: "I, Charles, Prince of Wales, do become your liege man of life and limb and of earthly worship, and faith and truth I will bear unto you, to live and die against all manner of folks." A minority of Welsh nationalists demonstrated against the ceremony, but most Welsh people favored the monarchy then, and still do today.

On the Anglesey side of the Menai Strait, a little further Northwest, stands Beaumaris Castle. Beaumaris means "the beautiful marsh" in Norman French, and sure enough it's built on low ground right by the sea. At high tide, it could be supplied directly by ship, and the water also provided a moat. Its walls are so thick that there's a warren of staircases and passages inside them, which are fun to explore. Edward's architect, James of St. George, was continuing to improve his techniques, and here built one entire castle inside another. But if you arrive at Beaumaris after going to Conwy and Caernarvon, you'll be struck by the fact that it's not so high. The reason is that it was never completed. Work began in earnest in 1295 and at first advanced rapidly. But in 1300, Edward turned his attention away from Wales and geared up for an invasion of Scotland. The craftsmen at Beaumaris weren't paid, and began to drift away from the site. Intermittent work was done in the following decades, every time a Welsh rebellion seemed likely, but stopped once and for all in 1330. Even unfinished, it's daunting.

The first bridge across the Menai Strait was also the world's first full-size suspension bridge. I mentioned Telford's little masterpiece at Conwy. Here is his big masterpiece. He designed and built it between 1819 and 1826 and it's still in use today, carrying a heavy load of traffic in both directions on a busy road. It's the crucial link in the road he built from London to Holyhead, the A5. Suspension bridges were an important conceptual breakthrough because they used far less material than conventional masonry bridges, and because there was no height limit. The deck of the Menai Bridge, 100 feet above the Strait, permitted high-masted sailing ships to pass beneath.

Across Anglesey Island from Beaumaris is Holyhead, the most northwesterly town in Wales, and the ferry port for Ireland. Just beyond the town, the land rises into high moorland that breaks off in dramatic sea cliffs. The area is honeycombed with the remains of ancient habitations. A series of stone rings on one of the hillsides are the remains of farmers' huts from the Roman era or even earlier. The cliffs are the nesting grounds of puffins, seagulls, cormorants, and guillemots. One bird, the chough, a kind of crow with an orange beak, is rare throughout Britain but is breeding well there, carefully monitored. The Royal Society for the Protection of Birds, RSPB, has organized the area as a sanctuary. Not surprisingly, this is a good place to see ornithologists in their natural habitat, with their powerful long-distance lenses and rugged bad-weather clothes.

South Stack Lighthouse stands on an island just offshore. It's a lighthouse worthy of the best adventure stories, because to get to it you have to climb down 410 steep steps, zig-zagging down the cliff-side, then cross a girder bridge that spans a high chasm where ocean waves crash against the rocks. In the days when this was a swaying rope bridge, the trip across must have been even more heart-in-mouth. Even today the wind, usually strong, moans in the girders. The lighthouse has been there since 1809. It's all white, and just over 90 feet tall—very imposing. When I visited as a child, there was still an actual lighthouse keeper. Now, regrettably, it's run by remote control from Essex, just outside London, hundreds of miles away. It's also haunted, a story I'll tell in the lecture on seafaring Britain.

Heading south from Anglesey Island, drive across the Llŷn Peninsula to the village of Llanystumdwy, the home of David Lloyd George, the only British prime-minister to come from Wales. The house where Lloyd George grew up is a modest little place, but is open to visitors. His widowed mother brought him up there with the help of her brother, a shoemaker and Baptist minister. The home radiates lower-middle-class respectability and a sense of moral rectitude. A picture of Abraham Lincoln hangs in the parlor; he was a hero to many mid-century British artisans, for his belief in free labor and his opposition to slavery. The museum attached to the house includes the shoemakers' workshop and the Victorian classroom where Lloyd George studied as a schoolboy.

Lloyd George began his career as a solicitor, but was a Member of Parliament for 55 years, from the time he was 27 until his death, always as a Liberal and always for the constituency of Caernarvon. An extremely gifted speaker, he appeared to have almost supernatural powers when it came to swaying audiences with a special blend of logic and emotion. A fascinating combination of energy, ability, charm, intrigue, and ruthlessness, he was also an incorrigible womanizer; qualities that have fascinated historians and biographers ever since.

He was Chancellor of the Exchequer in the government of Herbert Asquith in the early years of the 20th century, and ushered in the first elements of Britain's welfare state. At a time when working people had little access to health care, and faced chronic insecurity if unemployed or too old to work, he recognized the wisdom of giving them a greater sense of security. It would diminish the otherwise-powerful attraction of radical socialism. His leading parliamentary ally in those years was Winston Churchill, 11 years his junior, to whom he was a mentor. We think of Churchill as Britain's most famous conservative but for 20 years he was a prominent Liberal. Later, they fell out. Lloyd George said of Churchill in these later years: "He would make a drum out of the skin of his mother in order to sound his own praises." Stanley Baldwin, a Conservative prime minister of the 1930s who disliked both of them, remarked: "[Lloyd George] was born a cad and never forgot it. Winston was born a gentleman and never remembered it."

During World War I Lloyd George was Minister of Munitions, charged with increasing production. He showed his superiority to his boss, Asquith, by brilliant improvisation to achieve it. An intra-party coup in 1916 ousted the easy-going Asquith, leaving Lloyd George as prime minister. His coalition government, drawn from all the parties, brought the war to a successful conclusion by the truce of November 1918, again achieving prodigies of organization and logistics, in collaboration with French and American allies. But fissures in the governing coalition deepened after the war and Lloyd George resigned from the prime minister's office in 1922.

There are many statues of Lloyd-George: one outside his childhood home, one outside Caernarvon Castle, one in front of the National Museum in Wales, and, since 2007, one in front of the Houses of Parliament in London, a few yards from the statue of his old friend and rival Winston Churchill. Several Welshmen have been leaders of the opposition since Lloyd-George, but no other has yet become prime minister.

Heading south from Llanystumdwy, we reach Harlech, the fourth and final of the World Heritage castles I mentioned earlier in this lecture. It was built on a great rock outcrop beside the sea but now stands nearly a mile inland because the coast has been building up in this part of Britain. UNESCO describes Harlech as "one of the finest examples of late 13th and early 14th century military architecture in Europe." It too was built in the 1280s and was fought over during Edward I's wars in the 1290s. It was captured by Owen Glendower in the early 1400s, and besieged by Yorkists in the 1460s as they fought against the Lancastrians during the Wars of the Roses. It was also the very last place in Britain to be held by royalists against the forces of Parliament during the Civil Wars of the 1640s. Restored and stabilized in the 20th century, it now welcomes visitors, most of whom will find themselves humming the old tune "Men of Harlech" as they stride long the ramparts and battlements.

North Wales is often wet and windy—you need to be prepared with bad weather gear—but it's full of sights that bring to mind the area's turbulent history. Mountainous, picturesque, and dense with evidence of human activities over the last two millennia, it's also hospitable and welcoming. As I've suggested here, the great castles rank first among its attractions, closely followed by the mountains, the narrow-gauge railways, and the rugged coastline.

16

CARDIFF AND SOUTH WALES

Cardiff, featuring an ethnically and racially diverse population, is the capital of Wales. This lecture looks at sites in Cardiff and South Wales, including:

- Cardiff Castle.

- Civic buildings in Cardiff.

- Mining valleys.

- Swansea, the home of poet Dylan Thomas.

- The region's countryside, for which hiking boots and cameras are recommended.

Cardiff Castle

The first thing to see in Cardiff is Cardiff Castle, right in the city center. The first castle on the site was built soon after the Norman conquest, a fine example of the classic motte-and-bailey design. It still stands. Of greater interest, however, is the section of the castle that was converted during the 19th century into a pseudo-medieval fantasy house.

Cardiff Castle

The owner was John Crichton-Stuart. He may well have been the richest man in the world, though as a near contemporary of Andrew Carnegie and John D. Rockefeller, he certainly had rivals to the title. With his architect friend William Burges, he proceeded to transform Cardiff Castle into one of the most elaborate and ornate creations of the Victorian neo-Gothic revival.

Civic Buildings in Cardiff

Near the castle stands a set of three impressive civic buildings from the end of the 19th century. The first is the law courts, the second is City Hall, and the third is the National Museum of Wales. They were designed to project the pride and dignity of Cardiff.

Cardiff's civic buildings, backed by spacious parks, are close to the city's main shopping area, much of which has been improved by the exclusion of traffic. A mile away is the harbor, where urban renewal is in full form. As the British

Cardiff Town Hall

Cardiff Dock

coal industry died in the 1980s, so did Cardiff docks, becoming a desolate wasteland. The area's transformation since then is encouraging.

Nearby is the new Welsh assembly building. Devolution of power from London to the Welsh and Scottish capitals came in legislation of the 1990s, and was the impetus for its creation. The architect was Richard Rogers, and it was opened by the queen in 2006. On the plaza before the assembly building is an artful monument to merchant seamen from the area who died in wartime shipwrecks.

In the same complex is a major performing-arts building: the Wales Millennium Centre, from the beginning of this century. It includes an auditorium that holds nearly 2,000 people and two smaller concert halls for 250 and 300 people each, along with shops, rehearsal rooms, offices, and even some accommodation.

In front of the Millennium Center is a large open area, the Roald Dahl Plass. Dahl was the author of many wonderful children's books, such as *The Big Friendly Giant* and *Charlie and the Chocolate Factory*. This bowl-shaped plaza, often used for outdoor concerts, is named to honor his memory.

Mining Valleys

Aberfan

North of Cardiff are coal-mining valleys. Most of the mines have gone now, and this is an area of high unemployment. The remains of its mining history are all around, though most of the slag heaps have now been turned into grassy hills rather than being the ugly grey-black mounds of former years.

A few miles away, in the Taff River Valley, is the sad village of Aberfan, whose junior school was smothered by a landslide in October 1966. Nearly all the children in the village aged between 7 and 11 were killed, along with 28 adults. The site of the school has been transformed into an elegant memorial garden. Queen Elizabeth II, who first went to Aberfan a week after the tragedy, has returned three more times, most recently in 2012, to open a new junior school nearby.

Half a mile along the valley from this garden is the cemetery. The graves themselves are a painful sight, especially those bearing photographs of the children.

These South Wales mining valleys specialize in Methodism, male-voice choirs, and combative trade unions. They are also the source of many prominent Labour politicians. The nearby town of Tredegar, for example, was home of Aneurin Bevan, probably the most famous and emotional socialist in Welsh history.

Swansea

Moving west from Cardiff and the mining valleys of South Wales, you will soon arrive in Swansea. It was the home of the poet Dylan Thomas and is now the site of the Dylan Thomas Centre. It is housed in the old Guildhall, one of the most distinguished civic buildings in the city, centrally located and dating from the 1820s.

Another house, the Dylan Thomas Boathouse at Laugharne, another 40 miles west, is also now a museum. A wealthy admirer, Margaret Taylor, bought the house for Thomas in 1949, and he lived the last few years of his life there, from 1949 to 1953. The adjacent writing shed, where he worked, has been left deliberately messy.

The Countryside

Southern Wales contains wonderful countryside. On the country's southwestern tip, for example, the Pembrokeshire Coast National Park was created in the 1950s. The park is made up of sections designed to preserve an area of special geological interest.

The Pembrokeshire Coast Path, suggested in the early 1950s and officially opened in 1970, covers 186 miles of coastal cliffs and inlets. Nearly all its sections are lovely, and nearly all are challenging hikes. Don't worry about having to commit to the whole distance. A well-timed bus service enables you to walk short sections and then get a ride back to your starting point.

The Preseli Hills, in the northern section of the Pembrokeshire Coast National Park, are the source of the famous bluestones from which Stonehenge is made. The Preseli Hills are themselves rich in Neolithic remains. Not far away is Castell Henllys, an Iron Age site, on which a set of prehistoric round houses has been built, where archaeologists try to farm according to the original dwellers' methods.

The little city of St. David's is about halfway along the Pembrokeshire Coast Path. St. David is the patron saint of Wales. He lived in the 6th century and was the founder of a strict monastic order in the area.

Suggested Reading

Coombes, *These Poor Hands*.

Davies, *Cardiff and the Marquesses of Bute*.

Ferris, *Dylan Thomas*.

Thomas-Symonds, *Nye*.

Suggested Activities

1. Visit the Big Pit and Cardiff Castle on the same day, and then think about the gap between the very rich and the very poor.

2. Look at a map of Pennsylvania to find dozens of Welsh names, indicating one part of the great Welsh diaspora. Start at Bryn Mawr, the women's college in suburban Philadelphia.

CARDIFF AND SOUTH WALES

One of the great British films is *Tiger Bay*, from 1959. Set in Cardiff, the capital of Wales, it's the story of a little girl, played by Hayley Mills, who witnesses a murder. Out of loyalty to the murderer, a friendly and kind-hearted Polish sailor, she refuses to tell the police what happened. The story is chock full of moral ambiguity from start to finish, and contains what were, at the time, unusual scenes of multicultural life in Britain. Tiger Bay was the name of Cardiff harbor. Already before 1950 it was one of the most culturally diverse places in Britain, with large numbers of Greek, Indian, Scandinavian, Polish, and West Indian residents, a large transient population of sailors, and a high crime rate.

Cardiff today is nothing like that, though it still has an ethnically and racially diverse population. Today it's the capital of Wales, seat of its Parliament, but no longer a great industrial and shipping center. The first thing to see there is Cardiff Castle, right in the city center. The first castle on the site was built soon after the Norman Conquest, on an artificial hill, a fine example of the classic motte-and-bailey design. It still stands, in the midst of the castle grounds, and you can climb two steep staircases, one up the castle mound and a second up the tower itself. Of greater interest, however, is the section of the castle that was converted, during the 19th century, into a pseudo-medieval fantasy house.

The owner was John Crichton-Stuart, the 3rd Marquis of Bute. He may well have been the richest man in the world, though as a near-contemporary of Andrew Carnegie and John D. Rockefeller he certainly had rivals to the title. He was the owner of numerous South Wales coal mines, dozens of which dot the valleys whose rivers flow down to the South Wales coast. Welsh coal was the fuel of the industrial revolution, produced at a rate of 50 million tons per year in the late 1800s and early 1900s, distributed all over Britain and shipped in bulk to much of the rest of the world. Bute shocked the rest of the aristocracy by converting to Catholicism at the age of 21, when to do so still smacked of disloyalty to Protestant Britain. His tastes were scholarly rather than commercial, and with his architect friend William Burges, he proceeded to transform Cardiff Castle into one of the most elaborate and ornate creations of the Victorian neo-Gothic revival.

One room, the "Arab Room," has a gilded ceiling of dazzling complexity, with layer after layer of ornamentation. The ceilings of the office and the dining room are similarly intricate, with every inch heavily decorated, red and gold dominating. The family only spent a few weeks at Cardiff Castle each year, entertaining lavishly, but no expense was too high in the preparation of these rooms. In the great hall, too, every inch of every surface is decorated, with a wonderful carved wooden screen at one end, under the minstrels' gallery. Over the fireplace is an elaborate painted carving, all in bright colors. It shows a medieval Count of Glamorgan on horseback, riding out from his castle, through the arch and under the portcullis. His wife, or at any rate a comely lady, waves her handkerchief to him from above. Heralds blow trumpets decked with banners. In one corner a man's head is visible through prison bars. This is a reference to Robert, son of William the Conqueror, who was imprisoned by the younger brothers who succeeded him to the English throne, William II and Henry I. Over doorways flanking the fireplace sit carved monks at their scriptoriums. All the walls of the great hall are painted with scenes of chivalry. The ceiling is vaulted, and angels gripping heraldic shields stare down from the balustrade.

Equally magnificent, or equally ridiculous, depending on your taste and your judgment, is the library. Over the fireplace are five carved figures, each one holding a tablet that bears writing in one of the world's main alphabets. Two Gothic-arched doorways stand side by side at one end, their frames playfully carved with monkeys, two of whom have gotten hold of a book and are exploring its pages. Painted on the walls are cherubs, or putti, each bearing the name of one of the Marquis's favorite authors. Here too the dominant mood is one of exceptional richness, and an absorption in a highly-idealized past.

Throughout the formal parts of the house, every inch is decorated, with beautiful wall paintings, tiles, and patterns. My personal view is that it's a great national treasure, over which we should exult. What a good job that the early 20th-century Philistines, who despised everything about Victoriana, didn't desecrate it. There's just one room, the drawing room, in which the 18th-century interior has been preserved. It's decorous and decent, but will never set your heart racing, or bring a smile to your lips, like the Gothic rooms.

During World War II Cardiff, with its big port, was a target for German bombers, which inflicted a lot of damage. The city asked the 5th Marquis, grandson of the builder, to let it use the castle's immensely strong curtain wall as an air-raid shelter. He agreed, and the area is now open as part of the castle museum. It's huge, a great long stone corridor, where iron bed frames and wartime posters have been placed to give you more of a feel of life during the Blitz of 1940 and 1941. The posters are themselves little gems, deadly serious at the time but now nostalgic, about the importance of always carrying your gas mask, growing your own vegetables, and not gossiping about war news. My favorite is a "don't waste food" poster, which shows a big casserole with Churchill's face, above a saucepan with Hitler's face. The text reads: "Better pot-luck with Churchill today than humble pie under Hitler tomorrow." A powerful sound-track, of bombs whining down and exploding, completes the experience.

Near the castle stands a set of three impressive civic buildings from the end of the 19th century. The first is the law courts, the second is City Hall, and the third is the National Museum of Wales. They were designed to project the pride and dignity of Cardiff. It comes as no surprise to learn that they were paid for by the Marquis of Bute, though stylistically the City Hall is less medieval and more like a French-chateau. It has a dome and a great tower, both impressive. Inside are romanticized statues of ancient Welsh heroes such as Howell the Good, a 10th-century warrior and law-giver. Everything is elegant, white or pale brown swirled marble, and spacious.

The National Museum, Cardiff, another stupendous domed building, is next door. It too features great open staircases, massive central display spaces, and a radiant sense of its own importance. Among the paintings on the upper level are a collection of important Impressionists. It comes as almost a relief to learn that these van Goghs, Monets, and Renoirs came not from the Marquis but from a pair of rich, learned, and charitable sisters, Gwendoline and Margaret Davies. The daughters of another rich businessman, both born in the 1880s, they began collecting when the works were still new and controversial. They volunteered as nurses during World War I and later set up a house that was designed to be an arts center. This house, Gregynog Hall, in the central Welsh hills, is a pseudo-Tudor affair in black timber and whitewashed plaster, where annual music festivals attracted the biggest names of the interwar years: Edward Elgar, Ralph Vaughn-Williams, and Gustav Holst.

The sisters' importance to the National Museum is that they donated over 200 major works, whose collective effect is to make Cardiff one of the centers for the study of French art in Britain. There is much to enjoy at the museum, including a thorough geological history of the area, a robotic stuffed mammoth, and high-quality dinosaur skeletons. I single out for your special attention a painting of *Sir Thomas Mansel and His Wife, Jane Pole* from 1625, by an unknown artist. Mansel was a rich South Wales landowner, Member of Parliament, and courtier to King James I. His wife is much younger than he, they're both stiffly dressed in elaborate black and white costumes, but the way he holds her hand transforms the painting into a glimpse of tenderness behind the rigid protocol.

Cardiff's civic buildings, backed by spacious parks, are close to the city's main shopping area, much of which has been improved by the exclusion of traffic. A mile away, down the aptly named Bute Street, and passing through an ugly 1960s-era development named Bute-Town, you'll come to the harbor, where urban renewal is in full flower. As the British coal industry died in the 1980s, so did Cardiff docks, becoming a desolate wasteland. The area's transformation since then is encouraging. The first thing to command your attention there is also the principal survival from earlier days. It is the Pierhead Building, commissioned by you-know-who in the 1890s, and built in a mixture of styles, neo-Gothic, Renaissance, and neo-Jacobean. It was the business center of the dockyards, now converted into a visitor-center, far more elaborate than its utilitarian function might suggest, with pinnacles, turrets, oriel windows and a fine clock-tower. Even the gleaming tiles on the walls are distinguished.

Beside it stands the new Welsh Assembly building. Devolution of power from London to the Welsh and Scottish capitals came in legislation of the 1990s, and was the impetus for its creation. I mentioned in an earlier lecture that the new Scottish Parliament Building ran about 1,000 per cent over budget. This one came in at a sixth of the Scottish price (£70 million compared to £414 million) but was also late and also far more expensive than planned. Of the two, however, it is the better building. The architect was Richard Rogers, and it was opened by the Queen in 2006. You approach it up a series of slate steps and pass under its great canopy. On sunny days, the steps are just right for sitting to watch the passing scene. One section, *The Meeting Place on the Plinth*, is a functional work of art by the sculptor Richard Harris. The building's great glass front bespeaks openness and transparency, while the undulating wooden ceiling above suggests the movement of sea waves. Inside there's a spacious modern foyer—on a recent visit I saw a Welsh choir singing there—and behind it, the council chamber itself. The great wooden supports which curve into the textured wooden ceiling give you the sense that you're under an immense and dignified mushroom.

On the plaza before the assembly building is an artful monument to merchant seamen from the area who died in wartime shipwrecks. At first glance it looks like part of the hull of a shattered boat, composed of metal ribs covered with riveted plates. But you realize, on walking around to the other side, that it's also a human face, looking down into the water. It's an eerily effective way of blending the human and material tragedy of war. The artist, Brian Fell, who got the commission in 1994, taught himself hydraulic riveting to create the work's period mood.

In the same complex, part of the area's redevelopment, is a major performing-arts building, the Wales Millennium Centre, from the beginning of this century. It includes an auditorium that holds nearly 2,000 people and two smaller concert halls for 250 and 300 people each, along with shops, rehearsal rooms, offices, and even some accommodation. The materials are all Welsh, including many different colors of slate. A metallic façade is the most striking element of the design, bearing a line of poetry in both Welsh and English: "In these stones, horizons sing."

As night falls, you realize that the letters are actually windows, so that light from inside the building makes the writing even clearer than it was in daytime. The architect, Jonathan Adams, wrote that it was meant to evoke the Roman custom of placing inscriptions on public buildings:

> The inscription over the entrance of the Wales Millennium Centre is a revival of this classical tradition, and also a recognition of the formative influence of Roman culture upon our nation. We're lucky to have two languages; one that we share with half the world and one which belongs just to us. Words in songs, stories and poems have helped to make Wales the proud country that it is.

In front of the Millennium Center is a large open area, the Roald Dahl Plass. Dahl is the author of many wonderful children's books, such as *The Big Friendly Giant* and *Charlie and the Chocolate Factory*. Both his parents were Norwegian but they lived in Cardiff, whose strong links with Norway are underlined by the nearby Norwegian sailors' church. Dahl himself was born in Llandaff, nearby, and baptized at the Norwegian church. This bowl-shaped plaza, often used for outdoor concerts, is named to honor his memory.

Go north out of Cardiff and you enter the coal-mining valleys that made Lord Bute so wealthy. Most of the mines have gone, now, and this is an area of high unemployment. The remains of its mining history are all around you, though most of the slag heaps have now been turned into grassy hills rather than being the ugly grey-black mounds of former years. In the lecture on industrial Britain, earlier in this series, I described "The Big Pit" at Blaenavon, a superb coal-mining museum where you can go deep inside a disused coal mine with guides.

A few miles away, in the Taff River Valley, is the sad village of Aberfan, whose junior school was smothered by a landslide in October 1966. Nearly all the children in the village aged between 7 and 11 were killed: 116 of them, along with 28 adults. They were my contemporaries. I was 10 at the time and this was the event that started me reading newspapers and becoming aware of the wider world. After knowing about it all my life, I finally went to see Aberfan when I was 60. It's one of many places in Wales where you're always on a steep slope, up or down. It's easy to imagine the landslide, and hard to believe the folly of siting the school right beneath the slag heap. The site of the school, Pantglas, has been transformed into an elegant memorial garden. Queen Elizabeth II, who first went to Aberfan a week after the tragedy, has returned three more times, most recently in 2012, to open a new junior school nearby.

Half a mile along the valley from this garden is the cemetery, also on a very steep hillside, where a 116 stone arches, in two long rows, give unity to the area where the children were buried. The graves themselves are a painful sight, especially those bearing photographs of the children, in some cases of brothers and sisters both recorded as having died at the school.

These South Wales mining valleys specialize in Methodism, male-voice choirs, and combative trade unions. They are also the source of many prominent Labour politicians. The nearby town of Tredegar, for example, was home of Aneurin Bevan, probably the most famous and emotional socialist in Welsh history. Son of a coal miner, he too became a miner at the age of 13 and rose through the ranks of the miners' union. A spellbinding orator, he was a local leader during Britain's General Strike of 1926—which was the closest Britain ever came to socialist revolution—and he won a seat in Parliament in 1929. As Minister of Health in the post-World-War-II Labour government of Clement Attlee, Bevan supervised the creation and launch of the National Health Service. In his view, "no society can legitimately call itself civilized if a sick person is denied medical aid because of lack of means."

Winston Churchill, whose Conservative party opposed the National Health Service at first, quipped that Bevan was the "minister for disease." Its success since then, however, has prevented politicians from either main party from attempting to dismantle the National Health Service, and it's become one of the unquestioned foundations of British life. Access to affordable health care, of the sort Bevan achieved, is now as basic a right as access to 12 years of schooling. In my own life, spent half in Britain and half in the United States, I have found this difference one of the starkest between the two nations. Bevan himself was recently voted the most popular Welshman of all time.

From the same town of Tredegar came Neil Kinnock, another miner's son. He led the Labour Party in the 1980s, struggling to keep its moderate and radical factions in harmony. He detested Prime Minister Margaret Thatcher, and she despised him; they were polar antagonists on almost every question. Kinnock briefly featured in the American news in 1988 when Democratic presidential aspirant Joe Biden plagiarized one of his speeches, and was forced out of the race in disgrace.

Moving west from Cardiff and the mining valleys of South Wales, you soon arrive in Swansea. It was the home of the poet Dylan Thomas and is now the site of the Dylan Thomas Centre. It is housed in the old Guildhall, one of the most distinguished civic buildings in the city, centrally located and dating from the 1820s. The Centre was opened in 1995 by ex-US President Jimmy Carter, who admired Thomas's poetry. Since then it has served as a museum of manuscripts and artefacts from Thomas's life, a conference center, and a place that encourages new Welsh writers and holds regular readings.

Another house, the Dylan Thomas Boathouse at Laugharne, another 40 miles west, is also a museum. A wealthy admirer, Margaret Taylor, bought the house for Thomas in 1949, and he lived the last few years of his life there, from 1949 to 1953, to which era it has now been restored. The adjacent writing shed, where he worked, has been left deliberately messy. All around the table are screwed-up pieces of writing paper, a shorthand way of suggesting the anguished writer's struggle to get the words exactly right.

Dylan Thomas's poetry is beautiful, and formally precise. "Do not go gentle into that good night," a villanelle, is a plea to his dying father to struggle against death rather than succumb to it. "The force that through the green fuse drives the flower" is an intricate meditation on the implacability of nature in giving and in taking away life. "Fern Hill," by contrast, is a wonderful celebration of youthful enjoyment, commemorating the farm, owned by his aunt, where he spent happy days as a child.

Dylan Thomas was a schoolteacher's son, but he quit school early to become a journalist. Always an avid reader, he began writing excellent poetry—much of his best work was done in his teens. He won a London poetry prize when only 20, began to publish regularly, and was recognized as a major talent while still in his early 20s. T. S. Eliot and other luminaries admired him, and he had a gift for drawing the patronage, support, and money of wealthy and well-connected people in British life. The BBC asked him to give broadcasts in the 1940s, and he made a series of lecture tours of the United States in the early 50s. Records of him reading his own work, notably *A Child's Christmas in Wales*, were made in America and became very popular. In view of his reputation as a major Welsh poet it's odd, listening to them, that he has no trace of a Welsh accent. To get the most out of that work, listen to Richard Burton, another famous Welshman, reciting it instead.

Despite his genius, Dylan Thomas was an utterly irresponsible scoundrel. A reckless alcoholic, often blind drunk, irascible, argumentative, and an incorrigible womanizer, he borrowed money but didn't repay it, worked to avoid military service during World War II, and finally drank himself to death in his 30s. He sponged off the eminent historian A.J.P. Taylor for months at a time. Taylor hated him but his wife Margaret was sexually infatuated with him. Thomas was also a fearful procrastinator and spendthrift, never dependable. If Byron was the 19th century's most roguish, swashbuckling poet, Dylan Thomas took up his mantle in the 20th.

Southern and central Wales, no less than North Wales, is wonderful countryside. On the country's southwestern tip, for example, the Pembrokeshire Coast National Park was created in the 1950s. The park is made up of four sections designed to preserve an area of special geological interest. In fact, the geological term "Cambrian" comes from this area, where pioneering 19th-century geologists found rich fossil beds, sometimes including evidence of the soft tissue, as well as the skeletons, of extinct creatures. "Cambria" was the Roman name for Wales, and that name gives us the term "Cambrian," which refers to a geological time-period when, quite suddenly, there was an explosion in the diversity of life on our planet.

The Pembrokeshire Coast Path, suggested in the early 1950s and officially opened in 1970, covers 186 miles of coastal cliffs and inlets. Nearly all its sections are lovely, and nearly all are challenging hikes, because they require frequent descents off the clifftops to cross little river valleys as they flow down to the sea. Don't worry about having to commit to the whole distance. A well-timed bus service enables you to walk short sections and then get a ride back to your starting point. Ronald Lockley, who made the initial survey for this path, was an eccentric Welsh naturalist who had spent years on an offshore island, tracking migratory bird behavior and setting up observatories. His book *The Private Life of the Rabbit* educated his friend Richard Adams about rabbits' group behavior as he was writing the classic 1972 novel *Watership Down*.

The Preseli Hills, in the northern section of the Pembrokeshire Coast National Park, are the source of the famous bluestones from which Stonehenge is made. Stonehenge is 150 miles from here, and there's long been controversy over how stones weighing four tons could have been quarried and then moved so far. One possibility is that, during the ice-age, they were carried by the ice sheet and deposited much closer to the henge site, such that they should be classified as "glacial erratics." As always with Stonehenge, we're not quite sure. In any case, no definite quarry site has been identified.

The Preseli Hills are themselves rich in Neolithic remains. Two of them appear to be burial chambers, in both of which a large rock has been carefully lifted onto three or four stone uprights. These are Carreg Coetan and Pentre Ifan. Man-made earth mounds containing tomb chambers are thought to have been constructed around them. Not far away is Castell Henllys, an Iron Age site, on which a set of prehistoric round houses has been built, where archaeologists try to farm according to the original dwellers' methods.

The little city of St. David's is about half-way along the Pembrokeshire Coast Path. Saint David is the patron saint of Wales. He lived in the 6th century and was the founder of a strict monastic order in the area. His favor in God's eyes was shown during a particular sermon he preached against the Pelagian heresy. All at once, the ground where he stood rose up and became a hill, after which a white dove fluttered down from Heaven and settled on his shoulder. His remains, buried in the cathedral, became a major pilgrimage site in the Middle Ages. Pope Calixtus II declared, in the early 12th century, that two pilgrimages to St. Davids were the equivalent of one to Rome. That was good news for the local people, who created a lucrative pilgrimage business. Even warrior-monarchs like William the Conqueror and Edward I went to visit the shrine. That also means, of course, that the city went into decline after the Reformation. For your pilgrimage to Pembrokeshire I recommend hiking boots and cameras.

The mood of South Wales is different from that of North Wales. The area is more urban and bustling, with stronger links to England over the centuries. The Welsh language is less universally spoken, but you're still aware of being in a different country. To get the most of this sensation, go there on a day when the Welsh national rugby team is playing a match against England. The rivalry is as intense as any in the world, as is the pride the Welsh people feel in their distinctiveness.

17
THE NORTH
OF ENGLAND

T he north of England is an interesting area. Its regional accents are so different from those of the south that it's not always easy for people from one area to know what people from the other are saying. This lecture looks at notable sites in England's north, including:

- Liverpool.

- Manchester.

- The Pennine Hills.

- York.

- Carlisle and Berwick-upon-Tweed.

Three Graces

Liverpool

A good place to begin your tour of the north is in Liverpool. All of the most distinctive buildings in today's Liverpool are from the early 20th century. A dignified cluster at the waterfront is known as the Three Graces. The first of these, the Port of Liverpool Building, was opened in 1907, in the era of King Edward VII, when the British people still believed in their destiny and duty to dominate the rest of the world.

Nearby is the Royal Liver Building, from 1911. It's an office block, but it's historically important because it is generally recognized as the first reinforced concrete building in Britain.

The third of the Graces is the Cunard Building, an office block inspired by palaces of the Italian Renaissance but many times bigger. It was built during World War I and was headquarters of the most famous trans-Atlantic liner company. The *Queen Mary* and *Queen Elizabeth* were designed there, and this was the building to which passengers would report for their Atlantic crossings.

Two other buildings deserving of your attention are the two cathedrals, Anglican and Catholic, standing half a mile apart along the aptly named Hope Street.

Manchester

From Liverpool, it's 30 miles east to Manchester, another city worth visiting. This was a powerhouse city during the Industrial Revolution, serving as a world-leading manufacturing center.

Manchester's Town Hall, built in 1877, has been cleaned and looks marvelous. It's a Victorian Gothic building, designed to look as though it dates back to the Middle Ages. Inside, in the Great Hall, a series of pre-Raphaelite paintings by Ford Madox Brown tell the story of the city.

Manchester's Town Hall

The Pennine Hills

From the great industrial cities, you can drive northeast into the Pennine Hills. Be sure to stop off for an hour or two at Haworth, the village where the Brontë sisters spent most of their lives.

Another notable location is Ribblehead inside the Yorkshire Dales National Park. The limestone country there has many distinctive waterfalls. The best known is Malham Cove, a beautiful arc of rock, over which, when it's wet, the river falls 230 feet. The Pennine Way, a great footpath that meanders up the backbone of England, passes through Malham.

Hardraw Force

Not far away, also close to the Pennine Way, is another waterfall, Hardraw Force. It stands on private land, and the only way to get to it is through a pub, the Green Dragon, where you have to pay a small entry fee. It's worth the price, however, because the waterfall has created a dramatic overhang, where softer rock has eroded faster than the limestone band at the top.

York

The great ancient city of the English north is York. Archaeological findings show it to have been occupied for thousands of years, and it was already an old settlement when the Romans built a fort there, named Eboracum, in 71 CE.

It was the center of the Anglo-Saxon kingdom of Northumbria, but was overrun by the Vikings in 866. They called it Jorvik, which is now the name of a museum that mixes genuine artifacts from local excavations with costumed reenactors and animatronic Viking robots. York is also the site of one of the greatest cathedrals in Britain, York Minster, containing more medieval stained glass than any other church in the country.

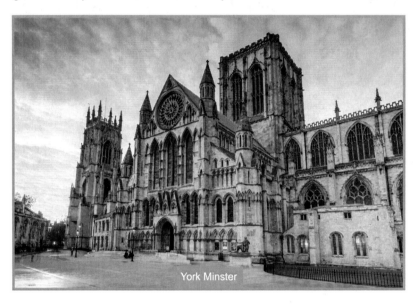
York Minster

York is also the home of the National Railway Museum, a mecca to enthusiasts who still grieve over the disappearance of regular-service steam locomotives in 1968. It is best museum of its kind in the world.

Carlisle and Berwick-upon-Tweed

From York, go north, all the way up to the border country between England and Scotland. Today, this is a pretty area, but a visit to Carlisle or to Berwick-upon-Tweed brings home the reality of a long, harsh history. For centuries, the border was contested ground. Warlords from both sides, English and Scottish, fought back and forth, and some towns changed hands repeatedly.

311

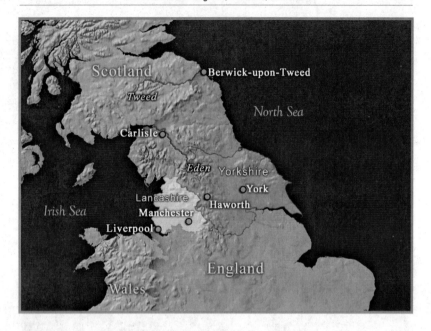

Carlisle Castle is a red sandstone fortress that stood on the front lines of the border wars for centuries. Founded by King William II in 1092 and built up over the centuries until it was immensely strong, it endured a succession of sieges during the Wars of the Roses.

On the other side of the country, at the North Sea shore, the Elizabethan-era fortifications at Berwick-upon-Tweed are even grander. They were built in the late 1500s to end an era in which the city had repeatedly changed hands between the English and the Scots, suffering frequent sieges and bombardments. Immense earthworks, strengthened with stone abutments, surround three-quarters of the city. They are designed in such a way that attackers, approaching, would have to cross open ground under withering crossfire.

Markers on these great fortifications explain that Elizabeth I, over the course of her reign, spent more money on the Berwick fortifications than on any other defense project. The battlements make a wonderful hike today, with

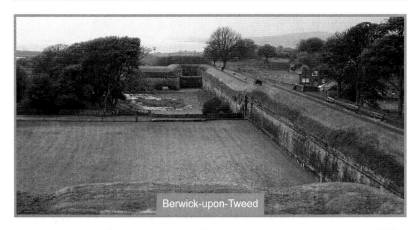

Berwick-upon-Tweed

great views over the sea, the city. They are, alarmingly, unprotected. Take care if you're there with young children to prevent them from falling.

Suggested Reading

Engels, *The Condition of the Working Class in England.*

Gaskell, *North and South.*

Kidd, *Manchester.*

Moffat, *The Reivers.*

Orwell, *The Road to Wigan Pier.*

Questions to Consider

1. Why was the Anglo-Scottish border the site of chronic low-level warfare for centuries before the 1600s?

2. What characteristics of the English north made it suitable for industrialization?

THE NORTH OF ENGLAND

The north of England has regional accents so different from those of the south that it's not always easy for people from one area to know what people from the other are saying. Yorkshire and Lancashire, the big counties on the east and west side of the central Pennine Hills each have distinctive accents. Different again, and often hard to follow if you're not from there, is the "Geordie" voice of people from Northumberland and Durham. Regional traditions remain strong; northerners regard themselves as superior to southerners. But within the north, neighboring towns often have bitter rivalries, fed by support for competing football teams, like those from Newcastle-upon-Tyne and Sunderland, or those from Manchester and Liverpool.

The Pennine Hills are the defining characteristic of the north. Not very high, especially by European and American standards, they are nevertheless wild. This is *Wuthering Heights* country. The rural areas are mainly upland sheep farms, crisscrossed by dry stone walls, and now largely protected as national parks. The valleys are the heartland of England's industrial revolution. In the 1800s the north was the dynamo of English industrialization, led by the cities of Manchester, Bradford, Halifax, and Leeds. It was a land of coal mines, blast furnaces, forges, and textile mills. One characteristic novel of the era, Elizabeth Gaskell's *North and South*, describes a gentle southern girl's amazement when her family moves from the soft rural south to the harsh and smoky north, to a town where working men are fighting the class war in deadly earnest. The region's reputation spread all over the world—Manchester, New Hampshire got its name from businessmen eager to emulate the energy of the English Manchester's industrial success.

In the 20th century, by contrast, the north succumbed to foreign competition. Globalization, and low wages in emerging industrial countries, undercut its supremacy, and one by one the mills, mines, and factories closed. It was severely environmentally degraded and then it began to suffer economic decline. A bad situation deteriorated further when Margaret Thatcher denationalized the heavy industries of the region, forcing its many unprofitable mines and factories to close. If you've seen the 1997 movie *The Full Monty*, you'll remember that the setting is Sheffield, an old iron and steel making town whose men are now mired in chronic long-term unemployment. Comical on the surface, its setting is one of dismay and decline.

Neither is the decline all that recent. Already by the 1930s the north was finding it hard to compete. One wonderful book about the area is George Orwell's *The Road to Wigan Pier*, a report of his travels in the region on behalf of his fellow English socialists. Among the many memorable passages is this one, where he compares the degraded landscape in the towns to the delightful landscape between them:

> The train bore me away, through the monstrous scenery of slag heaps, chimneys, piled scrap-iron, foul canals, paths of cindery mud criss-crossed by the prints of clogs … We passed row after row of little grey slum houses running at right angles to the embankment … But quite soon the train drew away into open country, and that seemed strange, almost unnatural, as though the open country had been a kind of park; for in the industrial areas one always feels that the smoke and filth must go on for ever and that no part of the earth's surface can escape them … In spite of hard trying, man has not yet succeeded in doing his dirt everywhere. The earth is so vast and still so empty that even in the filthy heart of civilization you find fields where the grass is green instead of grey.

Another place to see this juxtaposition of the green with the grimy is in the beautiful 1963 film *Billy Liar*, about a dreamy young man in a gaunt industrial town who escapes occasionally into the hills above.

Begin your tour of the north in Liverpool, where the local "scouse" accent sounds something like this.

Liverpool is a port whose River Mersey opens onto the Irish Sea. It has a long history of trade with the rest of the world, and became rich as a center of the Atlantic slave trade in the 1700s. Cotton from the American South poured in to Liverpool before moving to the textile towns of Lancashire and Yorkshire. Opening of the Liverpool and Manchester Railway in 1830 boosted this trade—it was the first railway in the world to have locomotives running at 30 MPH. In the 1840s and 1850s it became a heavily Irish town as refugees from the famine flocked in. A 100 years later, in the 1950s and 1960s, it became the center of a musical sensation, the "Mersey Beat," led by The Beatles.

All the most distinctive buildings in today's Liverpool are from the early 20th century. A dignified cluster at the waterfront is known as "The Three Graces." The first of these "graces," the Port of Liverpool Building, was opened in 1907, in the era of King Edward VII, when the British people still believed in their destiny and duty to dominate the rest of the world. It's a spectacular mix of styles that goes by the name of "Edwardian Baroque," blending a dome reminiscent of St. Paul's Cathedral with the columns of a Greek temple, all on a Wagnerian scale. Superbly restored since 2000, its dazzling white Portland stone is visible once again, and now you can visit the rotunda inside. Spend some time looking at the exterior decorations too, which include mermaids, anchors, shells, and ships' bells, along with a pair of dolphins supporting the globe.

Nearby is the Royal Liver Building, from 1911. It's an office block but it's historically important because it is generally recognized as the first reinforced concrete building in Britain. What a gorgeous place it is, with two proud towers and two domes just beneath and in front of them. The third of the graces is the Cunard Building, an office block inspired by palaces of the Italian Renaissance but many times bigger. It was built during World War I and was headquarters of the most famous trans-Atlantic liner company. The *Queen Mary* and *Queen Elizabeth* were designed there, and this was the building to which passengers would report for their Atlantic crossings.

I mentioned in an earlier lecture the modest homes in which the Beatles grew up, all fairly close to the center of Liverpool. The Cavern Club, where they played before becoming world famous, is still going strong as a live music venue. The other two buildings most deserving of your attention are the two cathedrals, Anglican and Catholic, standing half a mile apart along the aptly named Hope Street.

The Anglican cathedral was begun at the same time as The Three Graces, at the high-water mark of England's imperial self-confidence. Designed by a very youthful Giles Gilbert Scott and consecrated in the 1920s, its neo-gothic style makes it look much older than it is in fact. Be astonished by its sheer size. Cavernous, and built according to a unified design, it lacks the interior variety of the medieval gothic cathedrals, whose designs often changed over the 100 or more years of their building. It also lacks any sense of intimacy, and to enter is to feel dwarfed by something whose scale is overwhelming. To make matters worse, the walls and vaults are built of dark red sandstone, which seems to swallow up the available light. Even the massive stained glass windows can't compensate for the feeling of gloom and insignificance that besets you. White Portland stone would have made it much more hospitable. Despite these negative remarks, I still think it's impressive, and perhaps a transfiguration in stone of the hard-faced men who made Liverpool rich.

The Catholic Liverpool Metropolitan Cathedral was intended to be a rival in scale to its Anglican counterpart. In fact, Archbishop Downey, the Irish-born leader of Liverpool's Catholics from the 1920s to the 1950s, wanted it to be the best and biggest church in the world, outstripping even St. Peter's in Rome. He commissioned the non-Catholic Edwin Lutyens, star architect of the era, whose design aimed to do just that. Unfortunately, the harsh economic realities of the Great Depression, when building started, made it impossible, and building came to a stop when the Second World War began. Liverpool, a major dockyard and maritime center, suffered severe bomb damage.

Another start in the 1950s faltered so it wasn't until 1967 that the final work was done, 34 years after the foundations were laid, and according to yet another design, this time ultra-modernist. It looks like a cross between a vast Native American tipi and a space ship with a crown on top. In fact, one of its nicknames is "The Pope's Wigwam." The big open interior is circular with the altar in the center, to correspond with the Catholic Church's new idea of itself in the 1960s as less hierarchical and more communal. The circular lantern (or skylight) above the altar is finished in stained glass which creates a luminous glow in the interior, especially on sunny days.

As with so many daring modernist constructions, it was brave and distinctive but didn't work quite right. From the beginning the aluminum roof leaked, while mosaic tiles cracked and fell from the walls. No sooner had it been consecrated than repair crews had to get busy. There's a fascinating photo in a basement display about the Cathedral's history, which shows a member of the local archery club firing arrows at loose ceiling tiles to bring them down, rather than have them fall. The basement itself, immense, spacious, and vaulted, feels like part of a completely different building. That's because it's the one part of the original design that was finished according to Lutyens' original plans.

From Liverpool, travel 30 miles east to Manchester, another Lancashire City, but one whose local accent is very different from that of Liverpool.

It was the powerhouse city of the Industrial Revolution, the marvel of its age as it swelled from being a rustic village in the 1750s to a world-leading, state-of-the-art manufacturing center in 1800. Supporters of industrialization loved it; detractors hated it. Everyone agreed, however, that it was dirty, smoky, and by our standards unendurably polluted.

Friedrich Engels wrote a powerful condemnation of it in his book *The Condition of the English Working Class* from 1845. Here's what he had to say about Manchester's River Irk:

> [It is] a narrow, coal-black, foul-smelling stream, full of debris and refuse, which it deposits on the shallower right bank. In dry weather a long string of the most disgusting, blackish-green slime pools are left standing on this bank, from the depths of which bubbles of miasmatic gas constantly arise and give forth a stench unendurable even on the bridge forty or fifty feet above the surface of the stream.

I'm happy to be able to tell you that this is no longer an accurate description of the River Irk.

In the early 1800s, Manchester had no representation in Parliament. The factory owners were aggrieved because they thought their interests were not adequately represented, and the workers were aggrieved because they had no votes and were forbidden to create trade unions. The wave of fear that had swept through Britain after the French Revolution had led to passage of repressive legislation against workers' combinations. Agitation for political reform after 1815 led to great demonstrations. At one, on St. Peter's Fields, then an open area in the middle of Manchester, a pro-reform demonstration of unarmed men and women was attacked by mounted soldiers brandishing sabers. This was in August of 1819. Fifteen demonstrators were killed and several hundred slashed and maimed. The event shocked public opinion nationwide. It was nicknamed the "Peterloo Massacre," a parody of Waterloo where, four years before, British soldiers had won a great victory over Napoleon. The Peterloo Massacre is to England what Lexington and Concord are to America: symbolic moments in the struggle for freedom and democracy.

On the site was built Free Trade Hall, center of a great 19th century movement to get rid of tariff barriers. Unfortunately, Free Trade Hall is now a hotel, though its mid-Victorian façade has been preserved, and gives you a fine sense of the civic pride that went into its construction. Manchester's Town Hall, built in 1877, has been cleaned and looks marvelous. It's a Victorian Gothic building, designed to look as though it dates back to the Middle Ages and has a religious function, while actually being the home of down-to-Earth politicians. Inside, in the Great Hall, a series of Pre-Raphaelite paintings by Ford Madox Brown tell the story of the city. To tour the building is to discover a wonderful, almost fairyland quality to its staircases and hallways, all of which have been decorated far beyond what's necessary, in the name of civic pride. Statues of the city's dignitaries adorn every major corridor, and the polychromatic tiles are bright and intricate. The same is true of another spectacular neo-Gothic building nearby, the John Rylands Library, which is not only a pleasure to enter but also has one of the greatest collections in Britain, including an original Gutenberg Bible. It too feels as much ecclesiastical as civic or educational.

From the great industrial cities drive northeast into the Pennines, being sure to stop off for an hour or two at Haworth, the village where the Brontë sisters spent most of their lives.

Yorkshire too has its own distinctive voice.

Here, on a wild stretch of moorland, an hour to the north, you'll come to the starkly beautiful Ribblehead Viaduct, an object rich in history and controversy. It was built in the early 1870s when the Midland Railway company was looking for a way to extend its lines all the way to the Scottish border. Other companies had already taken the easier lowland routes up the east and west coasts, leaving the Midland to build this much more mountainous stretch between Settle and Carlisle. Ribblehead was one big challenge: tunnels were another. To build them, a workmen's settlement of nearly 2,000 people and 170 houses sprang up, of which only archaeological traces now remain. Itinerant canal and railway builders were called "navvies:" tough, hard-drinking men accustomed to harsh conditions. At Ribblehead they quarried local stone, made and fired their own bricks in makeshift kilns, and built the viaduct, completing it in 1875.

Railway enthusiasts loved the Settle to Carlisle line, of which this was the dramatic high point. It was the perfect place to take atmospheric photographs of steam locomotives working hard on the steep grades. They were dismayed when the railway decided to close the line in 1983, citing the very high cost of necessary repairs to the viaduct. Love of railway heritage is a quasi-religious passion to thousands of Britons, some of them influential, and they were able to gain parliamentary approval in 1989 to save the line and the viaduct. The repairs cost £3 million, the line reopened, and trains once more rumble across, albeit at low speed, including plenty of steam-locomotive-drawn weekend specials.

Ribblehead is inside the Yorkshire Dales National Park. The limestone country there has many distinctive waterfalls. The best known is Malham Cove, a beautiful arc of rock, over which, when it's wet, the river falls 230 feet. The Pennine Way, a great footpath that meanders up the backbone of England, passes through Malham. The impressive formations prompted the makers of *Harry Potter and the Deathly Hallows* to film a scene at Malham. Not far away, also close to the Pennine Way, is another waterfall, Hardraw Force. The catch with this one is that it stands on private land and the only way to get to it is through a pub, the Green Dragon, where you have to pay a small entry fee. It's worth the price, however, because the waterfall has created a dramatic semi-circular overhang, where softer rock has eroded faster than the limestone band at the top. As you approach the free-falling water, you're aware that millions of tons of rocks loom over your head, and that the place looks the way it does because they've been falling for centuries. The Green Dragon itself is an extremely attractive little pub, with low ceilings, a cozy fireplace, and eccentric but likeable decorations. I had lunch there after seeing the falls.

The great ancient city of the English north is York. Archaeological findings show it to have been occupied for thousands of years, and it was already an old settlement when the Romans built a fort there, named Eboracum, in 71 AD. It was the center of the Anglo-Saxon kingdom of Northumbria, but was overrun by the Vikings in 866. They called it "Jorvik," which is now the name of a museum that mixes genuine artifacts from local excavations with costumed reenactors and animatronic Viking robots, who act as warriors, blacksmiths, leather-makers and irritable women. Kids love it, and I recall feeling a guilty pleasure, years ago, when I boarded the museum's so-called "time-travel capsule," which hurtled me back in time to the crucial year 866. The Viking exhibits at the nearby Yorkshire Museum are more sober, but somehow more trustworthy, than the ones you'll see in Jorvik.

York is also the site of one of the greatest cathedrals in Britain, York Minster, containing more medieval stained glass than any other church in the country. The Great East Window, dates back to the early 1400s and consists of more than 300 panels, all recently restored. The Great West Window, with its superb stone tracery in the form of interwoven hearts (and nicknamed "the Heart of Yorkshire,") is even older, dating back to the 1330s.

Medieval remains are as clearly visible in York as in any other British city. An old crooked street, the Shambles, has a fine series of medieval and Tudor-era buildings whose upper floors are larger than their ground floors, so that they appear to lean toward each other over the narrow passage. Once a set of butchers' shops (hence the name the Shambles), they're now souvenir shops and restaurants, but the preservation of their exterior gives visitors a good sense of what medieval streets looked like. Best of all the medieval remnants are several miles of the old city walls. They were based on Roman originals, extended in the 12th and 14th centuries, and restored as a visitor-attraction in the 19th. Four great gatehouses or "bars," punctuate a walk around the walls, as does the Multangular Tower, which, by some estimates, dates back to the days of the Emperor Constantine.

Last but not least, York is the home of the National Railway Museum, a mecca to enthusiasts who still grieve over the disappearance of regular-service steam locomotives in 1968. I can't praise it too highly and it's certainly the best museum of its kind in the world. When I visited in 2013, the five preserved locomotives from the A4 class were all there. Mallard, the most illustrious of the five, is the all-time speed record holder for a steam locomotive, having reached 126 mph back in 1938. Clever marketers named this event "The Great Gathering." Thousands of men in late middle-age, which is to say, my exact contemporaries, crowded in and sighed with pleasure!

From York, go north, all the way up to the border country between England and Scotland. Today, this is a pretty area, rural and mild, but a visit to Carlisle or to Berwick-upon-Tweed brings home the reality of a long, harsh history. That's because, for centuries, the border was contested ground. These were the "marches." Warlords from both sides, English and Scottish, fought back and forth, and some towns changed hands repeatedly. To make matters worse, organized bandits called the reivers from the border country attacked the lands to their immediate south, creating a situation of chronic fear and uncertainty. The word "bereaved" comes from this experience: it means "having suffered an attack by the reivers." From this area of prolonged raiding we also have the word "blackmail," because demands for ransom, or forced payments for the right to be left alone, were common.

At Beamish, in County Durham, there's a wonderful example of a fortified farmhouse, which was designed with these attacks in mind. The family could withdraw into the thick-walled house, bar the entrances, and huddle inside, even if their cattle were seized by the raiders. Better than having family members carried off into slavery, which was the fate of many.

The archbishop of Glasgow got into such a rage about the Reivers in 1525 that he issued a memorable curse against them, more than a thousand words long, ordering it to be read out in all the churches of his diocese. Here's a fragment of it:

> I curse their head and all the hairs of their head; I curse their face, their eyes, their mouth, their nose, their tongue, their teeth, their skull, their shoulders, their breast, their heart, their stomach, their back, their womb, their arms, their legs, their hands, their feet, and every like part of their body, from the top of their head to the soles of their feet, before and behind, within and without ... May all the malevolent wishes and curses ever known, since the beginning of the world, to this hour, light on them. May the malediction of God, that fell upon Lucifer and all his fellows, that cast them from the high Heaven to the deep hell, light upon them.

It may well be the most vengeful and explicit official outburst in British history.

In 2001, a pair of artists named Gordon Young and Andy Altman collaborated on a project to engrave just over 300 words of the curse on a polished, 14-ton granite boulder, which was then sited in a pedestrian subway beneath a busy road in Carlisle. It sits on a pavement inscribed with the names of the leading Reiver families, and has itself become a bone of contention. Some Carlisle folk claimed that this cursing stone was bringing bad luck to the city. Foot and mouth disease broke out among cattle in the area, a flood damaged part of the city, and the local football team had such a bad season that it was relegated to a lower division. Might the stone have occult powers? The city council debated the question in 2005, decided to keep the cursing stone, and it's still there today, very much worth a visit. The bishop of Carlisle favored leaving it, but added that "the original curse was not a godly act" and that "we are called to bless, not curse, even our enemies."

Carlisle Castle, a hundred yards from the cursing stone, is a red sandstone fortress that stood on the front lines of the border wars for centuries. Founded by King William II in 1092 and built up over the centuries until it was immensely strong, it endured a succession of sieges during the Wars of the Roses.

It was often used as a prison, and intricate wall carvings still visible there are thought to be the work of either the prisoners themselves, or of bored prison guards. For a while the castle was commanded by Richard, Duke of Gloucester, who later became King Richard III. Royalists held it during an eight-month siege in the English Civil War until, after eating every horse, dog, and rat, they were starved into submission. Carlisle Castle was last fought over in 1745, during Bonnie Prince Charlie's uprising, but has remained in good condition ever since, continuously occupied as headquarters of the King's Own Royal Border Regiment.

On the other side of the country, the North Sea shore, the Elizabethan-era fortifications at Berwick-upon-Tweed are even grander. They were built in the late 1500s to end an era in which the city had repeatedly changed hands between the English and the Scots, suffering frequent sieges and bombardments. Immense earthworks, strengthened with stone abutments, surround three quarters of the city. They are designed in such a way that attackers, approaching, would have to cross open ground under withering crossfire. Elizabeth I, over the course of her reign, spent more money on the Berwick fortifications than on any other defense project, more even than she spent on defeating the Spanish Armada. The battlements make a wonderful hike today, with great views over the sea, the city, and the handsome Royal Border Bridge that carries the London-to-Edinburgh railway over the River Tweed. They are, alarmingly, unprotected. Take care if you're there with young children—there's nothing to stop them falling off the high parapet.

Peace finally descended over the marches after King James VI of Scotland became King James I of England. This union of crowns meant that the same authorities were at work on both sides of the border, and they set about stamping out the reivers once and for all. With the brutality characteristic of the era, leading reiver chieftains were rounded up, many were tried and executed, and by 1610 a semblance of peace had come to the area after centuries of fighting. It's a peace that you can still enjoy today, while visiting the picturesque remnants of the old chaos.

18

THE ENGLISH MIDLANDS

D ensely populated, the Midlands encompasses the counties of Staffordshire, Derbyshire, Leicestershire, Nottinghamshire, Lincolnshire, Warwickshire, Worcestershire, Herefordshire and Shropshire, along with parts of Northamptonshire and the former county of Rutland. At its center is Birmingham. The region has been industrial territory since the 1760s and a hub of Britain's network of canals. This lecture looks at some notable sites in the area, including:

- The Cotswolds.

- Nottingham.

- Birmingham.

- Several villages.

- Coventry.

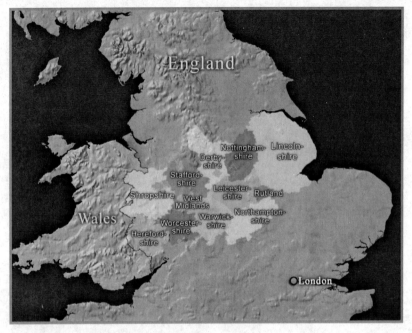

The Cotswolds

In the southern Midlands is the Cotswolds, an area of charming villages and gentle hills. It is the personification of rural England. This lecture begins its

Bottle-shaped brick kilns

visit with Stoke-on-Trent, a middle-sized Midlands town that used to be one of the most polluted places in the world. It and the towns around it are collectively referred to as the Potteries because they have been centers of pottery making for centuries. The bottle-shaped brick kilns that can still be seen all over the town have been eclipsed by newer and cleaner technology.

The arrival on the scene of Josiah Wedgwood transformed the area and gave it a position of world leadership that it held for two centuries. Wedgwood, who lived from 1730 to 1795, was the son of a small-scale pottery manufacturer. He thought big almost from the outset. He subdivided the manufacture, painting, glazing, firing, distribution, and sale of china and pioneered many marketing techniques, including "buy one, get one free."

A factory tour takes visitors along a series of elevated walkways, from which they can look down to watch each stage of the manufacturing process. The museum attached to the factory is a gem, guiding you through the stages of Wedgwood's innovations, his painstakingly thorough experiments, and his sharp eye for changing fashions among the British upper classes, whose patronage he cultivated.

Josiah Wedgwood

Birmingham

Birmingham, in the heart of the Midlands, is Britain's second-largest city. The Birmingham Museum and Art Gallery is a superb Victorian building that opened in 1885. It stands on Chamberlain Square.

Birmingham Museum

Birmingham was a major target for the German bombers in World War II and suffered severe damage. After the war, the city center had to be extensively rebuilt. Much of the concrete rebuilding of the 1950s and 1960s was praised by architects and hated by everyone else, so much so that there has been a second round of rebuilding since then.

Coventry

From Birmingham, it's a 25-minute train ride to Coventry, an ancient city whose most famous resident was Lady Godiva. Legend has it that she

Lady Godiva

rode naked through the town in protest against the heavy taxes imposed on the people by her husband, the earl of Mercia. There's a fine statue of her in the town square, with her long hair artfully preserving her modesty, and a superb romantic painting of her by John Collier in the town's Herbert Art Gallery.

Coventry was the site of a great medieval abbey but it was destroyed during the Reformation—just a few remains can still be seen at a partial excavation. The biggest remaining church in the town, St. Michael's, itself a superb medieval Gothic building, was designated as a cathedral in 1918 when Coventry became a diocese. German bombers destroyed it in a shattering air raid of November 14th, 1940.

The elegant spire somehow survived, along with a few fragments of the walls, and these ruins, now open to the sky, remain as consecrated ground. Descend a staircase in the old north transept, and you will enter the new Coventry Cathedral, built in the late 1950s and consecrated in 1962.

Coventry also features a museum of transport. The city was a bicycle and car-manufacturing center in the early 20th century, and the museum contains over 200 old cars, some highly exotic.

Coventry Cathedral

Coventry

Nottingham

Nottingham, like Coventry, was a bicycle town; it was the home of Raleigh bikes. Nottingham was also the home of writer D. H. Lawrence.

Robin Hood is also a notable (albeit debatable) figure from the area. According to the legends, Robin Hood was a loyal follower of King Richard the Lion-Heart, wrongly outlawed by bad Prince John, and dedicated to feuding with John's henchmen, the sheriff of Nottingham and Guy of Gisborne. The debate among folklorists and antiquarians about whether he existed continues. At Sherwood Forest and at Nottingham Castle, the displays about Robin Hood dodge the question of whether he actually existed. Instead, they leave it up to you to decide.

Nottingham Castle itself was started just after the Norman conquest and became an important royal site in the Middle Ages. It was converted into a mansion by the duke of Newcastle in the 1670s. When one of his descendants in the House of Lords voted against parliamentary reform in 1831, a mob of angry Nottingham workers broke in, smashed the furniture, and set it on fire.

Nottingham Castle

It was restored in the 1870s by a local philanthropist, who turned it into an art museum—the first municipal art gallery in Britain outside of London.

Villages

The southern area of the Midlands is more rural and encompasses the Cotswolds, which have a well-deserved reputation for exceptional beauty. They're not far from London, Birmingham, Bristol, or Oxford, and yet have preserved a relaxing feeling of remoteness and rusticity. Gently sloping hills and a warm yellow stone make the Cotswold towns little architectural gems.

Notable among the Cotswold towns are:

■ Bourton-on-the-Water, which has a shallow river, the Windrush, running right through its main street, crossed by a series of elegant low bridges. This area also features a model village.

■ Burford, whose main street runs down a long hill toward the Windrush. A Tudor market hall, now the Tolsey Museum, is halfway down the hill.

Burford

331

■ Broadway, which is 20 miles north. Before you get there, stop on a nearby hilltop to admire Broadway Tower. Broadway itself contains shops on the Cotswold Way, a 100-mile-long footpath that incorporates some of the area's best scenery.

Suggested Reading

Chinn and Dick, *Birmingham*.

Dolan, *Wedgwood*.

Teller, *The Rough Guide to the Cotswolds*.

Suggested Activity

1. Print a map of the British counties from the internet and try to fill in the names. Warning: It's a great deal more difficult than naming the American states because there are no straight lines.

THE ENGLISH MIDLANDS

T he Midlands is probably the least well-known part of Britain and the one that unwise travelers might be tempted to omit. It lacks the grandeur of London and the scenic magnificence of the Scottish Highlands, but it does have a fascinating heritage, much of which is now carefully preserved. It's my own home ground, and to me a source of particular pride.

Densely populated, the Midlands encompasses the counties of Staffordshire, Derbyshire, Leicestershire, Nottinghamshire, Lincolnshire, Warwickshire, Worcestershire, Herefordshire and Shropshire, along with parts of Northamptonshire and the former county of Rutland. At its center is the huge conurbation of Birmingham. The region has been industrial territory since the 1760s, center of the metal trades, engine, car, and railroad manufacture, and hub of Britain's network of canals. In the south Midlands, offsetting the industry, is the Cotswolds, an area of charming villages, and gentle hills, the personification of rural England.

Let's begin this visit in Stoke-on-Trent, a middle-sized Midlands town that used to be one of the most polluted places in the world. It and the towns around it are collectively referred to as "The Potteries" because they have been centers of pottery-making for centuries. The bottle shaped brick kilns that can still be seen all over the town have been eclipsed by newer and cleaner technology; they used to spew out choking smoke that seriously reduced local life expectancy. The combination of clay and coal in the ground nearby contributed to Stoke's early specialization.

The arrival on the scene of Josiah Wedgwood transformed it, and gave it a position of world leadership that it held for two centuries. Wedgwood, who lived from 1730 to 1795, was the son of a small-scale pottery manufacturer. He thought big almost from the outset. The living embodiment of the Protestant work-ethic, he drove himself hard and tried to whip unruly employees into shape. He subdivided the manufacture, painting, glazing, firing, distribution, and sale of china and pioneered many of the marketing techniques with which we are familiar today, like "Buy one, get one free," and "Full satisfaction or your money back."

Wedgwood is still a thriving business, making an array of styles, some dazzlingly attractive, nearly all very expensive, and setting standards for the rest of the industry. Their factory and museum in the village of Barlaston, just outside Stoke, should be on every visitor's list. It's a modern, state-of-the-art place, hospital-white and ultra-clean inside. The days of "potter's rot," the lung disease pottery workers used to contract from the toxic dust of the business, are long gone. The factory tour takes you along a series of elevated walkways, from which you can look down to watch each stage of the manufacture. At the beginning, one workman places lumps of clay in molds. Machines shape it into cups, plates, teapots, and jugs. Then they're sent into vast kilns that fire them at temperatures over 1,000 degrees centigrade.

The next stage is painting and decorating, and here the tour descends to ground level so that you can actually stand next to the skilled workers, mainly women, who are giving them the distinctive Wedgwood look. They're happy to chat as they work and explain the various problems they need to master. The uniformity of their gilding and flower painting is astonishing. Until you watch them you assume it must be done by machine. At the conclusion of the tour you even see craftsmen and craftswomen making elaborately shaped vases on traditional potters' wheels—for some shapes there's still no better way. The ease and confidence with which they do it belies the actual difficulties involved. Anyone who's tried to make a clay pot knows what I mean.

The museum that's attached to the factory is a gem, guiding you through the stages of Wedgwood's innovations, his painstakingly thorough experiments, and his sharp eye for changing fashions among the British upper classes, whose patronage he cultivated. He experimented tirelessly to get the right blend of materials, the right temperature in firing, the right glazes, and the right colors. In the museum, an immense wooden filing cabinet still contains the thousands of samples he generated during these experiments.

Incidentally, Wedgwood's famous old factory was about five miles up the canal in Etruria. Its remains stand beside a museum of the china industry that's housed in an old bone-grinding mill with working steam engines. This too must be part of your visit. Don't be deterred by the fact that you'll probably encounter junked cars and builders' rubbish in the area. The Etruria factory stands at the confluence of two canals, and that's not a coincidence. Wedgwood was plagued, in the early days of his business, by poor communications. Britain's roads were terrible in the mid-18th century, and china sent by pack horse was likely to break or be stolen. No wonder he was a fervent advocate for canals, or that he volunteered to be unpaid treasurer of the Trent and Mersey canal scheme which transformed the situation for the better in the 1770s.

Horses pacing along the canal bank could tow barges carrying 50-times their own weight. Once the canal was finished Wedgwood's raw materials could come in, and his finished product flow out, far more easily than ever before. Where the canals meet stands a statue of James Brindley, the canal-building genius who turned the idea into a reality. I talk more about Brindley—and canals, in general—in my lecture on sites associated with the Industrial Revolution.

Birmingham, in the heart of the Midlands, is Britain's second-largest city and I would like to invite Paul to say a word or two about it.

[Paul] I'd love to Patrick. Birmingham's people are known as "Brummies" and the local accent is strong. Like Stoke, it's a canal crossroads, and the transformation of the canals from commercial to leisure use has transformed the landscape around them. Gas Street Basin has an unpropitious sound, doesn't it? But this area, formerly of wharves, warehouses, muck, and profanity has been transformed into an upscale shopping district with cafes, restaurants, dance troupes, theaters, and the hall in which the City of Birmingham Symphony Orchestra performs to world-class standards. The area radiates civic pride.

Birmingham has been through successive changes in the last century. It was the constituency of Joseph Chamberlain, a high-minded Liberal mayor in the mid-19th century who aimed to improve the lives of his mainly poor constituents. A passionate advocate of universal education and free trade, Chamberlain made his fortune as a manufacturer of screws, then devoted himself to public service. He went on to play a major, and controversial, role in late Victorian and Edwardian politics. It was his son Neville Chamberlain who, half a century later, was the great advocate of appeasement, famously deceived by Hitler's false promises.

The Birmingham Museum and Art Gallery is a superb Victorian building that opened in 1885. It stands, aptly enough, on Chamberlain Square. Its clock tower, faintly reminiscent of Big Ben, is known locally as "Big Brum." As you enter, you pass the foundation stone, on which is engraved the slogan: "By the gains of industry we promote art." A common saying in the North and Midlands of Britain is: "Where there's muck there's brass," which is the same idea expressed in a slightly different idiom.

The highlight of the collection inside is an array of about 30 Pre-Raphaelite paintings, including many of the most famous ones by Burne-Jones, Rossetti, and William Holman Hunt. If I had to single out a favorite it would be Holman Hunt's *The Finding of the Saviour in the Temple,* in which the boy Jesus, dressed in a blue and white striped robe with a golden belt, is astonishing the priests and scribes by his knowledge and understanding of scripture. His mother Mary leans forward in relief to have found him. Every millimeter of the painting's surface is sharply delineated, the colors are rich, and the setting deliciously exotic. The gallery has a wide variety of masters too, from Canaletto, Gainsborough and Constable to Renoir and Degas. As with so many of Britain's Victorian galleries the building itself, opulent, confident and highly decorated, is a worthy setting for its contents.

Birmingham was a major target for the German bombers in World War II and suffered severe damage. My mother was born there in 1925, and she was there throughout the war years, spent hundreds of nights in an air raid shelter, and once returned to work in the morning to discover that the factory where she worked had been blown to pieces. After the war, the city center had to be extensively rebuilt. Much of the concrete rebuilding of the 50s and 60s was praised by architects and hated by everyone else, so much so that there's been a second round of rebuilding since then.

The results are uneven. Each architect appears to have acted as though no other buildings existed, and there has been seemingly no attempt to harmonize the styles or create a general look to the place. Some high-rise buildings have checker-box black, brown and white decorations, others are monoliths of glass. The Selfridges Building has an irregular, sinuously curving exterior decorated with circular aluminum discs on a blue background, and looks like an immense shiny beached whale. Worst of the lot, in my view, is the library at Centenary Square, a blue and gold monstrosity surrounded by a weird skin of metallic curlicues. Top-heavy, blockish, and painfully out of place, especially beside Birmingham's beautiful little war memorial, it just seems to say: "I don't care at all about the rest of you." I should add, however, that it won a major award from the Royal Institute of British Architects, so perhaps this is one of the many occasions, in talking about modern architecture, that I am wrong.

From Birmingham, it's just a 25-minute train ride to Coventry, where more modernist horrors await you. Coventry is nevertheless an ancient city, whose most famous resident was Lady Godiva. Legend has it that she rode naked through the town in protest against the heavy taxes imposed on the people by her husband, the Earl of Mercia. There's a fine statue of her in the town square, with her long hair artfully preserving her modesty, and a superb romantic painting of her by John Collier in the town's Herbert Art Gallery. A tailor named Tom was the only citizen to actually look at her; all the others averted their eyes out of gratitude. That's where we get the phrase "peeping Tom."

Coventry was the site of a great medieval abbey but it was destroyed at the Reformation; just a few remains can still be seen at a partial excavation. The biggest remaining church in the town, St. Michael's, itself a superb medieval gothic building, was designated as a cathedral in 1918 when Coventry became a diocese. German bombers destroyed it in a shattering air raid of November 14th, 1940, in which more than 550 people were killed, 4,000 houses damaged, and most of the central city destroyed. The elegant spire somehow survived, along with a few fragments of the walls, and these ruins, now open to the sky, remain as consecrated ground. Descend a staircase in the old North Transept and you will enter the new Coventry Cathedral, built in the late 1950s and consecrated in 1962. Some local politicians opposed it, on the grounds that the city still had a crying need for basic housing and social services, but a decision by the Home Secretary—whose letter is preserved on site—overruled them, and building began.

The architect was Basil Spence and his design has been argued over ever since. It's recognizable in shape as a cathedral, and relies on a mixture of modern and traditional materials. It was Spence's idea, a very good one, to leave the shattered remnants of the old building in place and to use the same type of sandstone on the exterior of the new. The best element, in my opinion, is the large stained glass multicolored window on the South side of the nave, and the series of colored glass walls angled obliquely into the structure.

Dominating the whole is an immense tapestry by Graham Sutherland, depicting Jesus on a green background. From the start, visitors claimed that his eyes would follow you wherever you were in the building. A statue of St. Michael slaying the devil, by Jacob Epstein, ornaments the exterior. For the consecration, the composer Benjamin Britten was commissioned to write his *War Requiem*. He used not just the text of the traditional Latin requiem for the dead, but also passages of poetry by the famous poet of World War I, Wilfred Owen. At Britten's request, there was no applause at the end of the performance, but critics were full of praise for the work itself.

Since its consecration, the new Coventry Cathedral has been prominent as a center for the British peace movement. Coventry's sister city in Germany is Dresden, which suffered incomparably worse bombardment at the hands of the British and American air forces in early 1945. When I last went to Coventry, the area around the new cathedral's chapter house was fenced off and a sign warned of falling masonry. Two or three tiles, recently detached from the walls, were lying inside the fenced area. Very sad.

Looking around the neighborhood of the cathedral, you can see some of the ugliest buildings ever created. One spot in particular can serve as a synecdoche for all the rest. The grand old late Victorian Council House, built of red sandstone in a neo-Jacobean style, overlooks a central garden. It's elegant and decorous. But just across the road a heartless modernist building has been raised, which is linked by a bridge that jams its way into the body of the Council House. The effect is as welcome as graffiti on Michelangelo's *David*, or five seconds of punk rock in the middle of a Mozart symphony.

Does Coventry have redeeming features? Yes: above all its museum of transport. The city was a bicycle and car-manufacturing center in the early-20th century, and the museum contains over 200 old cars, some highly exotic, including two jet-powered land-speed-record-breakers, others significant because of their ordinariness. I had a nostalgic moment when I saw a Hillman Imp, one of the cars previously built in Coventry. My family owned one in the early 1970s. It now seems comically dated and frail. There's also a rather grand double-decker bus on which my brother Malcolm served as a conductor during his college vacations. The bikes, motor-bikes, drag racers, and royal cars make up a wonderful and comprehensive exhibition, enabling you to leave Coventry with the conclusion that it's a very mixed bag, but that hope has not quite died.

Nottingham, like Coventry, was a bicycle town: the home of Raleigh bikes. In the late 1950s and early 1960s a literary movement called the "Angry Young Men" included the work of Alan Sillitoe from Nottingham. Among his best books is *Saturday Night and Sunday Morning*, about a young man who works at the Raleigh factory and gets into trouble by having affairs with other men's wives. It's an intense, atmospheric work, highly autobiographical, which was transferred effectively to the screen. Sillitoe wrote the screenplay and Albert Finney played the leading role. It was the movie that made him famous.

Sillitoe was a cranky working-class libertarian; he didn't like being told what to do or what to think; that's the theme of his great short story collection, *The Loneliness of the Long-Distance Runner* from 1959. Lionized in the Soviet Union for painting a bleak picture of British proletarian life, he was invited to address a Soviet writers' meeting in 1968. He bravely used the occasion, and the presence of Leonid Brezhnev, to denounce Soviet human rights abuses.

However, Alan Sillitoe may not be the first name that comes to mind when someone mentions Nottingham. Maybe not even the first writer, because this is also D. H. Lawrence's home ground. But surely Robin Hood should take pride of place? According to the legends, Robin Hood was a loyal follower of King Richard the Lion-Heart, wrongly outlawed by bad Prince John, and dedicated to feuding with John's henchmen, the sheriff of Nottingham and Guy of Gisborne. He wore Lincoln green clothes, lived in Sherwood Forest, stole from the rich, gave to the poor, and loved the high-born Maid Marian.

It's doubtful that there was a real person, but by 1500 Robin Hood had become a stock figure in May-Day plays and revels. He might have been a representation of the grievances of the old Anglo-Saxons against the Norman invaders. He might also have been the embodiment of chivalric virtue, of whom even the Norman elite could approve, at least in theory. The debate among folklorists and antiquarians continues. At Sherwood Forest and at Nottingham Castle, the displays about Robin Hood dodge the question of whether he actually existed. Instead, they leave it up to you to decide!

Sherwood Forest has diminished over the centuries and is now just a patch of woodland. However, by the Nottinghamshire village of Edwinstowe there is a wonderful old tree, the Major Oak, estimated at almost a

1,000-years old, and more than 30-feet around. It's a former winner of Britain's "Tree of the Year" award. For the last century, its heavy boughs have been propped up with scaffolding. Nearby is the Sherwood Forest Visitor Center, which explains the legends and all the local connections. The Sherwood Forest Country Park is a 450-acre woodland preserve that features many other oaks of more than 500 years' antiquity.

All over Nottinghamshire you'll encounter pubs named after Robin Hood and his Merry Men. You know the names: Little John, Friar Tuck, Will Scarlett, Alan-a-Dale, and Much the Miller's Son. There's also a good statue of Robin himself next to the gate-house of Nottingham Castle, made by a local sculptor, James Woodford. It caused controversy when first unveiled, in 1952, because it didn't look like Errol Flynn, who had played Robin Hood in a successful film from 1938. The man depicted is shorter, stockier, and wears a leather helmet rather than Errol Flynn's jaunty feathered cap. Vandals stole the statue's arrows until, in an exquisite act of historical irony, a latter-day sheriff of Nottingham with experience in the metal trades worked out how to use a hard alloy to keep them in place.

Nottingham Castle itself was started just after the Norman conquest and became an important royal site in the Middle Ages. Militarily obsolete by the time of the Civil War, it was converted into a mansion by the Duke of Newcastle in the 1670s. When one of his descendants in the House of Lords voted against parliamentary reform in 1831, a mob of angry Nottingham workers broke in, smashed the furniture, and set it on fire. It was a moldering ruin for 40 years after that but was restored in the 1870s by a local philanthropist, who turned it into an art museum—the first municipal art gallery in Britain outside of London.

Another super building in Nottingham is Wollaton Hall, a Tudor mansion from the 1580s built by a local business success, Sir Francis Willoughby. Its exuberant style links it to a series of "Prodigy Houses" that sprang up throughout England in the reign of Elizabeth I. The idea was to make them sufficiently attractive that the Queen herself would come to stay, with her retinue. In the event, Elizabeth I never came as far north as Nottingham, but Wollaton has survived. Purchased by the city in 1924, it is now a museum of natural history and industrialization.

So far in this lecture I've concentrated on Midlands cities: Stoke, Birmingham, Coventry, and Nottingham. The south Midlands is more rural and encompasses the Cotswolds, which have a well-deserved reputation for exceptional beauty. They're not far from London, Birmingham, Bristol, or Oxford, and yet have preserved a relaxing feeling of remoteness and rusticity. Gently sloping hills and a warm yellow stone make the Cotswold towns little architectural gems. Thatched rooves scattered among the cottages enhance an already charming scene. Bourton-on-the-Water, for example, has a shallow river, the Windrush, running right through its main street, crossed by a series of elegant low bridges. Ducks paddle about in the shallow water, graceful trees cast shade, while broad grassy parks give the houses room to breathe, each with its own calm dignity. You can feel your biorhythm slowing down in Bourton, and it's tempting to let the afternoon flow past in one of the pubs or teashops that dot the main street.

Having come this far, however, you should make the effort of visiting Bourton's Model Village. Built during the Great Depression, when the townsfolk must have had time lying heavy on their hands, it's a superb copy of the actual village, one-ninth scale but built of the same stone as the actual houses. Eighty years old by now, the stone of the models has had time to weather and gather moss and lichen, enhancing the verisimilitude. Miniature shrubs and trees, and cleverly managed gardens, also enrich the overall effect. There's even a model of the model village, creating one of those infinite regress series that fascinated us as eight-year-olds. My only quibble is that some renovation work in recent years, especially on the copy of the parish church, has cleaned it up too much, making it less believable than when it was darker and mossier. Even so, this is one of those oddly endearing British objects that leaves a permanent favorable mark on your psyche. Incidentally, Bourton has a little motor car museum, but it can't compete with the one in Coventry.

A second Cotswold village very much worth a visit is Burford, whose main street runs down a long hill toward the River Windrush, here a few miles downstream from Bourton. A Tudor Market Hall, now the Tolsey Museum, is half-way down the hill, nearly all of whose houses are made of the same warm stone. Wisteria grows lavishly over the cottages, coming out bright mauve in May and June. The town thrived in the late Middle Ages as a center of the wool trade, and prosperous merchants built a three-story gatehouse and chapel at the local Church of St. John the Baptist, in thanks for their good fortune.

You're aware, as a visitor, of the many times this church has been restored, extended, and repurposed; lots of interesting elements don't really add up to a coherent whole. The highlight is an elaborate tomb for Sir Lawrence and Lady Tanfield, local residents from the early 1600s who were also important at the court of King James I. Effigies of the couple lie side by side with hands crossed, while statues of their grandson and daughter kneel, one at each end, in prayerful vigil. The effect is stiff, slightly comical, and takes on a new dimension when you learn from the church guidebook that the couple were bitterly unpopular, and that the townsfolk burned his lordship in effigy each year for the next 200 years.

I mentioned in a previous lecture that, at the end of the English Civil War, the New Model Army became radicalized, and that some of its members, the Levellers, favored a drastic, democratic approach to politics, based on the principle of one-man, one-vote. Burford was the scene of a mutiny in the army's ranks, led by the Levellers. Commander Oliver Cromwell reacted by arresting 340 of them, and imprisoning them in the church. One scratched his name in the stone of the font, where you can still read "Anthony Sedley 1649 Prisner." Three of the ringleaders were led out and shot by firing squad, while the rest were forced to watch from the church's roof. This was the moment when Cromwell's flirtation with radical social change came to an end, and set him on the road to military dictatorship.

A third of these precious villages is Broadway, 20 miles further north, sometimes referred to as "The Jewel of the Cotswolds." Before you get there, stop on a nearby hilltop to admire Broadway Tower. It's a fake Saxon tower or "folly," built by James Wyatt in the 1790s for Lady Coventry, who lived 20y miles away and wondered whether she would be able to see the hill from her home in Worcester. In the 19th century, one of the Pre-Raphaelite artists, Edward Burne-Jones, rented it for a while as a studio. William Morris, a leader of the arts and crafts movement, often visited too, in the 1870s. He liked it so much that it inspired him to found the Society for the Protection of Ancient Buildings, precursor to the National Trust and English Heritage, which have done so much since then to care for Britain's rich architectural heritage.

If you're energetic enough, you can walk from the tower down to Broadway itself. They are both stops on the Cotswold Way, a 100-mile-long footpath that incorporates much of the area's best scenery. It's so lush and rustic in summertime that you could be forgiven for thinking you'd gone to the Shire, in *Lord of the Rings*, and that hobbits might step out to greet you at any moment. The Cotswold Way, open just since 2007, wanders from northeast to southwest, skirting the area's towns, keeping mainly to the high ground, and ending in the old spa town of Bath.

As you can see, there's much variety to the English Midlands, from the grimy old industrial towns to the gentle Cotswold vales. Continuously and densely settled for more than 2,000 years, it's a thoroughly domesticated landscape but also one that has been well-cared for and intelligently managed. To omit it from your travels would be, both literally and figuratively, to miss the heart of England.

BIBLIOGRAPHY

Ackroyd, Peter. *London: The Biography*. London: Vintage, 2001.

———. *Thames, Sacred River*. New York: Vintage, 2008.

———. *The Tudors: The History of England from Henry VIII to Elizabeth I*. London: St. Martin's Griffin, 2014.

Aitken, Bob. *The West Highland Way: Official Guide*. Ninth edition. London: Birlinn, 2013.

Amery, Colin. *Lutyens: The Work of the English Architect Sir Edwin Lutyens*. London: Arts Council, 1981.

Arnold, Catherine. *Globe: Life in Shakespeare's London*. London: Simon and Schuster, 2016.

Ashe, Geoffrey. *Arthurian Britain*. London: Gothic Image, 1997.

Atkinson, Harriet. *The Festival of Britain: A Land and Its People*. London: I. B. Tauris, 2012.

Bathurst, Bella. *The Lighthouse Stevensons*. Harper Perennial, 2005.

Bedoyere, Guy de la. *Roman Britain: A New History*. New York: Thames and Hudson, 2006.

Black, Jeremy. *London: A History*. New York: Carnegie, 2009.

Boorman, Derek. *A Century of Remembrance: One Hundred Outstanding British War Memorials*. Barnsley, UK: Leo Cooper, 2005.

Branigan, Keith. *Roman Britain: Life in an Imperial Province*. London: Reader's Digest Association, 1980.

Brown, David. *Anglo-Saxon England*. London: Bodley Head, 1978.

Bryson, Bill. *Notes from a Small Island: Journey Through Britain*. San Francisco, CA: Black Swan, 2015.

————. *Shakespeare: The World as a Stage*. London: William Collins, 2016.

————. *The Road to Little Dribbling: More Notes from a Small Island*. San Francisco, CA: Black Swan, 2016.

Bunyan, John. *Grace Abounding to the Chief of Sinners*. Abbotsford, WI: ANEKO Press, 2017.

Burke, John. *Roman England*. New York: Norton, 1984.

Campbell, Katie. *British Gardens in Time*. London: Frances Lincoln, 2014.

Cannadine, David. *The Decline and Fall of the British Aristocracy*. New York: Vintage, 1999.

Cannadine, David, et al. *The Houses of Parliament: History, Art, Architecture*. London: Merrell, 2000.

Care-Evans, Angela. *The Sutton Hoo Ship Burial* London: British Museum, 1986.

Charles, Prince of Wales. *A Vision of Britain: A Personal View of Architecture*. New York: Doubleday, 1989.

Chinn, Carl, and Malcolm Dick. *Birmingham: The Workshop of the World*. Liverpool: Liverpool University Press, 2016.

Clarke, Kenneth. *Gothic Revival: An Essay in the History of Taste*. London: John Murray, 1995.

Coombes, B. L. *These Poor Hands: The Autobiography of a Miner in South Wales*. Aberystwyth: University of Wales Press, 2010.

Cormack, Patrick. *Castles of Britain*. London: Crescent Books, 1982.

Crawford, Robert. *The Bard: Robert Burns, A Biography*. Princeton, NJ: Princeton University Press, 2009.

Darvill, Timothy. *Prehistoric Britain*. London: Routledge, 2010.

Davies, John. *Cardiff and the Marquesses of Bute*. Aberystwyth: University of Wales Press, 2011.

———. *A History of Wales*. London: Penguin, 2007.

Dolan, Brian. *Wedgwood: Entrepreneur to the Enlightenment* London: Harper Perennial, 2004.

Drabble, Margaret. *A Writer's Britain*. London: Thames and Hudson, 2009.

DuMaurier, Daphne. *Jamaica Inn*. London: Gollancz, 1936.

Edworthy, Niall. *Lords: The Home of Cricket*. London: Virgin Books, 1999.

Engels, Friedrich. *The Condition of the Working Class in England*. New York: Oxford World Classics, 2009.

Evans, G. R. *The University of Oxford: A New History. London: I. B. Tauris, 2013*.

Ferris, Paul. *Dylan Thomas: The Biography*. Ceredigion: Y Lolfa, 2006.

Flanders, Judith. *The Victorian City: Everyday Life in Dickens' London*. New York: Atlantic Books, 2013.

Foreman, Amanda. *Georgiana, Duchess of Devonshire*. New York: Random House, 1999.

Fraser, Antonia. *Cromwell, Our Chief of Men*. London: Phoenix, 2008.

Fraser, Rebecca. *The Story of Britain: From the Romans to the Present: A Narrative History*. New York: Norton, 2006.

Friday, Laurie. *Wicken Fen: The Making of a Wetland Nature Reserve*. London: Harley Books, 1997.

Fry, Michael. *Edinburgh: A History of the City*. London: Pan, 2010.

Gale, Matthew. *Tate Modern, The Handbook*. London: Tate Publishing, 2016.

Gaskell, Elizabeth. *North and South*. New York: Penguin Classics, 1996.

Girouard, Mark. *Hardwick Hall*. London: David and Charles, 1989.

Goodier, Steve. *Literary Walks: Lake District Walks with Links to Wordsworth and Beatrix Potter*. Helsby, UK: Northern Eye Books, 2014.

Hannavy, John. *Britain's Industrial Heritage*. Wellington, UK: Pixz Books, 2015.

Higham, Nicholas and Martin J. Ryan. *The Anglo-Saxon World*. New Haven, CT: Yale University Press, 2013.

Horton, Rosalind, and Sally Simmons. *One Hundred and Eleven Places in Cambridge that You Should Not Miss*. Emons Verlag GmbH, 2017.

James, Henry. *English Hours: A Portrait of a Country*. London: Tauris Parke, 2011.

Jenkins, Simon. *Britain's 100 Best Railway Stations*. London: Viking, 2017.

———. *England's Cathedrals*. London: Little Brown, 2016.

———. *England's Thousand Best Churches*. London: Allen Lane, 1999.

Johnson, Paul. *Cathedrals of England, Scotland, and Wales*. New York: Harper Collins, 1990.

———. *The Offshore Islanders: A History of the English People*. Phoenix, AZ: Orion, 1998.

Jones, Nigel. *Tower: An Epic History of the Tower of London*. London: St. Martin's Press, 2013.

Jones, Robin. *Cornwall's Secret Coast*. Wellington: PiXZ Books, 2014.

Kidd, Alan. *Manchester: A History*. Lancaster, UK: Carnegie, 2012.

Kildea, Paul. *Benjamin Britten: A Life in the Twentieth Century*. London: Penguin, 2014.

King, Alex. *Memorials of the Great War in Britain*. Oxford, England: Berg, 1998.

King, Dorothy. *The Elgin Marbles: The Story of the Parthenon and Archaeology's Greatest Controversy*. London: Hutchinson, 2006.

Knight, Roger. *The Pursuit of Victory: The Life and Achievement of Horatio Nelson*. London: Penguin, 2006.

Knowles, David. *Bare Ruined Choirs*. New York: Cambridge University Press, 1984.

Licence, Amy. *Living in Squares, Loving in Triangles: The Lives and Loves of Virginia Woolf and the Bloomsbury Group*. Stroud, England: Amberley Publishing, 2016.

Linnick, Anthony. *A Walker's Alphabet: Adventures on the Long-Distance Footpaths of Great Britain*. London: Author House, 2011.

Lodge, David. *Changing Places*. New York: Vintage, 2011.

Lonely Planet Great Britain. London: Lonely Planet, 2017.

Loyn, H. R. *The Vikings in Britain*. New York: St. Martin's Press, 1977.

Lycett, Andrew. *Conan Doyle: The Man Who Created Sherlock Holmes*. London: Weidenfeld and Nicolson, 2008.

MacKenzie, Alister. *The Spirit of St. Andrews*. Three Rivers Press, 1998.

Marshall, Ian. *Old Trafford: 100 Years at the Theatre of Dreams*. London: Simon and Schuster, 2011.

McCarthy, Fiona. *Byron: Life and Legend*. London: John Murray, 2014.

Meeres, Frank. *A History of Norwich*. London: Phillmore and Co., 2016.

Mill, John Stuart. *Autobiography*. New York: Penguin Classics, 1989.

Moffat, Alistair. *The Reivers: The Story of the Border Reivers*. London: Birlinn, 2017.

Morris, Marc. *Castle: A History of the Buildings that Shaped Medieval Britain*. London: Channel 4 Books, 2003.

Nairn, Ian. *Nairn's London*. London: Penguin Modern Classics, 2014.

Ocran, Nana. *London's Parks and Gardens*. London: Metro Publications, 2006.

Orwell, George. *The Road to Wigan Pier*. New York: Houghton Mifflin/Harcourt, 1958.

Ovenden, Mark. *London Underground by Design*. London: Penguin, 2013.

Panayi, Panikos. *Spicing Up Britain: The Multicultural History of British Food*. London: Reaktion Books, 2010.

Parker, Steve. *Museum of Life*. London: Natural History Museum, 2010.

Paterson, Michael. *Life in Victorian Britain*. London: Robinson, 2008.

Phibbs, John, and Joe Cornish. *Capability Brown: Designing English Landscapes and Gardens*. New York: Rizzoli International Publications, 2016.

Prebble, John. *Glencoe: The Story of the Massacre*. London: Penguin, 1978.

———-. *The Highland Clearances*. London: Penguin, 1982.

Price, Katherine. *Kew Guide*. London: Royal Botanic Gardens, 2014.

Reynolds, Graham. *Constable's England*. New York: Metropolitan Museum of Art, 1983.

Robinson, John Martin. *Buckingham Palace: The Official Illustrated History*. London: Royal Collection, 2001.

———. *Windsor Castle: The Official Illustrated History*. London: Royal Collection, 2001.

Rose, Sarah. *For All the Tea in China: How England Stole the World's Favorite Drink and Changed History*. London: Penguin, 2011.

Rosenthal, Michael. *British Landscape Painting*. London: Phaidon Press, 1982.

Russell, Bertrand. *Autobiography. London: Harper Collins, 1975.*

Schama, Simon. *A History of Britain: At the Edge of the World: 3000 BC–1603 AD*. New York: Talk Miramax Books, 2000.

————. *A History of Britain: The British Wars, 1603–1776*. London: BBC Books, 2001.

Shenton, Caroline. *Mr. Barry's War: Rebuilding the Houses of Parliament After the Great Fire of 1834*. Oxford: Oxford University Press, 2016.

Smiles, Samuel. *Lives of the Engineers*. 1861.

Stafford, Fiona. *Jane Austen: A Brief Life*. New Haven, CT: Yale University Press, 2017.

Starkey, David. *Crown and Country: A History of England Through the Monarchy*. London: Harper, 2011.

————. *Magna Carta: The Medieval Roots of Modern Politics*. London: Quercus Books, 2015.

Tames, Richard. *An Armchair Traveller's History of Cambridge. London, Armchair Traveller's Bookhaus, 2013.*

Taylor, Alan. *Glasgow: The Autobiography*. Edinburgh: Birlinn, 2017.

Taylor, Arnold J. *The Welsh Castles of Edward I*. London: Hambledon Continuum, 1984.

Teller, Matthew. *The Rough Guide to the Cotswolds*. London: Rough Guides, 2015.

Thomas-Symonds, Nick. *Nye: The Political Life of Aneurin Bevan*. London: I. B. Tauris, 2016.

Tinniswood, Adrian. *His Invention So Fertile: A Life of Christopher Wren*. New York: Oxford University Press, 2001.

Toye, Richard. *Lloyd George and Churchill: Rivals for Greatness*. London: Macmillan, 2007.

Traquair, Peter. *Freedom's Sword: Scotland's Wars of Independence.* London: Collins, 1998.

Uglow, Jenny. *The Lunar Men: Five Friends Whose Curiosity Changed the World.* New York: Farrar Straus and Giroux, 2002.

The Ultimate Trans-Pennine Trail Guide: Coast to Coast Across Northern England by Bike or on Foot. London: Ultimate Guide Series, 2017.

Wallis, Steve. *Thomas Hardy's Dorset Through Time.* Stroud, England: Amberley Publishing, 2012.

Wambu, Onyekachi. *Empire Windrush: Fifty Years of Writing About Black Britain.* London: Phoenix, 1999.

Way, Twigs. *Gertrude Jekyll.* London: Shire Publications, 2012.

Weightman, Gavin. *The Industrial Revolutionaries: The Making of the Modern World, 1776–1914.* New York: Grove Press, 2010.

Wheatley, Keith. *National Maritime Museum Guide to Maritime Britain.* London: Caxton, 2000.

Whitehead, Stephen R. *The Brontes' Haworth: The Place and the People the Brontes Knew.* York, England: Ashmount Press, 2006.

Williams, Gareth. *A Monstrous Commotion: The Mysteries of Loch Ness.* London: Orion Press, 2015.

Wilson, A. N. *Charles Darwin: Victorian Mythmaker.* New York: Harper, 2017.

———. *A Life of Walter Scott: The Laird of Abbotsford.* London: Pimlico, 2002.

Wilson, Andrew. *Narrow Gauge Railways of North Wales.* London: History Press, 2003.

————. *Turner in His Time*. London: Thames and Hudson, 2006.

Worden, Blair. *The English Civil Wars: 1640–1660*. London: Phoenix, 2010.

IMAGE CREDITS

Page:

NOTES

NOTES

NOTES

NOTES